AIA METRIC BUILDING
AND CONSTRUCTION GUIDE

AIA METRIC BUILDING AND CONSTRUCTION GUIDE

Edited by

SUSAN BRAYBROOKE

for
The American Institute of Architects

This book was prepared in full collaboration with the National Bureau of Standards, Center for Building Technology, and the American National Metric Council, Construction Industries Coordinating Committee

A WILEY-INTERSCIENCE PUBLICATION

JOHN WILEY & SONS, **New York** • **Chichester** • **Brisbane** • **Toronto**

Library of Congress Cataloging in Publication Data:

Main entry under title:
AIA metric building and construction guide.

   Includes index.
   1. Building—Handbooks, manuals, etc. 2. Metric
system—Handbooks, manuals, etc. I. Braybrooke, Susan.
II. American Institute of Architects. III. Center for
Building Technology. IV. American National Metric
Council. Construction Industries Coordinating Committee.

TH151.A14   690   78-31997

ISBN 0-471-03812-1
ISBN 0-471-03813-X pbk.

Printed in the United States of America

10 9 8 7 6 5 4 3 2 1

FOREWORD

Chapter by chapter, the specialist authors of this manual have examined metrication in the light of daily professional requirements. They have attempted to anticipate everyday problems that metrication poses for the architect and planner, and have provided concise directions logically arranged.

The tables—given a place near every drawing board and desk—will be most easily and accurately employed after reading the discussion chapters. The short time invested will earn dividends in speed and confidence, thanks especially to the clear and specific examples in computation and graphics.

The introduction chronicles our 200 years of failure as a nation to begin speaking this international language of peace and progress. It does not say that metrication is an idea whose time has come, nor will I. We know instead that it is sadly overdue, and the price the United States is paying for further delay is rising every day.

As the construction industry's representative on the U.S. Metric Board, I commend the American Institute of Architects for leadership in taking this first important and practical step.

F.R. DUGAN, FAIC
U.S. METRIC
Board

PREFACE

The measurement of the environment is something most of us are only too glad to take for granted. We develop sufficient technical understanding, and assimilate whatever level of working competence we need to function effectively in our chosen walk of life, and otherwise give this matter little conscious thought, that is, until we are asked to change our approach. One of the essential underpinnings of civilized life, our system of weights and measures is revealed to us in its full complexities only when, as now, our nation declares its intention of moving—slowly and somewhat belatedly but, it appears, deliberately and inexorably—toward the adoption of the International Metric System of Measurement, known as SI.

For those involved in the construction industry the change will be a profound one, ultimately affecting every aspect of their work. But, over and above the intrinsic logic and coherence of the system itself, are other tremendous advantages. Better coordinated products, improved communication among different branches of the industry, a reduction in on-site cutting and fitting, and simplification of project documentation and cost estimating are only a few of the advantages cited as the beneficent corollaries of change.

Yet, while these virtues may be accepted in principle (although certainly not unanimously), contemplation of the change itself is to many a horrifying proposition which they would rather ignore, hiding their heads in the sand, until it is forced upon them.

Because many architects undoubtedly share this feeling, the AIA and John Wiley have collaborated to produce this book. In it we have tried to relate the metrication process to all aspects of construction with which architects will have to deal, setting out guidelines for the use of SI units in architecture and engineering, and for the conversion process itself, and including essential information on dimensional coordination and the effects of metrication on such activities as architectural drafting, surveying, and the establishment of codes and standards. While this does not claim to be the definitive work on the subject, it can qualify as a reliable, essential, and accessible primer of information in a form that architects will actually be able to read and use.

If anyone should deceive himself or herself into thinking that the change to metric will be easy, this is most assuredly a delusion. The compilation of this book has itself revealed some inkling of the complexities involved, and it has called for the research, deliberations, and editorial judgment of a great many people, only some of whom there is space to mention here.

My first thanks must go to Dudley Hunt, FAIA, of John Wiley & Sons, and to Michael Barker, James Dowling, Arthur Duncan and Robert Packard, AIA, of The American Institute of Architects, whose personal commitment to this book went far beyond the call of duty. To the authors of the individual chapters thanks are also due, especially to Hans J. Milton, FRAIA, and Cornelius Wandmacher, whose pioneering work in this field formed the basis for much of the material in this book, over and beyond the sections to which their names are appended. The AIA Metric Conversion/Dimensional Coordination Task Force monitored progress of the book, and Rudolph Dreyer, AIA, Chairman, and Anna Halpin, FAIA, now a Vice President of the AIA, are owed special recognition for their consistent involvement in the detailed development of the text. To James Gross and his colleagues at the Center for Building Technology I am grateful for a body of technical material and meticulous technical review of the manuscript. To the American National Metric Council and its Construction Industries Coordinating Committee I owe the benefit of advice and support and a review of current activity as it developed. To M. J. Jacobs, who typed the manuscript, and to J. Dyck Fledderus, who prepared a number of the drawings, I am indeed grateful for their significant contributions to the final quality of the book. In the preparation of Chapter 2 significant portions of the content were derived from the *American National Metric Council Editorial Guide,* Third Edition.

If I shall be personally sorry to say good-bye to the rod, pole, and perch, I recognize my attachment to them as sentimental and nostalgic rather than rational, and it is to the logic and coherence of the SI system, and the good effects that these can have on the practice of architecture, that this book is dedicated.

SUSAN BRAYBROOKE

New York, New York
March 1980

CONTENTS

AIA METRIC BUILDING AND CONSTRUCTION GUIDE

1

AN INTRODUCTION TO INTERNATIONAL METRICATION

DR. MALCOLM O'HAGAN

Executive Director, U.S. Metric Board

"Metrication" is the term now commonly used to describe the process of changing to the metric system of weights and measures. The lexicographer will tell you that the proper word is "metrification," but Lord Ritchie Calder, the first Chairman of the British Metrication Board, being of positive disposition, did not take kindly to the term, claiming that there was no *if* about Britain going metric. Hence the abbreviated but bold term "metrication."

It is fair to say at this time that the *if* no longer applies in the United States, and we are therefore not presumptuous in adopting the same posture. A look at world trends and past and recent events in the United States points to an affirmative answer.

The metric system was a product of the French Revolution, an intellectual substitution for the agrarian and haphazard, although practical, systems of weights and measures prevailing at the time. The simple logic and coherence of the metric system were recognized and appreciated, and it won gradual acceptance throughout Europe and in the French and Spanish colonies. By 1875 the metric system had gained international endorsement and was standardized in the Treaty of the Meter signed by 17 countries. The United States was one of the signatories to the treaty and has participated in the development of the metric system since that time. In 1960 the international nature of the metric system was solidly established when, after fundamental revision by the General Conference on Weights and Measures, the system was modernized and given the name Système International d'Unités (SI). Those of us who were taught the metric system in school learned the traditional CGS or MKSA version, and it is important to recognize that it is to SI that we are now converting.

Although the United States and Great Britain appreciated the logic of the metric system and both were signatories to the Treaty of the Meter, the inch-pound system was firmly entrenched in the New World and throughout the British Empire. It was John Quincy Adams in his capacity as Secretary of State who made the first serious study of the metric system for the United States. In response to a request from the Senate he submitted in 1821 a classic treatise on the subject entitled *Report Upon Weights & Measures*. Although Adams was fully aware of the benefits of the metric system, he concluded that the time was not yet ripe for its adoption, since it was not standardized in Europe nor had it been adopted by England, our principal trading partner.

Since the Adams *Report* sporadic attempts have been made to make the United States a metric nation. Use of the metric system was actually legalized in

THE EVOLUTION OF SI

the United States on July 28, 1866, in an act signed by President Andrew Johnson. The act provided that "No contract, or dealing or pleading in any court, shall be deemed invalid or liable to objection because the weights or measures expressed or referred to therein are weights or measures of the metric system." In other words, the act permitted, but did not encourage, use of the metric system. Our forefathers apparently decided that the foot and the pound were good enough for them.

THE DEBATE OVER METRICS

The century-long metric debate in the United States has been at times intense and emotional. A few zealous opponents equated the metric system with god-lessness and lack of patriotism. Some were even moved to poetry in defense of the customary system of measurement. Around 1880 the Institute for Preserving and Perfecting the Anglo-Saxon Weights and Measures developed a theme song that went in part as follows:

> Then down with every metric scheme
> Taught by the foreign school,
> We'll worship still our father's God
> And keep our father's "rule."
> A perfect inch, a perfect pint,
> The Anglo's honest pound,
> Shall hold their place upon the earth,
> Till time's last trump shall sound!

Most of the arguments for and against the change were, however, the same as those we have been hearing during the past decade, with those in favor touting the virtues of the metric system and the need for international uniformity, and those opposed pointing to the cost of conversion and to the difficulty and confusion involved in learning a new system.

What is interesting about those early debates is the optimism expressed in certain quarters. Upon returning from a European tour in 1902, Dr. Stratton, the first Director of the National Bureau of Standards, said, "It will be a close race between the United States and Great Britain as to which shall first adopt the metric system. . . ." As it turns out, it might have been more appropriate for him to speculate about a race to be last to convert. The chairman of the Congressional Committee before which Dr. Stratton was testifying said, "I believe that the metric system is coming just as surely as the tides are going to continue to rise and fall." Little did he realize how long it would take the metric tide to come in.

But is it really coming in, or are we also victims of our own optimism? Why can we say now with greater assurance that the United States finally is serious about adopting the metric system?

THE INTERNATIONAL TREND TOWARD METRICATION

Although many of the same arguments for and against the metric system are still heard today, a changing domestic and international environment places those arguments in a different context. There are five major factors that have fostered a more favorable climate for conversion:

1 The adoption by the General Conference on Weights and Measures of the International System of Units (SI).
2 The emergence of multinational corporations with global operations.
3 The decision of our trading partners in the English-speaking countries to convert to SI.
4 The increased importance of international commerce and communications.
5 The signing of the Metric Conversion Act of 1975.

Following World War II Japan completed its conversion to the metric system. A decade later, India adopted the system. In 1960 world interest in the metric system was heightened when the General Conference on Weights and Measures adopted the modernized version of SI. Adoption of SI by the General Conference on Weights and Measures presented the world with a truly coherent system of units for the first time in its history. And the world responded favorably. In 1965 the British government announced that it would abandon the system of weights and measures it had spawned and spread throughout the Commonwealth in favor of the modernized metric system. South Africa initiated its conversion program in 1967, and Australia and Canada followed suit in 1970. A year later the European Economic Community issued a directive requiring the use of SI units in trade and commerce within the Common Market by 1978. The European countries will therefore be obliged to phase out some of their traditional metric units in favor of the modernized SI units. It would seem, therefore, that the world is finally converging on a common standard for weights and measures, and it is not too late for the United States to be a leader in the move to SI. It is worth remembering that unit names like kelvin, newton, pascal, and joule are as new to the rest of the world, including Europe, as they are to us.

Another significant factor favoring U.S. metrication is the growth of corporations with global operations. A common language of measurement facilitates communication and technology transfer and is the basis for international engineering and product standards. Since SI is becoming that common language, it is not surprising that such organizations in the United States are in the vanguard of the change to metric.

DEVELOPMENT OF WORLDWIDE MARKETS

Coupled with the growth in such worldwide operations is the increase in international commerce. About fifty years ago our exports amounted to less than $5 billion. In 1978, they were approximately 142 billion, a nearly thirtyfold increase. But while our exports have been growing, in recent years our market share has been declining. For example, in 1958 the U.S. share of world exports of manufactured goods was 28%. By 1978 our share had been reduced to 17%, a decrease of almost 40%. In the 10-year period from 1963 to 1973 U.S. exports doubled in dollar value, as compared with a fivefold increase in Japan, a fourfold increase in Italy, and a threefold increase in West Germany, France, and Canada. Although the United States still maintains its position as the industrial and technological leader of the world, its economic and industrial supremacy is being seriously challenged, and even eroded.

Finally, we are now operating in a favorable legislative climate. The overwhelming support in the House of Representatives (300 to 63) and the unanimous Senate consent to the Metric Conversion Act and ratification of the U.S. Metric Board demonstrate that Congress endorses a program of planned and coordinated voluntary conversion.

But as President Ford pointed out when he signed the bill, "legislation cannot solve all our problems. Indeed if the legislation is not founded on public acceptance it will have less than no effect at all." What is the state of public acceptance upon which successful conversion will hinge? A Gallup Poll conducted in January 1977 indicated that 75% of the public were aware of the metric system, compared with 54% in 1973 and only 29% in 1965. However, of those professing awareness, 40% were opposed to the United States adopting the metric system, and only 29% favored its adoption. The results clearly indicate that public support for conversion is less than enthusiastic. Gallup attributed the resistance in part to widespread ignorance of the metric units themselves and of how the system works, for, whereas 75% were aware of the metric system, fewer than 7% could hazard a guess as to how many liters there are in a gallon, or the distance of a kilometer. A major responsibility of the U.S. Metric Board will be to

NEED FOR PUBLIC SUPPORT AND PUBLIC EDUCATION

correct this dismal state of affairs. The most effective way to learn the metric system, however, is through exposure to metric products. Over the next 5 years such products will enter the market at an accelerating rate.

Already film, cigarettes, skis, and drugs are designated in metric terms. Soft drinks are now being sold in $\frac{1}{2}$-liter, 1-liter, and 2-liter bottles, and by 1980 all wine and spirits must be sold in metric quantities. General Motors has announced that it expects to complete its conversion program by 1982 with all its cars of metric design at that time. General Motors made its commitment to metric conversion in 1973, as did IBM, and the decisions of these two companies were pivotal. Other corporate giants, particularly multinationals, such as Rockwell International, Honeywell, International Harvester, Xerox, Chrysler, and Ingersoll-Rand, were quick to join the bandwagon. By now most major companies are seriously confronting the issue and laying plans for an orderly conversion.

The automobile, off-road vehicle, and steel industries are in the vanguard of the U.S. change to metric. The decisions of the major corporations inevitably affect the operations of the smaller companies who are their suppliers, and so the metric ripple emanating from the multinationals is slowly encompassing all of American industry. In general, metric implementation is being geared to the introduction of new products, this being the most sensible and least costly conversion strategy. Metrication will expand to all activities in due course as the appropriate conditions develop, and it is possible that the United States will be categorized as metric as early as 1985.

Planned and coordinated action is the key to a sound conversion program. It was for this reason that the American National Metric Council (ANMC) was established in 1973 by the American National Standards Institute. The council now operates as an independent nonprofit and nonadvocate coordinating body and information clearinghouse. Through a structure of sector and coordinating committees ANMC is developing coordinated conversion plans for major segments of the U.S. economy (see Chapter 11), including the design and construction industries.

One can hardly deny that the final push is underway. The United States is indeed committed to adopting SI, and substantial progress has already been made in that direction. How the conversion program will proceed from here is hard to project, since progress will depend on many factors, including the economic and political climates, and will demand a spirit of cooperation and a commitment by all.

2

FUNDAMENTALS OF THE INTERNATIONAL SYSTEM OF UNITS (SI)

SUSAN BRAYBROOKE

Editor

The International System (SI) is a logically developed language of measurement, whose units relate to each other in simple ways and whose symbols are the same in all languages. There are seven base units from which all other SI units are derived by means of simple one-to-one relationships. There are three kinds of SI units: the seven base units, two supplementary units, and a large number of derived units (Tables 2.1, 2.2, 2.3, and 2.4 and Figure 2.1).

The principal merits of SI might be stated in the following way:

Simplicity.   The identification of a small number of essential base units that may be expanded directly into various sets of derived units.

Coherence.   Direct one-to-one relationships between base units and derived units without the use of intervening multipliers.

Uniqueness.   No duplication of derived units, that is each derived unit is used in the same form and with the same name in all branches of technology to which it is applicable.

Symbolization.   Unmistakable identification of units and of unit multipliers (prefixes) by widely recognized symbols.

Decimalization.   Simplified computation and recording similar to the decimal monetary system; utilization of the concept of powers of 10.

Versatility.   Units applicable to various requirements with convenient unit multiples and submultiples to cover a wide range of sizes.

Universality.   Worldwide language in respect to terminology and unit symbols.

Reproducibility.   Description of base units in terms of reproducible physical phenomena with least possible dependence on artifacts.

Despite the advantages of SI, some non-SI units, whose use is compatible with SI, have been retained for convenience or because of their widespread use and acceptance (Table 2.5).

Specific rules for use, type style, and punctuation have been established by the General Conference on Weights and Measures (CGPM); the Secretary of the

ADVANTAGES OF THE INTERNATIONAL SYSTEM

RULES AND CONVENTIONS FOR USING SI

This chapter was developed with the aid and permission of the American National Metric Council, National Bureau of Standards Center for Building Technology, and Professor Cornelius Wandmacher.

Table 2.1 SI Base Units

Physical Quantity	Unit	Symbol
length	meter	m
mass	kilogram	kg
time	second[b]	s
electric current	ampere[b]	A
thermodynamic temperature	kelvin	K
luminous intensity	candela[b]	cd
amount of substance	mole[a]	mol

[a]Not used in building construction. [b]In use in United States.

Table 2.2 SI Supplementary Units

Physical Quantity	Unit	Symbol
plane angle	radian	rad
solid angle	steradian	sr

Table 2.3 Derived Units with Compound Names

Physical Quantity	Unit	Symbol
area	square meter	m^2
volume	cubic meter	m^3
density	kilogram per cubic meter	kg/m^3
velocity	meter per second	m/s
angular velocity	radian per second	rad/s
acceleration	meter per second squared	m/s^2
angular acceleration	radian per second squared	rad/s^2
volume rate of flow	cubic meter per second	m^3/s
moment of inertia	kilogram square meter	$kg \cdot m^2$
moment of force	newton meter	$N \cdot m$
heat flux density	watt per square meter	W/m^2
thermal conductivity	watt per meter kelvin	$W/(m \cdot K)$
luminance	candela per square meter	cd/m^2

Table 2.4 Derived Units with Special Names

Physical Quantity	Unit	Symbol	Derivation
frequency	hertz[b]	Hz	s^{-1}
force	newton	N	$kg \cdot m/s^2$
pressure, stress	pascal	Pa	N/m^2
work, energy, quantity of heat	joule	J	$N \cdot m$
power	watt[b]	W	J/s
electric charge	coulomb	C	$A \cdot s$
electric potential	volt[b]	V	W/A
electric capacitance	farad[b]	F	C/V
electric resistance	ohm[b]	Ω	V/A
electric conductance	siemens[b]	S	Ω^{-1}
magnetic flux	weber[b]	Wb	$V \cdot s$
magnetic flux density	tesla[b]	T	Wb/m^2
inductance	henry[b]	H	Wb/A
temperature	degree Celsius	°C	K
luminous flux	lumen[b]	lm	$cd \cdot sr$
illumination	lux	lx	lm/m^2
activity	becquerel	Bq	s^{-1}[a]
absorbed dose	gray	Gy	J/kg[a]

[a]Not used in building construction. [b]In use in United States. (Hertz replaces cycles per second and siemens replaces mho, without changing their values.)

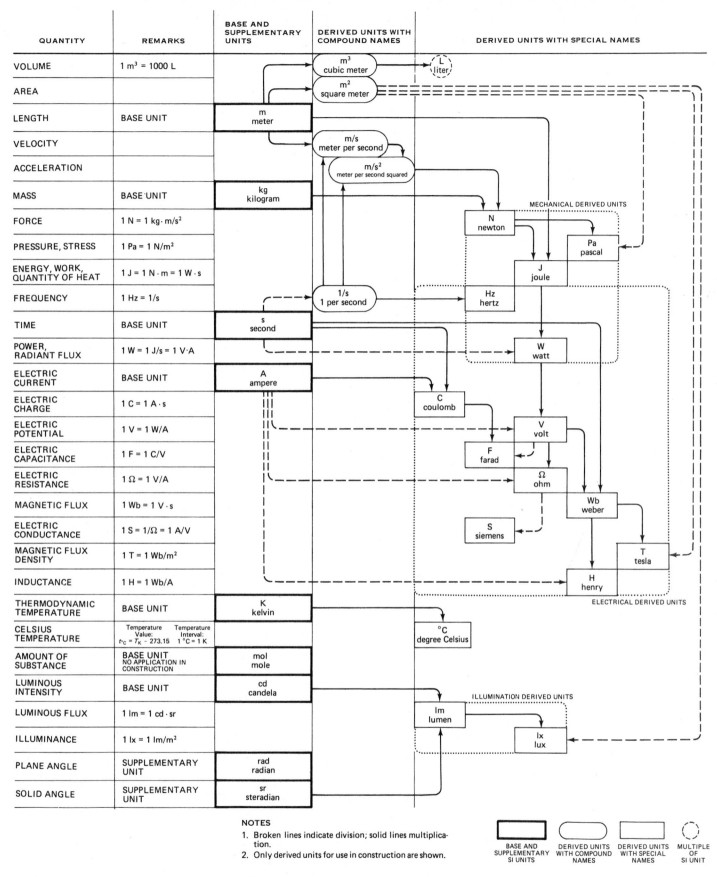

Figure 2.1 SI base and derived units, and their relationships.

Hans J. Milton, FRAIA, Technical Consultant, National Bureau of Standards; Gaithersburg, Maryland

Table 2.5 Non-SI Units Used with SI

minute	min
hour	h
day	d
nautical mile	n mile
knot	kn
kilometer per hour	km/h
revolution per minute	r/min
degree (angle)	°
minute (angle)	′
second (angle)	″
kilowatt-hour	kW·h

Department of Commerce is responsible for determining preferred usage in the United States.

Standard, upright lower-case letters are used for unit names and symbols, except when the symbols are derived from proper names, such as ampere (A), hertz (Hz), newton (N), or pascal (Pa), where the first letter of the symbol is capitalized. The one exception to this general rule is the use of the capital letter L as the symbol for liter, because the lower-case l was thought by standards-writing bodies in the United States to be easily confused with the numeral 1. Symbols are not followed by a period or full stop, except when they occur at the end of a sentence. Unit names are used in the plural to express numerical values greater than 1. All other values take the singular form of the unit name. Thus the following are correct: 100 meters, 1.1 meters, 0.5 meter, ½ liter, −0.2 degree Celsius, −1 degree Celsius. The plural of a unit name is formed by adding an "s." Exceptions are hertz, lux, and siemens, which remain unchanged, and henry, which becomes henries. Symbols are the same in both singular and plural.

Prefixes denoting decimal multiples and submultiples (allowing SI units to express magnitudes from the subatomic to the astronomic) are governed by the same general rules concerning capitalization and punctuation (see Table 2.6).

It is important to note that mega, giga, and tera (M, G, T) are capitalized in symbol form to avoid confusion with established unit symbols, but they maintain the lower-case form when spelled out in full. No space is left between the prefix and the letter for the unit name: mL (milliliter), mm (millimeter), kA (kiloampere).

Preference is given to the use of decimal multiples that are related to the base units by multiples of 1000 (Table 2.6). As far as is possible, prefixes denoting magnitudes of 100, 10, 0.1, and 0.01 should be avoided. Certain multiples of SI units likely to be extensively used have been given special names (Table 2.7).

The prefix symbol is considered to be part of the unit symbol and is attached to it without a space or dot: km, *not* k m, k-m, or k.m.

A space is left between a numeral and the unit name or symbol to which it refers: 20 mm, 10^6 N. In angular measure, where the unit degree (°) is used, no space is left between the numeral and the degree symbol: 27°. Parts of a degree are preferably expressed in decimals (26.27°). The customary angular units of minute (′) and second (″) will be continued in use for cartography only. For temperature measurements the symbol for degree Celsius (°C) is inseparable with no space between the two parts; it is also preferable to leave no space between the numeral and the unit: 20°C.

When a numeral is used as an adjective, it is preferable to use a hyphen instead of a space between the number and the unit name, but not between number and the symbol: a 12-meter (12 m) yacht.

In the United States and Canada the decimal point is a dot on the line, but in some other countries a comma or a raised dot is used.

Table 2.6 SI Prefixes

Multiplication Factor	Prefix	Symbol	Pronunciation U.S.	Meaning In the United States	In Other Countries
$1\ 000\ 000\ 000\ 000\ 000\ 000 = 10^{18}$	exa	E	ex'a (a as in about)	One quintillion times	Trillion
$1\ 000\ 000\ 000\ 000\ 000 = 10^{15}$	peta	P	as in petal	One quadrillion times	Thousand billion
$1\ 000\ 000\ 000\ 000 = 10^{12}$	tera	T	as in terrace	One trillion times	Billion
$1\ 000\ 000\ 000 = 10^{9}$	giga	G	jig'a (a as in about)	One billion times	Milliard
$1\ 000\ 000 = 10^{6}$	mega	M	as in megaphone	One million times	
$1\ 000 = 10^{3}$	kilo	k	as in kilowatt	One thousand times	
$100 = 10^{2}$	hecto	h	heck'toe	One hundred times	
$10 = 10$	deka	da	deck'a (a as in about)	Ten times	
$0.1 = 10^{-1}$	deci	d	as in decimal	One tenth of	
$0.01 = 10^{-2}$	centi	c	as in sentiment	One hundredth of	
$0.001 = 10^{-3}$	milli	m	as in military	One thousandth of	
$0.000\ 001 = 10^{-6}$	micro	μ	as in microphone	One millionth of	
$0.000\ 000\ 001 = 10^{-9}$	nano	n	nan'oh (an as in ant)	One billionth of	Milliardth
$0.000\ 000\ 000\ 001 = 10^{-12}$	pico	p	peek'oh	One trillionth of	Billionth
$0.000\ 000\ 000\ 000\ 001 = 10^{-15}$	femto	f	fem'toe (fem as in feminine)	One quadrillionth of	Thousand billionth
$0.000\ 000\ 000\ 000\ 000\ 001 = 10^{-18}$	atto	a	as in anatomy	One quintillionth of	Trillionth

1. Although hecto, deka, deci, and centi are SI prefixes, their use should generally be avoided except for the SI unit multiples of area and volume and the nontechnical use of centimeter, as for body and clothing measurement. The preferred prefixes used in building design and construction are mega, kilo, milli and micro, while tera, giga, nano, and pico are sometimes used.
2. Femto, atto, eka and peta will probably not be used.

Decimal notation is preferred with metric measurements, but simple fractions are acceptable (except on drawings), such as those where the denominator is 2, 3, 4, 5, 8, and 10. Simple fractions are not, however, recommended.

Examples   0.5 g, 1.75 kg, and 0.7 L are preferred; $\frac{1}{2}$ g, $1\frac{3}{4}$ kg, and $\frac{7}{10}$ L are acceptable (except on drawings)

A zero before the decimal point should be used in numbers between 1 and −1 to prevent the possibility that a faint decimal point will be overlooked.

Example   The oral expression "point seven five" is written as 0.75.

Since the comma is used as the decimal marker in many countries, a comma should not be used to separate groups of digits. Instead, the digits should be separated into groups of three, counting both to the left and to the right from the

Table 2.7 Multiples of SI Units with Special Names

Physical Quantity	Name	Symbol	Magnitude	
volume	liter	L	10^{-3} m³	$= 0.001$ m³
mass	metric ton	t	10^{3} kg	$= 1000$ kg
	(megagram)	Mg		
area	hectare	ha	10^{4} m²	$= 10\ 000$ m²
pressure	millibar[a]	mbar[a]	10^{2} Pa	$= 100$ Pa

[a]Used for meteorological purposes only.

decimal point, and a space used to separate the groups of three digits. The space should be fixed width, equal to that formerly occupied by the comma.

Examples   4 720 525
                0.528 75

If there are only four digits to the left or right of the decimal point, the space is acceptable but is not preferred.

Examples   6875 or 6 875
                0.1234 or 0.123 4

However, in a column with other numbers that show the space and are aligned on the decimal point, the space is necessary.

Example   14.8
                   3 780
                 +12 100
                 ‾‾‾‾‾‾‾‾

Compound units are those formed by combining simple units by means of the mathematical signs for multiplication and division, and the use of exponents.

When writing symbols for units such as square millimeter or cubic meter, the symbol for the unit should be followed by the superscript ^{2} or ^{3}, respectively: thus 26 mm^2 and 14 m^3.

For a compound unit that is a quotient, "per" should be used to form the name (kilometer per hour) and a slash (/) to form the symbol (km/h). There is no space before or after the slash. Compound units that are quotients may also be written by using negative exponents (km · h^{-1}).

Considerable information on SI is contained in ANSI/ASTM E380-76 *Standard for Metric Practice* and in ANSI/ASTM E621-78, *Recommended Practice for the Use of Metric (SI) Units in Building Design and Construction.*

DEFINITIONS OF HARD AND SOFT CONVERSION

The term ex*act* or *direct conversion* denotes a precise conversion from a customary reference value to its exact equivalent in SI units, generally expressed to the number of decimal places needed to satisfy legal, scientific, or statistical requirements. (For example, 1 U.S. gallon = 3.785 412 liters; 12 feet = 3657.6 millimeters.) The degree of accuracy of exact conversion is hardly ever required in building design and construction, and in fact should be avoided, since it provides unnecessarily cumbersome values. Exact conversion is, however, the starting point for determining rounded metric values (soft conversion) and preferred metric values (hard conversion).

The term *soft conversion* represents a change in description, but does not generally imply any significant change in requirement, material, or product, other than the rounding of the descriptive value to the nearest sensible number. The change is one made on paper—or in the "software"—hence the name. [For example, the description of a gallon container is changed to 3.78 L (a 0.14% decrease) or 3.8 L (a 0.38% increase); a length of 12 ft is changed to 3660 mm (a 0.07% increase) or 3650 mm (a 0.21% decrease)—all such changes are probably well within permissible tolerances.]

The term *hard conversion* represents a definite change from an existing physical measurement or quantity to a different, new, and generally "preferred" metric value. Since hard conversion indicates a change in "hardware" as well as in software, it will normally lead to incompatibility between customary and metric properties or product characteristics [For example, a 1-gal container is replaced by a 4-L container (a 5.6% increase); and a length of 12 ft is replaced by a "preferred metric dimension" of 3600 mm (a 1.57% decrease), requiring the modification of design details and production and assembly operations.]

Preferred metric values are selected numerical values with special characteristics or relationships that take on a particular significance in the conversion to SI because of the opportunities they provide for standardization and more rational approaches. A variety of preferred number systems can be constructed to suit particular ends, and a number of such systems are already in widespread use in the metric building world.

In a decimally measured environment, the numbers which represent powers of 10, such as 1, 10, 100, 1000, have a special place in sets or series of numbers. They often provide preferred reference values, such as originating and/or terminating values in sequences. For example, the internationally agreed fundamental unit of size for use in building—the building module—is established as 100 mm.

Preferred dimensions for use in coordinated building design and building product sizing are based upon selected preferences of this fundamental 100-mm module, which is also referred to as "M." The module has been endorsed as the basic unit of size for use in metric dimensional coordination in the United States by the Construction Industries Coordinating Committee of the American National Metric Council and its sector committees, as well as the Metrication and Dimensional Coordination Task Force of the American Institute of Architects.

While the practical application of metric dimensional coordination is discussed in Chapter 6, it must be appreciated that preferred dimensions in the context of dimensional coordination are ideal or reference dimensions, rather than actual dimensions. The actual dimensions will have to take into account allowances for joints, tolerances, and deviations. [For example, a "coordinating" preferred dimension for a building product may be 400 mm (4M); but as that dimension would have to include half a joint width on either side, the actual dimension must be less. If the design joint thickness is 10 mm, the "manufacturing target dimension" will be 390 mm.]

PRINCIPLES OF ROUNDING

This section does not discriminate between *rules for rounding of numbers* (e.g., as outlined in Section 4.4 of ASTM E380-76) and *conversion and rounding of measurement values.* Rules for rounding should apply regardless of the measurement system used. For example:

When the first digit to be discarded is less than 5, the number should be truncated at the last digit to be retained.

Example 3.5432 rounded to four digits becomes 3.543; if rounded to three digits, 3.54; and, if rounded to two digits, 3.5.

When the first digit to be discarded is greater than 5, or 5 followed by at least one digit other than 0, the last digit retained should be increased by one unit.

Example 8.9876 rounded to four digits becomes 8.988; if rounded to three digits, 8.99; and if rounded to two digits, 9.0.

When the first digit to be discarded is exactly 5, or 5 followed by zeros only, the last digit should be rounded upward if it is an odd number and downward if it is an even number.

Example 1.215 rounded to three digits becomes 1.22; 1.225 rounded to three digits becomes 1.22.

(An exception may be made only in the case of a preferred number: for example, while 1.245 would be rounded to 1.24, the choice of 1.25 might be preferable if this is a preferred number in the specific measurement context.)

CONVERSION AND ROUNDING

Suitable rounding of metric values obtained by converting untolerated customary values is necessary so that "workable" numbers are obtained for use in the permanent metric environment. The following approaches are suggested:

Where customary values are expressed by a combination of units, such as feet and inches or pounds and ounces, conversions should be based on the smaller unit:

Examples   14 ft 5 in = 173 in   4 lb 12 oz = 76 oz

Multiply the customary unit by the conversion factor. Round the resulting value, which may have a number of decimal places, to an equivalent significance of digits. Generally, where a value is measured with a scale or measuring instrument, rounding should be to a value that represents a measurable gradation on such an instrument.

Examples   173 in × 25.4 (mm/in) = 4394.2 mm, which rounds to 4394 mm for 1 mm gradations, 4395 mm for 5 mm gradations, 4390 mm for 10 mm gradations, and 4400 mm for 100 mm gradations. The maximum variation from the exact equivalent is 0.13% for a hard conversion to 4400 mm.

When a customary value represents a maximum (upper limit) or a minimum (lower limit) that must be respected, the rounding must be in the direction that does not violate the original limit.

These recommendations do not apply to the conversion of degrees Fahrenheit to degrees Celsius.

3

SI UNITS
IN ARCHITECTURE

HANS J. MILTON, FRAIA

Technical Consultant, Center for Building Technology
National Bureau of Standards
U.S. Department of Commerce

and

ROBERT T. PACKARD, AIA

Director, Documents/Architectural Graphic Standards Division
The American Institute of Architects

During the transition to the use of SI units, the architect will be faced with a construction world using both metric and U.S. customary units. It will frequently be necessary to convert measurements or values either from customary to metric, or the reverse. This conversion process will involve either simple rounding to retain equivalent values, or rationalization to alternative values in preferred numbers serving the same functional purpose but no longer interchangeable. Very seldom will a direct conversion yield a simple number. Historically, however, construction dimensions have been selected for numerical simplicity because of a need for data that can be easily measured, verified, memorized, and communicated. Wherever practicable, the metric building world should be based on similar numerical simplicity.

CONVERSION APPROACHES

Different approaches to conversion are defined in Chapter 2. The architect needs to be aware that exact conversion, using precise conversion factors, results in complex values. Exact conversion is rarely needed in design and construction, but is a basis for determining appropriate rounded or new preferred sizes. Soft conversion, or rounding within permissible tolerances, will allow either customary or metric dimensioned products to be used. But the use of rounded figures—a "metric veneer"—should be limited because they offer no real advantage, other than a uniform metric terminology, over customary values. Hard conversion, however, is a rational approach to the selection of new preferred and rationalized values. In construction hard conversion to metric dimensions, sizes, and product ranges provides many advantages, such as reduction in the range of products, elimination of conflicting standard or code requirements, and a simpler numerical system.

PREFERRED DIMENSIONS

The use of hard conversion to achieve preferred metric dimensions, and dimensional coordination between products, elements, and buildings, is strongly recommended. In considering preferred dimensions, which are discussed in more detail in Chapter 6, it is obvious that certain numbers offer advantages because they are easily added and divided.

An example is 600 mm, which is divisible by the preferred dimensions 100, 200, and 300 mm, as well as 120 and 150 mm. Other preferred dimensions include 800, 1200, 1800, and 2400 mm. An understanding of preferred dimensions can lead to the optimization of dimensions and sizes in buildings. Although experience has shown that nonmodular dimensions will be required in building design and construction, for example, in wall and floor thicknesses, attention to such dimensions can still allow their integration into an overall modular grid.

CONVENIENT AND PREFERRED VALUES

Several mathematical concepts can be applied during metric conversion to obtain convenient or preferred values. These concepts are discussed in detail in NBS Technical Note 990, "The Selection of Preferred Metric Values for Design and Construction."

The convenient numbers concept is based on preferences for numbers that are multiples of 5, 2, and 1 and their powers to 10 in descending order (Table 3.1). The preferences can be applied to establish a succession of convenient number preferences, with less and less rounding from the exact equivalent. Convenient number preferences for a number, such as 67.413, are shown in Table 3.2.

The decision as to which preference to use must be based on considerations relative to the quantity being converted and the degree of precision considered necessary.

SERIES OF VALUES

Although convenient number preferences are most suitable for the conversion of individual values, additional considerations are necessary when a series of values is under examination, such as in a range of products or properties.

Arithmetic series proceed in equal increments, such as 1, 2, 3, 4, 5, or 2, 4, 6, 8, 10. This concept is applicable to addition or subtraction from a constant base value, and numbers in the series may be selected from convenient numbers, described earlier.

Geometric series proceed by multiplying the previous numbers by a constant factor or ratio. An example is the progression of integral powers of 2, or doubling series 1, 2, 4, 8, 16, 32, etc. Geometric series are useful where this type of regularity is appropriate, such as areas, volumes, forces, pressures or stresses, powers, concentrations, flow rates, or speeds. Note that for cross-sectional area a preferred number series may be better.

At the international level the International Organization for Standardization (ISO) has issued standards for geometric number series relating to the decimal system. These *ISO Preferred Number Series* have many applications in a metric measurement environment, for example, for cross-sectional areas or certain properties of materials. They are already in common use in photography. Series

Table 3.1 Convenient Number Preferences Based on Whole Multiples (*n*) of Numbers Shown in the Matrix

| Preference | Numerical Range | | | | |
	0.1–1.0	1.0–10	10–100	100–1000	1000–10 000
1	$n \times 0.5$	5	50	500	5000
2	$n \times 0.2$	2	20	200	2000
3	$n \times 0.1$	1	10	100	1000
4	$n \times 0.05$	0.5	5	50	500
5	$n \times 0.02$	0.2	2	20	200
6	$n \times 0.01$	0.1	1	10	100
7	$n \times$ —	—	—	5	50

Table 3.2 Convenient Number Preference for Rounding of a Value (67.413)

Preference	Numerical Range 10–100	Rounded Figure	Percent of Change
1	$n \times 50$	50	−25.83
2	$n \times 20$	60	−11.00
3	$n \times 10$	70	+ 3.84
4	$n \times 5$	65	− 3.58
5	$n \times 2$	66	− 2.10
6	$n \times 1$	67	− 0.61

can have 5, 10, 20, or 40 intervals between successive powers of 10; for example, the ISO R-10 series in the range 100 to 1000 has the following terms: 100, 125, 160, 250, 315, 400, 500, 630, 800, 1000. Note that the factor between successive terms is 0.25, or 25%. A full discussion of the concepts is contained in NBS Technical Note 990.

SI UNITS FOR BUILDING

Metric (SI) units for use in architecture and typical applications for specific units are contained in the American Society for Testing and Materials Standard ANSI/ASTM E621-78, "Standard Practice for the Use of Metric (SI) Units in Building Design and Construction," based on NBS Technical Note 938 with a similar title. The differences between the two documents are minor, except that NBS Technical Note 938 uses the American spelling "meter" and "liter," which has also been adopted in this *Guide*, whereas ASTM uses the international English spelling "metre" and "litre."

Precise conversion factors have been included in this chapter to assist in the first step of conversion activity, the establishment of exact equivalents. But rounding is necessary to avoid meaningless precision. For example, in the general measurement of length in building design, production, or construction, whole millimeters (mm) only are used. In many applications, specification to the nearest 10 mm is all that is warranted, such as in footings, so that conversions to a number of decimal places are not needed.

MEASUREMENT OF LENGTH

The SI base unit of length is the meter. Decimal fractions or multiples of the base unit can be expressed with prefixed units to retain numerical simplicity; for example, 0.025 m can be shown as 25 mm, and 147 500 m as 147.5 km.

All activities in the construction industry, from precision measurement of coating thicknesses to specification of long travel distances, can be expressed with just four units (Table 3.3). In the interest of clarity, it is wise to avoid prefixes not specifically recommended for construction.

The general unit for dimensioning buildings, components, and tolerances is the millimeter (mm). Dimensions up to 32'-9½" can be expressed by a simple four-digit number in millimeters; similarly, dimensions up to 328'-1", by a

Table 3.3 Common SI Units for Length as Used in Construction[a]

Unit Name	Symbol	Comment	Computer Symbol
meter	m	also spelled "metre"	M
millimeter	mm	0.001 m	MM
kilometer	km	1000 m	KM
micrometer	μm	0.000 001 m	UM

[a]The centimeter is not recommended for construction.

five-digit number. Consistently using just one measurement unit instead of feet, inches, and different common fractions of inches ($\frac{1}{2}$, $\frac{1}{4}$, $\frac{1}{8}$, $\frac{1}{16}$, etc.) greatly facilitates calculations and measurements and provides more speed and accuracy in documentation and laying-out.

Use of the meter (m) is limited to large dimensions, such as site distances, overall dimensions, and levels. Meters are also used in engineering computations, estimating, and land surveying. The kilometer (km) is used for transportation and in surveying and mapping only. The micrometer (μm) occurs only in precision measurement, such as coating thickness.

The recommended linear basic module for metric construction is 100 mm. Chapter 6 provides details on the application of this module in dimensional coordination. The metric module, which is in worldwide use, is very close to the traditional 4 in (101.6 mm) module generally used for light construction.

Scales of drawing relate to units of length. Meters should be used on all drawings with scale ratios between 1:200 and 1:2000; millimeters, on drawings with scale ratios between 1:1 and 1:200.

Conversion factors for length are shown below:

Customary to Metric

1 mile (mi) = 1.609 344 kilometers (km)
(international)
1 chain   = 20.1168 meters (m)
1 yard (yd) = 0.9144 meter
1 foot (ft) = 0.3048 meter
            = 304.8 millimeters (mm)
1 inch (in) = 25.4 millimeters

Notes 1 U.S. survey foot = 0.304 800 6 meter. All conversion factors, except that for chain, are exact.

Metric to Customary

1 meter   = 3.280 84 feet or 1.093 61 yards
1 millimeter   = 0.039 370 1 inch
1 kilometer   = 0.621 371 mile or 49.709 6 chains
1 micrometer (μm) = 0.000 039 37 inch or 0.039 37 mil

MEASUREMENT OF AREA

There is no SI unit base for area. Rather, area units are derived from units for length, as follows (Table 3.4).

At times, area is expressed by linear dimensions such as 40 mm × 90 mm, 300 × 600. Normally the width is written first, and the depth or height second.

The square centimeter is not recommended for construction. Such measurements may be converted to square millimeters (1 cm² = 100 mm²) or to square meters (1 cm² = 10^{-4} m² = 0.0001 m²).

Table 3.4 Area Units Derived from Units for Length

Unit Name	Symbol	Comment
square meter	m²	1 m² = 10^6 mm²
square millimeter	mm²	
square kilometer	km²	for land areas only
hectare[a]	ha	1 ha = 10 000 m²

[a]The hectare, although not an SI unit, is acceptable for use with SI in the surface measurement of land and water areas only.

Conversion factors for area are shown below:

Customary to Metric

1 square mile (mi²)	= 2.590 00 square kilometers (km²)
(U.S. statute)	
1 acre	= 0.040 468 7 hectare (ha)
	= 4046.87 square meters (m²)
1 square yard (yd²)	= 0.836 127 square meter
1 square foot (ft²)	= 0.092 903 square meter
1 square inch (in²)	= 645.16 square millimeters (mm²)

Note Conversion factor for square inch (in²) is exact.

Metric to Customary

1 square kilometer	= 0.386 101 square mile
	(U.S. statute)
1 hectare	= 2.471 04 acres
1 square meter	= 10.7639 square feet
	= 1.195 99 square yards
1 square millimeter	= 0.001 550 square inch

There is no SI base unit for volume; units are derived from units for length, by cubing. The liter (L) is a special name for a volume of one thousandth of a cubic meter (m³)—equal to the nonpreferred cubic decimeter (dm³)—and will be in common use for the description of volumes of fluids or capacities (Table 3.5).

In construction the cubic meter (m³) is used for volume and capacity of large quantities of earth, concrete, sand, and so on. It is preferred for all engineering purposes.

The section modulus is also expressed as a unit of length to the third power (m³ and mm³).

MEASUREMENT OF VOLUME AND SECTION MODULUS

Table 3.5   Units for Volume Derived from Units for Length

Unit Name	Symbol	Comment
cubic meter	m³	1 m³ = 1000 L
cubic millimeter	mm³	
liter	L	volume of fluids
milliliter	mL	1 mL = 1 cm³
cubic centimeter	cm³	1 cm³ = 1000 mm³

Conversion factors for volume and section modulus, and for liquid capacity, are listed below:

Volume and Modulus of Section

Customary to Metric

1 acre-foot	= 1233.49 cubic meters (m³)
1 cubic yard (yd³)	= 0.764 555 cubic meter
100 board-feet (board-ft)	= 0.235 974 cubic meter
1 cubic foot (ft³)	= 0.028 316 8 cubic meter (m³)
	= 28.316 85 liters (L)
1 cubic inch (in³)	= 16 387.1 cubic millimeters (mm³)
	= 16.2871 milliliters (mL) or cubic centimeters (cm³)

1 cubic meter	$= 0.810\ 709 \times 10^{-3}$ acre-foot
	$= 1.307\ 95$ cubic yards
	$= 35.3147$ cubic feet
	$= 423.776$ board-feet
1 cubic millimeter	$= 61.0237 \times 10^{-6}$ cubic inch

Liquid Volume (Capacity)

Customary to Metric

1 gallon (gal) (U.S. liquid)	$= 3.785\ 41$ liters (L)
1 quart (qt) (U.S. liquid)	$= 946.353$ milliliters (mL)
1 pint (pt) (U.S. liquid)	$= 473.177$ milliliters
1 fluid ounce (fl oz) (U.S.)	$= 29.5737$ milliliters

Note 1 gallon (U.K.) = approx. 1.2 gallons (U.S.).

Metric to Customary

1 liter	$= 0.035\ 314\ 7$ cubic foot (ft³)
	$= 0.264\ 172$ gallon (U.S.)
	$= 1.056\ 69$ quarts (U.S.)
1 milliliter	$= 0.061\ 023\ 7$ cubic inch (in³)

MEASUREMENT OF MASS

The International System of Units, SI, makes a clear distinction between the concepts of mass and force (mass times acceleration). The SI base unit of mass is the kilogram (kg), an original unit in the metric system. Unlike other SI units, the kilogram is based on a prototype and cannot be derived without reference to the International Prototype kilogram maintained under specified conditions at the International Bureau of Weights and Measures (BIPM) near Paris, France.

Force is a derived unit ($kg \cdot m/s^2$) which has been given a distinct name and symbol: newton (N). There is no unit for weight, which is technically a variable force due to gravitational attraction, and hence should always be stated in newtons (see Chapter 4).

The SI units for mass and units for use with SI are given in Table 3.6.

Masses in construction will generally be expressed in kilograms (kg). The kilogram will also be used in derived units, such as mass per unit length (kg/m), mass per unit area (kg/m²), and mass per unit volume or density (kg/m³).

Large masses may be expressed in the non-SI unit metric ton (t), which equals 1000 kg or 1 Mg (megagram).

Small masses for test specimens and laboratory investigations will be expressed in grams (g).

Table 3.6 SI and Other Acceptable Units for Mass

Unit Name	Symbol	Comment
kilogram	kg	most used
gram	g	
metric ton	t	1 t = 1000 kg

Customary to Metric

1 ton (short)	= 0.907 185 metric ton (t)
	= 907.185 kilograms (kg)
1 pound (lb)	= 0.453 592 kilogram
1 ounce (oz)	= 28.3495 grams (g)
1 pennyweight	= 1.555 17 grams

Note   1 long ton (2240 lb) = 1016.05 kilograms or 1.016 05 metric tons.

Metric to Customary

1 kilogram	= 2.204 602 pounds (avoirdupois)
	= 35.2740 ounces (avoirdupois)
1 metric ton	= 1.102 31 tons (short, 2000 lb)
	= 2204.62 pounds
1 gram	= 0.035 274 ounce
	= 0.643 015 pennyweight

MEASUREMENT OF TIME

The SI base unit for time is the second, from which other units of time are derived. In construction measurements, such as flow rates, the use of minutes is not recommended, so that cubic meters per second, liters per second, or cubic meters per hour will normally be used. Time symbols are as follows:

second	s
minute	min
hour	h
day	d
month	
year	a (365 days or 31 536 000 seconds)

For clarity, international recommendations for writing time and dates are as follows:

Time	express by hour/minute/second on a 24-hour day:
	03:20:30
	16:45
Date	express as year/month/day:
	1978-06-30
	1978 06 30 (second preference)
	19780630 (computer entry)

MEASUREMENT OF TEMPERATURE

The SI base unit of temperature is the kelvin, which has its zero point at absolute (zero) temperature. The permitted unit degree Celsius (°C) predates the kelvin and has an identical temperature interval, but 0°C is the freezing point of water. Thus a temperature shown in degrees Celsius plus 273.15 degrees is the same temperature in kelvin. The degree Celsius is in common use for construction, not kelvin. However, in compound units with a temperature component it is more appropriate to use the kelvin (K), such as watt per meter kelvin, W/(m · K).

1 degree Fahrenheit (1°F) = 0.555 556 degree Celsius (°C)
= 5/9 degree Celsius or 5/9 kelvin (K)

Metric to Customary (Temperature Interval)

1 degree Celsius = 1 kelvin
= 1.8 degrees Fahrenheit

Note   The term "centigrade" is not part of SI and should not be used. The correct unit name is degree Celsius.

SI UNITS IN ENGINEERING

CORNELIUS WANDMACHER

Chairman, Engineering Design Subsector
Construction Industries Coordinating Committee
American National Metric Council

The International System of Units (SI) is a logical, evolutionary step toward a significantly improved system of measuring units, which will provide all branches of engineering and science with a much more effective means of exchanging ideas, information, and data.

ENERGY RELATIONSHIP

Of greatest significance in the changeover to SI is the direct, coherent relationship between mechanical, thermal, and electrical energy.

In SI the ''ampere'' is identified as one of seven base units and is defined in terms of force units. Specifically the SI definition says:

The *ampere* (A) (already defined in Chapter 2) is that constant current which, if maintained in two straight, parallel conductors of infinite length and of negligible cross section, placed 1 meter apart in a vacuum, would produce between these conductors a force equal to 2×10^{-7} newton per meter of length. (See Figure 4.1.)

Thus a key, straightforward tie-in between all mechanical and electrical systems is provided since the ''newton,'' the new absolute force unit, is defined as follows:

One *newton* (N) is that force which gives to a mass of 1 kilogram (kg) an acceleration of 1 meter per second squared (m/s²). Hence $1.0 \text{ N} = 1.0 \text{ kg} \cdot \text{m/s}^2$.

Energy in all forms (including work and quantity of heat) may therefore be measured in terms of the ''joule,'' defined as:

One *joule* (J) is the work done when the point of application of a force of 1 newton moves a distance of 1 meter along the line of action of the force. Hence $1.0 \text{ J} = 1.0 \text{ N} \cdot \text{m}$.

Power, the rate of utilization of energy, or the rate of heat transfer, is defined in terms of the ''watt'' in similar manner:

A *watt* (W) is the power which in 1 second gives rise to the energy of 1 joule. Conversely, a joule is a watt-second.

A further step in formulating SI was to take the value of the magnetic constant, the permeability of space, as $\mu = 4\pi \times 10^{-7}$ henry per meter (H/m), thus making

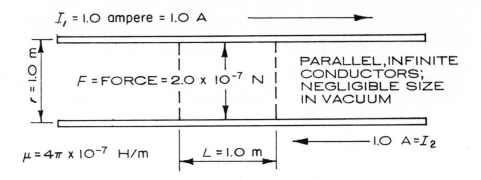

Figure 4.1 Graphic representation of the definition of the ampere. The newton appears as the absolute unit of force.

the electromagnetic part of SI equivalent to the MKSA, or rationalized unit Giorgi system. (See Figure 4.1.)

Since the customary coherent relationships with other electrical quantities will still prevail, the observations made above in respect to work, energy, quantity of heat, and power may be summarized, strictly from a "units" point of view, as follows:

$$N \cdot m = J \quad J/s = W \quad J = W \cdot s \quad W = A \cdot V \quad J = A \cdot V \cdot s$$

MASS

The preferred unit multiples of mass are milligram, gram, kilogram, and megagram (or metric ton), which are written respectively as:

$$mg \quad g \quad kg \quad Mg \text{ (or t)}$$

As previously mentioned, the kilogram (kg) is the SI base unit for mass, but all other units of mass are formed by applying prefixes to "gram." The metric ton (t) appears to be carried forward at this time in deference to widespread common usage. Actually the metric ton is 1000 kg and hence is really 1.0 Mg, a recognition which probably will be achieved generally in the years ahead. Thus in SI use of the term "megagram" (Mg) is preferable. The name "tonne" is *not* recommended for use in the United States.

A valuable aspect of SI is that for all practical purposes 1 cubic meter (1.0 m³) of fresh water has a mass of 1 metric ton (1.0 t), and 1 liter (1.0 L) of fresh water has a mass of 1 kilogram (1.0 kg).

Machines and devices for ascertaining the mass of a body or an amount of material should be calibrated in grams, kilograms, or metric tons, and decimal parts thereof.

Weight is predominantly a concept of the customary "gravitational" system. Since SI is an absolute system dealing with mass and with the forces related to the acceleration of a mass, there is no special name for a unit of weight in SI.

Weight is a particular force due solely to gravitational attraction on a mass and should be viewed as such in the following discussion.

FORCE

Since SI is a coherent system and since the fundamental law of physics ($F \propto ma$) states that force is dependent solely on mass and on acceleration,

$$1.0 \text{ kg accelerated at } 1.0 \text{ m/s}^2 \rightarrow 1.0 \text{ force unit} \rightarrow 1.0 \text{ newton (1.0 N)}.$$

The use of the name "newton" for the unit of force should fix in the mind the full significance of the distinctions between mass and force.

Normally a mass to be supported or moved will be specified or labeled in terms of kilograms (kg), but all forces acting upon a structure of a machine part, either gravitationally or laterally (including wind, sway, and impact), should be specified or determined ultimately in terms of newtons (N). Distributed forces should be stated in terms of newtons per meter (N/m) or newtons per square meter (N/m²), as the case may be. The most useful multiples will probably be kN and MN; occasionally the submultiple mN will be applicable.

Correspondingly, forces or moments, applied by testing machines, dynamometers, or similar devices, should be specified, determined, and/or recorded in terms of newtons or newton meters (N·m), and so on. Deflection calibrations will generally be expressed in terms of millimeters (mm) or mirometers (μm), and angular deformations will be expressed in terms of radians or in decimal degrees.

If a mass is likely to be hoisted at an acceleration of substantial magnitude, it is, of course, essential to determine and state the rating of the equipment in terms of newtons.

UNIT SYSTEMS: A COMPARISON

The technical manner in which mass and force (and thereby "weight") are handled in various unit systems may be summarized as shown in Table 4.1. In this comparison and in all related discussions, the symbol lb denotes mass in the same manner as kg denotes mass, and the symbol lbf denotes force in the same manner as the non-SI unit kilogram-force (kgf)—also called kilopond (kp) in some countries—denotes force.

From Table 4.1 it will be observed that the mass and force quantities in the several systems are related by the following factors:

Based on customary gravitational usage:

Mass: $1.0 \text{ slug} \approx 32.17 \text{ lb} \approx 14.59 \text{ kg} \approx 1.488 \text{ kgf/(m/s}^2)$
Force: $1.0 \text{ lbf} \approx 32.17 \text{ pdl} \approx 4.448 \text{ N} \approx 0.4536 \text{ kgf}$

Based on SI usage:

Mass: $1.0 \text{ kg} \approx 2.205 \text{ lb} \approx 0.068\,52 \text{ slug} \approx 0.1020 \text{ kgf/(m/s}^2)$
Force: $1.0 \text{ N} \approx 7.233 \text{ pdl} \approx 0.2248 \text{ lbf} \approx 0.1020 \text{ kgf}$

The *force* definitions are:

The "newton" is the force required to accelerate 1 kilogram mass at the rate of 1.0 m/s^2.

The "poundal" is the force required to accelerate 1 pound of mass at the rate of 1.0 ft/s^2.

The "pound-force" is the force required to accelerate 1 pound of mass at the rate of 32.1740 ft/s^2.

Table 4.1 Comparison of Unit Systems

Quantity	Mass, Length, Time (absolute)		Force, Length, Time (gravitational)		Customary Combined System
	SI	English	Metric	English	
Mass	kg	lb	kgf/(m/s²)	lbf/(ft/s²) (slug)	lb (alt: lbm)
Force	kg·m/s² N (newton)	lb·ft/s² pdl (poundal)	kgf (alt: kp)	lbf	lbf
Coherence factor	1.0	1.0	1.0	1.0	1/32.17

The related definitions for the *derived mass* units are:

The "slug" is that mass which, when acted upon by 1 pound-force, will be accelerated at the rate of 1.0 ft/s².

The gravitational metric unit of mass is that unit of mass which, when acted upon by 1 kilogram-force, will be accelerated at 1.0 m/s². There seems to be no generally accepted name or symbol for this gravitational unit of mass, except the inference to the kilogram.

The "kilogram" and the "pound" are base units, *not* derived units as are the slug and the gravitational metric unit of mass. Both the kilogram and the pound relate directly to an artifact of mass which, by convention, is regarded as dimensionally independent—thus the name "base unit."

Note It has been customary in traditionally metric countries to use, under the metric gravitational system (sometimes called the metric technical system), the kilogram-force (kgf), but this unit is not a part of SI and is therefore being abandoned in countries moving to SI. A recent decision by the European Economic Community removes the legal status of the kilogram-force, thereby making it unacceptable in EEC specifications and standards.

A graphic representation of the key relationships between mass, force, and weight in SI is given in Figure 4.2.

EXAMPLES OF MASS AND FORCE

Example 1 A block with a mass of 1.0 kg resting on a flat surface is prevented from accelerating in free fall toward the center of the earth at 9.8 m/s² by its support. In effect we have imposed an acceleration upward of 9.8 m/s². The mass of 1.0 kg is accelerated at 9.8 m/s² by its support, which results in a reaction force of 9.8 N. $F = m \cdot a$; 9.8 N = 1.0 kg × 9.8 m/s². Simply stated, the 1.0 kg of mass weighs 9.8 N, but the description above will serve for the following examples.

Example 2 The same 1.0 kg block on a smooth, frictionless surface is accelerated horizontally at 4 m/s². The force required is 4 m/s² × 1 kg = 4 N.

Example 3 We now hang the 1.0 kg block from a cable. In its static condition the cable imposes a force of 9.8 N by preventing the block from falling freely. It is in effect being accelerated upward at 9.8 m/s², or, again, it weighs 9.8 N. If we increase the acceleration upward by lifting the block up at an acceleration of 3 m/s², we have a resultant acceleration of 9.8 + 3 = 12.8 m/s². The force on the cable will now be 12.8 m/s² × 1.0 kg = 12.8 N.

Example 4 If we drop the 1.0 kg mass by lowering the cable at the rate of 3 m/s², the force on the cable is reduced to 6.8 N, that is (9.8 − 3) m/s² × 1.0 kg = 6.8 N.

Example 5 If the 1.0 kg block shown in Examples 1 and 2 is placed on an inclined plane with a 30° angle (slope of $1 : \sqrt{3}$), the 9.8 N gravitational force resolves into two components: 4.9 N along the sloping plane, and 8.5 N normal to the smooth surface. In addition, the force required to achieve 5.0 m/s² acceleration along the plane is 5.0 N; thus a total force of 4.9 N + 5.0 N = 9.9 N is required to achieve the upward sliding motion shown.

Example 6 A 1.0 kg disk 1.2 m in diameter being rotated on an axis at the center of the disk at an acceleration of 5 rad/s² would require a force couple

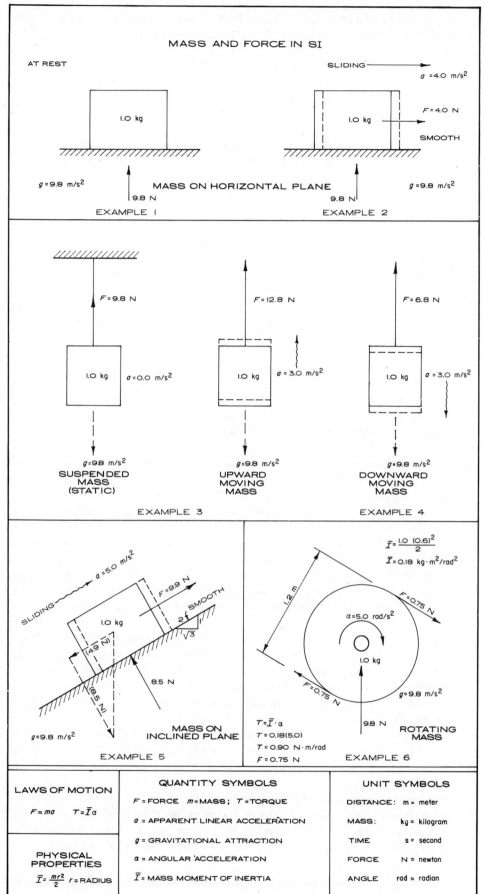

Figure 4.2 Graphic representation of typical examples of mass and force.

tangent to the disk of 0.75 N × 1.2 m. In other words, the torque T is equal to the mass moment of inertia $\bar{I}$ times the angular acceleration α.

$$\bar{I} = m \cdot r^2/2 = 1.0 \text{ kg } (0.6 \text{ m})^2/2 = 0.18 \text{ kg} \cdot \text{m}^2$$
$$T = \bar{I} \cdot \alpha = 0.18 \text{ kg} \cdot \text{m}^2 \times 5 \text{ rad/s}^2 = 0.90 \text{ kg} \cdot \text{m}^2/\text{s}^2 = 0.90 \text{ N} \cdot \text{m}$$
$$T = F \cdot d; \quad 0.90 \text{ N} \cdot \text{m} = F \times 1.2 \text{ m}$$
$$F = 0.75 \text{ N}$$

MOMENT (BENDING, TORSIONAL)

Bending moment and torsional moment are concepts of statics. Both involve the product of a force and a perpendicular distance, the latter being termed the moment arm. Thus the primary SI unit is the newton meter, which may be symbolized as $N \cdot m$, $kN \cdot m$, and so on.

Note the word order used above, giving first emphasis to the force in newtons. This is recommended to indicate that the symbol should be written as $N \cdot m$ and *not* mN, to eliminate any chance of confusion with a prefixed unit notation which would be read as "millinewton."

Also it should be noted that bending moment ($N \cdot m$) is a product of a force and a distance *perpendicular* to its line of action. Hence the units of static moment should *never* in themselves be further interpreted into "joules," which pertain only to work and energy considerations. Nor should torsional moment be stated in joules unless rotation occurs.

TORQUE

When rotation occurs as a result of an applied moment, the condition is one requiring the application of the principles of dynamics. In such cases the key factor is torque, which is based on a product of force and distance moved along the line of action of the force. This product is expressed in newton-meters per radian ($N \cdot m/\text{rad}$),* which is equal to joules per radian (J/rad).

PRESSURE, STRESS, ELASTIC MODULUS

These may be stated directly either in pascals (Pa) or in newtons per square meter (N/m^2). Common multiples are kPa, MPa, GPa or kN/m^2, MN/m^2, GN/m^2. In appraising the current use of the "pascal" it is essential to observe that this important new SI unit was adopted by the General Conference on Weights and Measures (CGPM) as recently as 1971.

It should be noted also that MN/m^2 is equal to N/mm^2. The latter form is sometimes used for stress. However, it is generally preferred practice to use the prefix in the numerator only; hence the forms MPa and MN/m^2 are recommended. For a comparative analysis of the physical properties of representative construction materials, stated in both inch-pound units and SI units, see Table 4.2.

Another unit of pressure measurement is the "bar," which is 10^5 Pa. This has been favored in some earlier scientific and metric engineering activities, such as meteorology, fluid power, and thermodynamics, because it approximates 1 atm. As will be noted, the bar is 100 kPa and 0.1 MPa, which is a departure from the 10^3, 10^6, 10^9 ternary intervals usually preferred. The millibar, 10^2 Pa, is a further aberration of preferred usage. Since the use of the bar appears *not* to be expanding in other metric countries, there is little point in encouraging additional use here. The kPa and MPa are much preferred wherever SI is being introduced.

MOMENT OF INERTIA

The mass moment of intertia of any body relating to rotation about a given axis is the second moment of the particles of that mass about the given axis and as such is given generally in kilogram-square meters per radian squared ($kg \cdot m^2/\text{rad}^2$).* The radius of gyration is normally given in meters per radian (m/rad).*

---

*The radian may be omitted where only complete revolutions are of concern or where dynamic conditions are equated instantaneously with static conditions.

Table 4.2 Comparative Analysis of Some Approximate Physical Properties[a] for Representative Engineering Materials
Note Values given below are *rounded* in each system and are *not* direct conversions.

| | In Terms of U.S. Customary Units | | | | | | | In Terms of Preferred SI Units | | | | | | |
Coefficient of Linear Expansion α (10⁻⁶ in/in °F)	Allowable Stresses (lbf/in² × 10³)			Elastic Modulus (lbf/in² × 10⁶)		Weight Density w (lb/ft³)	Material	Mass Density ρ (kg/m³)	Elastic Modulus (GPa = GN/m²)		Allowable Stresses (MPa = MN/m²)			Coefficient of Linear Expansion a μm/(m·K)
	σ_f^b	σ_c^c	τ_s	E	G				E	G	σ_f^b	σ_c^c	τ_s	
6.5	20	20	10	30	12	490	Mild steel	7850	200	80	140	140	70	11.7
6.9	24	24	15	30	12	490	High-strength steel	7850	200	80	165	165	100	12.4
6.0	3	10	2	15	6	450	Cast iron	7200	100	40	20	70	15	10.8
9.3	8	8	5	17	6.4	560	Copper	8960	120	45	55	55	35	16.7
10.4	12	8	6	13	5	520	Brass	8300	90	35	80	55	40	18.7
13.0	16	15	8	10.3	4	170	Aluminum	2700	70	27	110	100	55	23.4
							Timber							
1.7	1.3	0.8	0.05	1.2	—	27	Softwood	430	9	—	9.6	5.5	0.3	3.1
2.5	1.8	1.2	0.10	1.6	—	48	Hardwood	770	12	—	12.4	8.3	0.7	4.5
6.2	1.2	1.0	0.15	2.5	—	150	Concrete (reinf.)	2400	17	—	8.3	6.9	1.0	11.2
—	—	0.03	—	—	—	105	Soil	1680	—	—	—	0.2	—	—
4.4	—	0.3	—	—	—	165	Rock	2640	—	—	—	2.0	—	7.9
—	—	—	—	—	—	62.4	Water	1000	—	—	—	—	—	

[a]For use *only* for comparing representative values in the respective unit systems; *not* intended for design. For design purposes see other standard references such as ANSI, AISC, ACI, and IFI.
[b]Extreme fiber bending.
[c]Short compression block; in timber, parallel to grain.

Second moment of area (I) and section modulus (S) of the cross section of structural sections or machine parts are usually preferred in terms of 10^6 mm⁴ and 10^3 mm³, respectively, for consistency with other dimensions of sections, which usually will be given in millimeters. (For illustrative data on physical properties of rolled steel structural shapes and conversion factors see Tables 4.2, 4.3, 4.4, and 4.7.)

Presentation Table of Structural Steel Design Properties. The structural steel industry and the American Institute of Steel Construction (AISC) have not set any target dates for change to SI. However, committees have been working on the subject so that the conversion can be implemented in a short period of time after a date is established. The American Iron and Steel Institute has published an SI Metric Practice Guide for the industry. In all probability the structural shapes will be presented in an SI Manual of Steel Construction in a form similar to that shown in Tables 4.3 and 4.4.

Building Codes Listing of Floor Loads. Allowable floor loads can be posted in terms of mass in either kilograms or kilograms per square meter. Building codes can specify these floor loads in either way, but it will probably be more convenient to show them in force units of kilonewtons and kilopascals instead of mass units.

Example 7: Beam Design Problem Select a beam to span 6 m carrying a uniformly distributed mass of 800 kg/m². The width of the contributing mass distribution is 2 m.

Solution

$$M = \frac{1}{8}\left(15.7\,\frac{kN}{m}\right)(6\ m)^2 = 70.6\ kN\cdot m$$

$$S_x = \frac{70.6 \times 10^3\ N\cdot m}{230 \times 10^6\ N/m^2} = 307 \times 10^3\ mm^3$$

Select W310 × 28.3 with $S_x = 349 \times 10^3$ mm³.

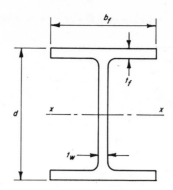

Table 4.3 Wide-Flange Beams: Dimensions and Properties[a]

Designation of Nominal Size (mm)	Mass (kg/m)	Area of Section A (mm²)	Depth of Section d (mm)	Flange Width b_f (mm)	Flange Thickness t_f (mm)	Web Thickness t_w (mm)	About X-X Second Moment of Area I (10⁶ mm⁴)	About X-X Section Modulus S (10³ mm³)	About X-X Radius of Gyration r (mm)
W310 × 44.5	44.5	5670	313	166	11.2	6.6	99.1	633	132
× 38.7	38.7	4940	310	165	9.7	5.8	84.9	547	131
× 28.3	28.3	3590	309	102	8.9	6.0	54.1	349	122
W250 × 38.5	38.5	4910	262	147	11.2	6.6	59.9	457	110
× 32.7	32.7	4190	258	146	9.1	6.1	49.1	380	108
W200 × 31.3	31.3	3970	210	134	10.2	6.4	31.3	298	88.6
× 26.6	26.6	3390	207	133	8.4	5.8	25.8	249	87.1

[a]The values in this table are direct conversions from the customary units of sections presently rolled (soft conversion).

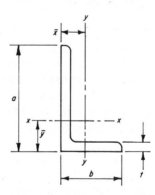

Table 4.4 Unequal Leg Angles: Dimensions and Properties (illustrative)[a]

Size and Thickness $a \times b \times t$ (mm)	Mass (kg/m)	Area A (mm²)	Axis X–X I (10⁶ mm⁴)	Axis X–X S (10³ mm³)	Axis X–X r (mm)	Axis X–X $\overline{y}$ (mm)	Axis Y–Y I (10⁶ mm⁴)	Axis Y–Y S (10³ mm³)	Axis Y–Y r (mm)	Axis Y–Y $\overline{r}$ (mm)
L200 × 100 × 15	33.7	4300	17.58	137.0	64.0	71.6	2.99	38.4	26.4	22.2
× 12	27.3	3480	14.40	110.0	64.3	70.3	2.47	31.3	26.7	21.0
× 10	23.0	2920	12.20	93.2	64.6	69.3	2.10	26.3	26.8	20.1
L100 × 75 × 12	15.4	1970	1.89	28.0	31.0	32.7	0.90	16.5	21.4	20.3
× 10	13.0	1660	1.62	23.8	31.2	31.9	0.78	14.0	21.6	19.5
× 8	10.6	1350	1.33	19.3	31.4	31.0	0.64	11.4	21.8	18.7

[a]The values in this table are metric equivalents of customary sizes with dimensions adjusted to rationalized values (hard conversion).

The problem solution is as simple as that. To elaborate on each step for the purpose of detailing the process, however, the solution is as follows. To determine the force on the beam from this mass, we multiply by the gravitational constant $g = 9.8$ m/s². With $F = mg$, the load per lineal meter of beam is:

$$(800 \text{ kg/m}^2 \times 2 \text{ m}) \, 9.8 \text{ m/s}^2 = 15\,700 \text{ kg/s}^2$$
$$= 15\,700 \text{ N/m} \quad (\text{N} = \text{kg} \cdot \text{m/s}^2)$$
$$= 15.7 \text{ kN/m}$$

Using 350 MPa yield point steel and 230 MPa (MN/m²) allowable stress, we find that the required section modulus is:

$$S_x = \frac{70.6 \text{ kN} \cdot \text{m}}{230 \text{ MN/m}^2}$$
$$= \frac{70.6 \times 10^3 \text{ N} \cdot \text{m}}{230 \times 10^6 \text{ N/m}^2}$$
$$= 0.307 \times 10^{-3} \text{ m}^3$$

To put this into the format of a future steel manual's section property tables, which will probably list section modulus as 10^3 mm³, we perform this operation:

$$0.307 \times 10^{-3} \text{ m}^3 \left(\frac{10^3 \text{ mm}}{\text{m}}\right)^3 = 307 \times 10^3 \text{ mm}^3$$

Referring to our future SI metric steel manual, we select a W310 $\times$ 28.3, which has a section modulus S_x of 349×10^3 mm³. This is a W12 $\times$ 19 in the current AISC manual. We have just described the section as 310 mm nominal beam depth $\times$ 28.3 kg/m mass, instead of 12 in. nominal depth $\times$ 19 lb/ft mass.

ANGULAR MEASURE

The "radian" (rad), although not a base unit, is specifically identified as a "supplementary unit" and as such is the preferred unit for measurement of plane angles. The customary units of degrees, minutes, and seconds of angular measure are considered to be outside SI, but are acceptable where there is a specific practical reason to use them, as in cartography. If degrees are to be used, a statement of parts of degrees in decimals is preferred. The SI unit of solid angle is the "steradian" (sr).

FLUID MECHANICS

Fluid mechanics utilizes the physical concepts of density (mass per unit volume), dynamic viscosity, kinematic viscosity, surface tension, potential energy, and pressure in dealing with the flow of relatively incompressible fluids at constant temperatures. There is a proper SI expression for each of these quantities, derived from base units in accordance with applicable physical relationships.

HEAT TRANSFER IN BUILDINGS

Heat transfer calculations, involving heat loss, heat gain, or thermal insulating properties of materials, will be simplified in SI because of the coherent relationships between units used. Heat transfer units are generally derived from the unit for temperature (kelvin or degree Celsius), the unit for energy and quantity of heat (joule), the unit for heat transfer rate (watt), and the units for time (second), length (meter), area (square meter), and mass (kilogram).

Table 4.5 shows some of the principal units that will be used in heat transfer calculations, and indicates the reduction in the variety of units that will be achieved by going SI.

Table 4.5 Units for Use in Heat Transfer Calculations

Quantity Name	SI Unit	Unit Name	Conversion Factor	
Energy, quantity of heat (E, Q)	J (W·s)	joule	1 Btu (int.)	= 1.055 056 kJ
			1 kWh	= 3.6 MJ
			1 therm	= 105.5056 MJ
Heat flow rate (P, q)	W (J/s)	watt	1 Btu/h	= 0.293 071 W
			1 Btu/s	= 1.055 056 kW
			1 ton (refrig.)	= 3.516 800 kW
Specific energy, calorific value (mass basis)	J/kg	joule per kilogram	1 Btu/lb	= 2.326 kJ/kg
Irradiation, intensity of heat flow, heat loss from surfaces	W/m²	watt per square meter	1 Btu/ft²·h	= 3.152 481 W/m²
			1 W/ft²	= 10.763 91 W/m²
			1 Btu/ft²·s	= 11.348 93 kW/m²
Specific heat capacity (mass basis)	J/(kg·K)	joule per kilogram kelvin	1 Btu/lb·°F	= 4.1868 kJ/(kg·K)
Thermal conductivity (k-value)	W/(m·K)	watt per meter kelvin	1 Btu·in/h·ft²·°F	= 0.144 228 W/(m·K)
			1 Btu·in/s·ft²·°F	= 519.2204 W/(m·K)
			1 Btu/h·ft·°F	= 1.730 73 W/(m·K)
Thermal conductance, coefficient of heat transfer (c, U-value)	W/(m²·K)	watt per square meter kelvin	1 Btu/h·ft²·°F	= 5.678 26 W/(m²·K)
Thermal resistance, thermal insulance (R)	m²·K/W	square meter kelvin per watt	1 °F·h·ft²/Btu	= 0.176 110 m²·K/W

TEMPERATURE

As an absolute system, SI basically refers to the "kelvin" thermodynamic temperature scale with its zero point at the absolute zero value. On this scale either a temperature value or a temperature interval is known as a kelvin (K).

The Celsius temperature scale, for which the zero reference is the freezing point of water, will also be used for ambient temperatures. The kelvin scale uses a temperature interval that is identical to the degree Celsius. Although the Celsius temperature scale was previously referred to in the United States as "centigrade," this name should no longer be used.

$$°C = 5/9(°F - 32) \qquad °F = (9/5 \cdot °C) + 32$$
$$K = °C + 273.15 \qquad °R = °F + 459.67$$

Conversion of Temperature Tolerance Requirements

Tolerance (°F)	±1	±2	±5	±10	±15	±20	±25
Tolerance (K or °C)	±0.5	±1	±3	± 6	± 8	±11	±14

For a comparison of temperature scales see Figure 4.3.

Figure 4.3 Temperature conversion via single-line graphic representation.

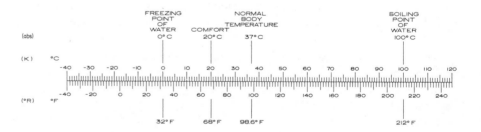

TIME

The SI base unit of time is the "second" (s), which is preferred in most technical expressions and calculations. It is of interest to note that the second is the one SI base unit which for many generations has had complete international acceptance.

Use of the hour (h), as in 5 km/h, and the day (d), as in m³/d, will occur in special cases, but the use of the minute (min) will be de-emphasized in favor of the second (s). For this reason the statement of speeds of rotating machinery will move toward a preference for revolutions per second (r/s), except in the case of slowly rotating machinery, where revolutions per minute (r/min) may continue to be used in order to keep the quantity in integers.

HEATING DEGREE-DAYS

For heating design purposes and the determination of suitable insulation, North America has used the concept of heating degree-days, founded on a base temperature of 65°F (18.33°C).

It is likely that 18°C (64.4°F) will be used as the metric base temperature if the heating degree-day concept is carried over into the metric environment.

COMPARISON OF ALTERNATIVE ENERGY SOURCES

The change to SI will simplify the direct comparison of alternative energy sources, if the quantity of heat (energy) is measured in joules (J). Table 4.6 provides an approximate indication of relative energy values.

Table 4.6   Energy Values for Alternative Energy Sources

Energy Source and Quantity	Value (mega joules, MJ)
1 kg of dry wood (8600 Btu/lb)	20
1 kg of bituminous coal (25 800 000 Btu/ton)	30
1 L of kerosene (135 000 Btu/gal)	37.6
1 L of crude oil (5 800 000 Btu/barrel)	38.5
1 m³ of natural gas (1050 Btu/ft³)	39
1 kWh of electricity	3.6
1 therm (100,000 Btu)	105.5

THERMAL CONDUCTIVITY

The thermal conductivity, or k-value, of a material is defined as the amount of heat energy conducted through a unit area of unit thickness in unit time with unit temperature difference between the two faces. In SI the unit $W/(m \cdot K)$ replaces $Btu \cdot in/h \cdot ft^2 \cdot °F$, but if unit time is considered useful, the alternative expression is $J/(s \cdot m \cdot K)$, because 1 W = 1 J/s. Unit thickness has been canceled out against unit area; otherwise the expression would be $J \cdot m/(s \cdot m^2 \cdot K)$, which directly resembles the customary expression in terms of constituent units.

OVERALL HEAT TRANSFER

Conductivity generally increases with the level of absolute temperature. Some typical thermal conductivities (k-values) at 300 K are:

Material or Substance	$k = W/(m \cdot K)$
Copper	386
Aluminum	202
Steel	55
Concrete	0.9–1.4
Glass	0.8–1.1
Brick	0.4–0.7
Water	0.614
Mineral wool	0.04
Air	0.0262

In heat transfer through a composite element, such as a building wall, a sequence of conduction and convection coefficients may be involved. As in other "series type" problems the approach to determining the combined or "overall" coefficient U is based on the sum of the resistances, which is the sum of the reciprocals of the conductances in the path of the heat transfer.

The following definitions can be used to identify the coefficients:

$$K = \text{thermal conductance;} \qquad K = \frac{kA}{L} \frac{W}{m \cdot K} \times \frac{m^2}{m} = W/K$$

$$R = \text{thermal resistance;} \qquad R = \frac{L}{kA} \frac{m \cdot K}{W} \times \frac{m}{m^2} = K/W$$

Frequently, the above factors may be stated in terms of unit areas. Any data taken from reference tables should be checked carefully.

The overall heat transfer relationship can be stated as

$$q = U \cdot A \cdot \Delta T$$

where q = heat transfer rate   W (= J/s)
     A = cross-sectional area of heat transfer path m^2
    ΔT = overall temperature differential   K
     U = overall heat transfer coefficient $W/(m \cdot K)$

To determine U it is often necessary to use the relationship:

$$\frac{1}{U} = R_1 + R_2 + R_3, \text{ etc.;} \qquad \frac{1}{U} = R_T$$

Alternatively, this may be stated as:

$$R_T = \frac{1}{h_i} + \frac{L_2}{k_2} + \frac{L_3}{k_3} + \frac{L_4}{k_4} + \frac{1}{h_e}$$

Example 8: Calculation of Heat Loss Through a Wall   An exterior building wall consists of 100 mm of brick, 200 mm of dense concrete, and 20 mm of gypsum plaster, for which the thermal conductivities are, respectively, $k = 0.50$, 1.50, and 1.20 $W/(m \cdot K)$. The surface heat transfer (film) coefficients are as follows: (interior) $h_i = 8.1$ and (exterior) $h_e = 19.0$ $W/(m^2 \cdot K)$. What is the heat loss through a 2400 mm (2.4 m) by 6000 mm (6.0 m) panel of this wall when there is a temperature difference of 30°C (30 K)?

Computation of thermal resistance:

$$R_T = \frac{1}{8.1} + \frac{0.100}{0.50} + \frac{0.200}{1.50} + \frac{0.020}{1.20} + \frac{1}{19.0} = 0.5261 \ m^2 \cdot K/W$$

$$U = \frac{1}{R_T}; \qquad U = 1.901 \ W/(m^2 \cdot K)$$

$$q = U \cdot A \cdot \Delta T$$

$$q = 1.901(2.4 \times 6.0)30 = 821 \ W = 821 \ J/s$$

ACOUSTICS   SI units have been applied in acoustics to define frequency (hertz), sound power (watt), sound intensity (watt per square meter), and sound pressure level (pascal).

The reference quantities for the dimensionless logarithmic unit decibel (dB) are also expressed in SI units.

(a) Sound power reference quantity: 1 pW = 10^{-12} W

$$\therefore \text{Sound power level (dB)} = 10 \log_{10} \frac{\text{actual power (W)}}{10^{-12}}$$

(b) Sound intensity reference quantity: 1 pW/m² = 10^{-12} W/m²

$$\therefore \text{ Sound intensity level (dB)} = 10 \log_{10} \frac{\text{actual intensity (W/m}^2)}{10^{-12}}$$

(c) Sound pressure reference quantity: 20 μPa = $2 \times 20 \times 10^6$ Pa

$$\therefore \text{ Sound pressure level (dB)} = 20 \log_{10} \frac{\text{actual pressure (Pa)}}{20 \times 10^6}$$

ELECTRICITY AND MAGNETISM

Electrical engineering, for many years, has used metric (SI) units as practical electrical units. These units are all coherent in that they are formed directly from SI base and derived units on a unity (one-to-one) basis, as shown in Figure 2.1.

The only changes involve the use of the term "siemens" (S) for electrical conductance, instead of the previous name "mho," and the replacement of the cycle per second with the SI unit hertz (Hz).

The kilowatt-hour (kWh) is not an SI unit but will probably be retained for the measurement of electrical energy consumption because of its long history and extensive use. The recalibration of existing electricity meters from kilowatt-hours to megajoules (MJ), on the basis of 1 kWh = 3.6 MJ, hardly seems justified at this time. However, the kilowatt-hour should not be introduced into new areas.

Table 4.7 shows the principal units for electricity and magnetism and their derivation.

ILLUMINATION ENGINEERING

The SI units for luminous intensity, the candela (cd), and for luminous flux, the lumen (lm), are already in general use in the United States.

Illuminance (luminous flux per unit area) will be expressed in the derived SI unit lux (lx), which is a special name for the lumen per square meter (lm/m²). The lux (lx) and kilolux (klx) replace the footcandle, which is also known as the lumen per square foot.

Similarly, the SI unit of luminance, the candela per square meter (cd/m²), replaces the candela per square foot, the lambert, and the footlambert.

Conversion factors are:

1 lx	= 0.092 903 footcandle	1 footcandle	= 10.7639 lx
1 klx	= 92.903 footcandles		
1 cd/m²	= 0.092 903 cd/ft²	1 cd/ft²	= 10.7639 cd/m²
	= 0.291 964 footlambert	1 footlambert	= 3.426 259 cd/m²

Table 4.7 Units for Electricity and Magnetism

Quantity	Unit Name	Symbol	Derivation	Remarks
Electric current	ampere	A		SI base unit
Current density	ampere per square meter	A/m²		
Magnetic field strength	ampere per meter	A/m		
Electric charge quantity of electricity	coulomb	C	(A·s)	
Electric charge density	coulomb per cubic meter	C/m³		
Electric potential, electromotive force	volt	V	(W/A)	
Electric field strength	volt per meter	V/m		1 V/m = 1 N/C
Electric capacitance	farad	F	(C/V)	
Permittivity	farad per meter	F/m		
Electric resistance	ohm	Ω	(V/A)	
Electric conductance	siemens	S	(A/V)	Replaces "mho"; also equals $1/\Omega$
Electric power	watt	W	(V·A)	Also equals J/s
Magnetic flux	weber	Wb	(V·s)	
Magnetic flux density	tesla	T	(Wb/m²)	1 T = 1 V·s/m²
Inductance	henry	H	(Wb/A)	1 H = 1 V·s/A
Permeability	henry per meter	H/m		

ABANDONED UNITS

For various reasons many derived and specialized units will fall into disuse as the changeover to SI progresses. Some, like British thermal unit (Btu) and horsepower (hp), will be dropped because they are based on the inch-pound (English) system.

But many former metric units, of the c.g.s. variety, are no longer recommended. These include the erg, dyne, poise, stokes, gauss, oersted, maxwell, stilb, and phot. In addition a number of traditional metric units are outside SI, and their use is deprecated. These include the kilogram-force, calorie, micron, torr, fermi, metric carat, stere, and gamma.

REPLACING ACRONYMS WITH SI UNIT SYMBOLS

With the increased emphasis on internationally recognized unit symbols in SI and an official statement of preferred style of usage, the custom of coining acronyms to describe compound units is unnecessary and is disapproved. This fact is apparent when recommended SI usage is compared, as in the following examples, with customary counterparts: km/h, *not* mph; m³/s or L/s, *not* gpm; J, *not* Btu or therm; A, *not* amp; Pa, *not* psi.

SIGNIFICANT DIGITS

When numerical conversions are to be made, it is important to keep in mind the all-too-frequently neglected principles of "significant digits."

In general, the result of any multiplication, division, addition, or subtraction cannot be given in more significant digits than are present in any one component of the *original data*. This condition pertains regardless of the number of decimal places in which a conversion factor is given.

In reference tables conversion factors should be stated to a substantial number of decimal places to cover a wide range of uses. It is the responsibility of the user to interpret the resultant decimal number to the extent applicable.

The following example illustrates this point briefly, showing that the rule about significant digits works both ways—from SI to customary units, and from customary to SI.

Question   What is the equivalent of 3 miles in terms of kilometers?

Conversion Factor	Direct Multiplication	Significant Equivalent
miles to kilometers = 1.609	3 mi = 4.827 km	3 mi ≈ 5 km
Or, in reverse form:		
kilometers to miles = 0.6214	5 km = 3.107 mi	5 km ≈ 3 mi

SINGLE-LINE, DUAL-SCALE CHARTS

Conversions also can be interpreted on a single-line, dual-scale, graphical representation.

An important advantage of conversion by graphical representation is that it keeps the user mindful of significant digits. Any chart scale should be selected initially on the basis of the significant digits in the original data and the anticipated results. No readings beyond those reasonably available by normal interpolation from a chart should be considered significant.

ROUNDING OF NUMBERS

The utmost discretion in rounding is essential, since in the changeover from one measuring system to another the units dealt with in the two systems are frequently of substantially different size. For example, a quantity rounded to the nearest meter has an implied precision of ±0.5 m, while a quantity rounded to the nearest foot has an implied precision of ±0.5 ft. Obviously the two are quite different. If a quantity in feet (to the nearest foot) is to be converted to meters, any rounding should be to the nearest 0.3 m.

Table 4.8 Key Conversion Factors: SI to U.S. Customary Units[a] (illustrative)

Length[b]			Area			Volume[c]		
mm =	0.039 370	in	mm² =	0.001 550 0	in²	mm³ =	0.000 061 024	in³
m =	3.280 8	ft	m² =	10.764	ft²	m³ =	35.315	ft³
m =	1.093 6	yd	m² =	1.196 0	yd²	m³ =	1.3080	yd³
km =	0.621 37	mi	km² =	0.386 10	mi²	L (liter) =	0.264 17	gal
			ha =	2.471 0	acres	L (liter) =	1.056 7	qt

Mass			Force[d]			Pressure-Stress[e]		
g =	0.035 274	oz	N =	3.597 0	ozf	kPa =	0.145 04	psi
kg =	2.204 6	lb	N =	0.224 81	lbf	kPa =	0.334 56	ft H₂O
kg =	0.068 521	slug	N =	7.233 0	pdl	kPa =	7.500 6	mm Hg
Mg =	1.102 3	tons (short)	N =	0.101 97	kgf	MPa =	0.101 97	kgf/mm²

Moment			Engery-Work-Heat[f]			Power[g]		
N·mm =	0.141 61	in·ozf	J =	0.737 56	ft·lbf	W =	0.737 56	ft·lbf/s
N·m =	8.850 7	in·lbf	kJ =	0.947 82	Btu	W =	3.412 1	Btu/h
N·m =	0.737 56	ft·lbf	kJ =	0.238 85	kcal	kW =	1.341 0	hp
			J =	1.00000	W·s			
			kJ =	0.277 78	W·h			

[a] For SI to U.S. customary units, multiply by factor shown; for U.S. customary to SI units, divide by factor shown. For more complete information on interpretation and use of these conversions factors and for additional significant digits, see ANSI Z 2101 (ASTM E 380, IEEE Std. 268).
[b] The U.S. survey foot is 1200/3937 meter, exactly.
[c] The factors for "gallon" and for "quart" are based on liquid measure.
[d] pdl = poundals, lbf = pound-force, etc.
[e] The factor for "ft H₂O" is 4°C, and that for "mm Hg" is at 0°C.
[f] The factors for "Btu" and "calorie" are based on the International Table.
[g] The factor for "hp" is based on 550 ft·lbf/s.

Another example is the case of allowable stresses. Structural steel computations in customary units are generally considered sufficiently accurate if determined within the nearest 100 psi. Since 1.0 psi is equal to 6.89 kPa, it would be just as acceptable if stresses in SI units were rounded to the nearest 0.7 MPa. A suitable, perhaps slightly conservative approach would be to give allowable stress to the nearest 0.5 MPa.

Decisions on rounding as applied to specified loads, span, or section modulus—once a level of accuracy of three or four significant digits is determined—would be made on the same basis.

In making the changeover to SI, critical decisions about new rounded values will be required for many factors widely used in technical work. In some instances the new rounded value in SI may be closer to the actual value than the present value in customary units. A striking example of this fact is found in the value of the modulus of elasticity of steel:

ROUNDED VALUES

Usually quoted value: $E = 30 \times 10^6$ psi

$$E = \frac{30 \times 10^6 (9.8)144}{2.205(0.3048)^2} = 206.7 \text{ GPa}$$

The unit checkout for this example is as follows:

$$\frac{\text{lb}}{\text{in}^2} \cdot \frac{\text{kg}}{\text{lb}} \cdot \frac{\text{m}}{\text{s}^2} \cdot \frac{\text{ft}^2}{\text{m}^2} \cdot \frac{\text{in}^2}{\text{ft}^2} = \frac{\text{kg}\cdot\text{m}}{\text{m}^2\cdot\text{s}^2} = \frac{\text{N}}{\text{m}^2} = \text{Pa}$$

On this basis the most widely used values will probably be:

(1) $E = 200$ GPa   (29.0×10^6 psi)
(2) $E = 205$ GPa   (29.7×10^6 psi)

both of which are closer to the usual actual value for mild steel.

NUMERICAL CONSTANTS

Many frequently used formulas include numerical constants which are sometimes used without a full appreciation of all the factors they represent. Such constants should always be examined in relation to their origin.

Dimensionally sensitive constants result from any combination of the given units of physical properties of matter involved and/or a variety of given conditions, as shown in the following example.

A device constant such as K in the expression $Q = Kh^{1/2}$, used for determining fluid flow through a calibrated meter, may be found as:

$$K \sim Qh^{-1/2} \qquad K \sim \frac{m^3}{s} \cdot m^{-1/2} \qquad K = \frac{m^{2.5}}{s}$$

NEW FORMS OF FAMILIAR EQUATIONS

In the changeover to SI many customary expressions will take on important new significance. The familiar Bernoulli equation is an example. Although this is an energy equation, it is normally written and used in the form

$$\frac{p}{w} + \frac{V^2}{2g} + z = \text{constant}$$

In this customary framework energy is measured in terms of head. But in SI the Bernoulli equation should be written directly in terms of energy per unit of mass, expressed as joules per kilogram (J/kg):

$$\frac{p}{\rho} + \frac{V^2}{2} + gz = \text{constant}$$

In the use of such expressions and equations for physical phenomena, it is good practice to accompany the numerical solution with a related unit checkout, such as:

$$\left(\frac{N}{m^2} \cdot \frac{m^3}{kg} \right) + \frac{m^2}{s^2} + \left(\frac{m}{s^2} \cdot m \right) = \left(\frac{N \cdot m}{kg} \right) = \frac{J}{kg}$$

which recognizes that the newton (N) is, by definition, kilogram-meters per second squared (kg·m/s²) and that in SI the mass density ρ will be given in terms of kilograms per cubic meter (kg/m³), while all pressures will be in pascals (Pa), which is the special name for newtons per square meter (N/m²).

5

SI UNITS IN SURVEYING

DR. CHARLES A. WHITTEN

Chairman, Survey Sector
American National Metric Council

The surveying profession is very sensitive to the national program for the increasing use of the metric system and the ultimate conversion to it. The services and products of this profession, one of the oldest in human history, are used in some way by everyone. To describe the impact of full conversion to the use of SI in surveying, it is important to consider the effects on each of its five major branches: geodetic, topographic, hydrographic, engineering (or construction), and land surveying.

Geodetic surveys provide the fundamental horizontal and vertical control networks for the entire country. The unit of length for these surveys has always been the meter. Ferdinand R. Hassler, the first Superintendent of the Coast Survey (later the Coast and Geodetic Survey and now the National Ocean Survey), brought an iron meter bar to the United States in 1805, 2 years before the Coast Survey was established. This iron meter bar was one of a group of 16 prepared by a European Committee of Weights and Measures and had been standardized at Paris in 1799 under the direction of Lenoir. This iron bar, identified as the "Committee Meter" or C.M., was the national reference standard until 1890, when two of the then-new International Prototype Meter bars, 90% platinum and 10% iridium, were brought to the U.S. Coast and Geodetic Survey. These bars were transferred to the National Bureau of Standards in 1901 when that Bureau was organized. These prototype bars served as the standard until 1960, when the General Conference on Weights and Measures defined the meter in wavelengths of krypton-86.

It is against this historical background that the technological development of precise measurement of lengths during the last 100 years has taken place. In the nineteenth century, bars 4 or 5 m in length, either compensated for in temperature, or submerged in ice, were used to measure base lines 8 to 10 km in length. Near the end of the nineteenth century, steel tapes were perfected, and early in this century 50 m Invar tapes were first used as standard equipment. In the 1950s electronic distance measuring was introduced. Distances of 40 to 60 km could be measured with uncertainties of only a few millimeters. In this decade near-earth satellites are used to fix earth-centered positions (in three dimensions) with uncertainties on the order of one or two tenths of a meter. Estimates for the next decade are that these uncertainties in three dimensions will be under 20 mm. Then distances or differences of elevation between points 500 or more km apart can be determined to a precision of 4 parts in 10^8.

The geodetic horizontal and vertical networks consist of monumented points spaced 2 to 20 km apart. Factors such as land value and density of population are used in determining the spacing. Rectangular coordinates and elevations

GEODETIC SURVEYING

listed to three decimal places of the meter are available in data banks. At the present time the National Geodetic Survey (NGS) provides state plane coordinates in feet (two decimal places) for the horizontal control points. However, this agency, in cooperation with the other North American geodetic agencies, is establishing a new earth-centered datum with an estimated project completion date of 1983. After that date NGS will provide plane coordinates in meters only.

The use of SI units will have an impact on some of the techniques used for geodetic measurements. The meter, with appropriate decimals, is the fundamental unit for distances, coordinates, and elevations. The millimeter, with appropriate decimals, is the unit for error studies, movement of the earth's crust, structural deformation, and so on. If Invar or steel tapes are used for measuring short distances, the units of tension will be newtons (Figure 5.1). Atmospheric pressure, which heretofore has been expressed in millimeters (or inches) of mercury, will be shown in pascals for the reduction of electronic distance measurements or astronomic position determinations. Temperature will be recorded in degrees Celsius with formulae and correction tables provided as needed. Sexagesimal units (degrees, minutes, and seconds) will continue to be used when measuring angles, bearings, and/or azimuths. The circles of some surveying instruments are divided in grads or gons (hundredth parts of a right angle), but the correlation of longitude with time is lost if these centesimal systems are used. Decimals of degrees (or minutes or seconds) may be used when appropriate.

The measurement of absolute or relative gravity is considered to be a geodetic activity. The gal is a unit which may be used under SI for a limited time. However, geodesists and geophysicists use milligals and microgals when measuring small differences of gravity. The mean value for the acceleration of gravity used for engineering purposes is 9.8 m/s². To meet the needs of those who measure small differences, the term "nanogravimetry" has been proposed, with units of nanometers per second squared (nm/s²). Ten such units are equal to a microgal.

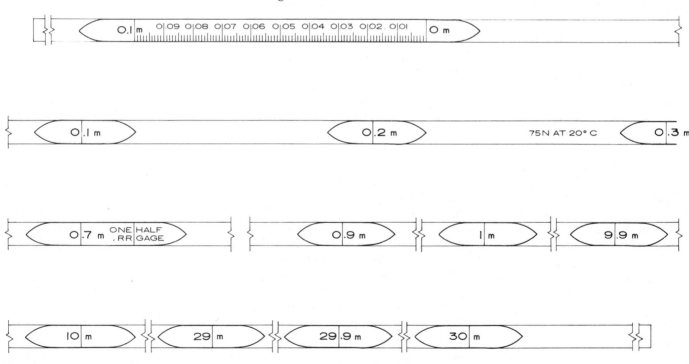

Figure 5.1 Markings on a 30-meter tape with a 1-decimeter "add-increment." The tape is standard at 20 degree Celsius with a tension of 75 newtons.

This branch of surveying uses geodetic positions and elevations to control the compiled maps. Photogrammetric techniques using instruments such as stereocomparators, or applying numerical methods of analytical aerotriangulation are the most efficient means of producing a map which shows the form of the earth's surface, the natural drainage systems, the ground cover—forests, cultivated fields, or deserts—and the location of highways, railroads, pipelines, transmission lines, and other features associated with urban development and economic growth. At the present time English units are used for most topographic surveying and mapping. However, the U.S. Geological Survey (USGS) has issued a policy statement on the preparation of metric base maps for the national mapping program. The USGS plans to use 1:25 000, 1:50 000, 1:100 000, 1:250 000, 1:500 000, and 1:1 000 000 scales in the various topographic series. Exceptions are to be made for Puerto Rico, which will continue on 1:20 000, and those states which desire to have complete coverage at 1:24 000 before converting to the metric system. Most of Alaska is presently mapped at 1:63 360, but the last sizable unmapped area is being mapped at 1:50 000, and the long-range plan calls for converting to 1:50 000 scale throughout the state. For the national mapping program, basic contour intervals will be 1, 2, 5, 10, 50, or 100 m.

Increasing use of the metric system will require greater coordination between map producers and cooperation between these producers and their clients. Topographic map producers include not only the federal agencies such as USGS but also state, county, city, and private groups. The users are primarily engineers and scientists. However, there has been an increasing demand for large-scale topographic maps for recreational purposes.

The greatest opportunity for coordination is in the selection of scales. Ideally, the scales used with SI should follow the rational number series—1, 2, 5—but scales using the 1, 2.5, 5 series also have widespread acceptance. The USGS selected the latter series for the national mapping program. The inch-foot scales used by architects and engineers should be replaced by the 1, 2, 5 series. The following are a few examples:

Inch-Foot Scale	Recommended Scale
1 in = 80 ft	1:100
1 in = 100 ft	1:1000
1 in = 200 ft	1:2000
1 in = 400 ft	1:5000
1 in = 500 ft	1:5000

For very large-scale mapping, such as site plans, contour intervals of 0.1, 0.2, or 0.5 m should be used. The cartographer should select the contour interval appropriate for the scale and the land form to be mapped unless otherwise specified.

Most of the nautical charts for waters bordering the United States are produced by the National Ocean Survey and the Defense Mapping Agency Hydrographic Center. The data used in the compilation of these charts are the records from both old and new hydrographic surveys. The cartographer will find both English and metric units in the records. An effort is always made to obtain the latest shifts of shorelines or changes in depth which may have resulted from storms or normal erosion and accretion. The ultimate use of the metric system will not have a critical impact on the producers of charts. Depths can be shown in meters (or decimal fractions) as easily as in feet or fathoms. Most "large-ship" users of nautical charts are familiar with metric charts because other countries producing such charts use the metric system. Large numbers of the general public use small-craft nautical charts for recreational purposes and will have to become familiar with the metric units. The National Ocean Survey has issued a few metric nautical charts but has not as yet set a schedule for the conversion of all its nautical charts to the metric system.

The selection of scales and contour intervals (if used) for nautical charting is similar to that for topographic mapping.

ENGINEERING SURVEYS

Many of the techniques used by engineers when making construction surveys are similar to those employed by geodesists. Corrections for temperature, atmospheric pressure, and tension of tapes are essentially the same. The SI units should be used.

There may be some concern about the unit of length. It has been recommended that architects and structural engineers use the millimeter as the basic unit. The surveyor, in support of their work, will probably use the meter as the fundamental unit. Divisions on tapes, readout of electronic distance-measuring equipment, level rods, and so on are in meter and decimal fractions. Only when the surveyor is responsible for the site plan would he or she choose to use millimeters.

The specifications for an engineering survey should indicate the number of decimal places of a meter to be used for measurements, for example, three decimals when steel is involved, two decimals for highway, pipeline, or transmission line surveys, and perhaps one decimal for topographic control. There may be superprecise surveys, such as calibration bases, networks for guidance or tracking of missiles, high-speed rail systems, and deformation of structures, for which tenths of millimeters or four decimal places of the meter should be specified.

A casualty of engineering surveying under the use of the metric system may be the practice of "stationing." Most of the logical reasons for using the 100 ft station breakdown, such as the standard 100 ft tape, a practical distance for point delineation of curves, or an acceptable spacing for cross sections, do not apply as well to 100 m stations. Furthermore, under SI usage the recommended division is 1000, and the use of 100 is discouraged. If a breakdown along a survey or project route is useful for construction or maintenance, the kilometer spacing with the third decimal place to show the nearest meter should be adequate for identification.

LAND SURVEYING

The impact of metrication will be greater on land surveying than on any of the branches. Most of the wealth of our country is secured by or invested in property or the improvements upon it. The land surveyor has the responsibility for defining and identifying such properties. The impact will be not on his (or her) engineering ability to measure, his legal skills to trace the ownership of bounding properties, or his analytical ability to correlate conflicting evidence, but on his knowledge of the units of measure used in the original survey, his treatment of existing land records, and his association with his clients.

Fortunately, most of the units used in the original Colonial grants and in the later rectangular public land system are of British origin. Those for length are the foot, the rod (pole, perch, or gad), the chain, and the statute mile. Those for area are the acre, section, and township. The factors for converting these units to metric equivalents are based on the 1866 metric law, which defines 39.37 inches as equal to 1 meter. A point of interest not often seen in print is that the same law lists 3280 feet plus 10 inches as equal to 1 kilometer. This reduces to 39 370 inches equals 1 kilometer, providing evidence of the care and exactness with which these equivalents were defined in 1866. The entire surveying community—all five of its branches—is insistent that the "survey" foot and the associated factors be used whenever converting English (or customary) units to metric equivalents.

Land grants of the French crown were usually described in terms of the arpent.

The arpent is a unit of area, approximately 0.85 acre. If "arpent" is used as a linear term, it refers to the side of a square arpent. The exact value depends on local origin and custom. To determine the proper value to use, local authorities should always be consulted. In Louisiana, Mississippi, Alabama, and northwestern Florida 1 arpent = 0.847 25 acre or 0.342 87 hectare. In Arkansas and Missouri 1 arpent = 0.8507 acre or 0.3443 hectare. Some land records in Michigan also refer to the arpent.

Land records in some of the southwestern states use the vara, an old Spanish unit of length which was approximately 33 inches. As with the use of the arpent, local authorities should be consulted. For example, a Texas law of 1919 defines 36 varas as equal to 100 feet or 1 vara equal to 33.3333 inches, while in California the values range from 32.953 to 33.372 inches.

A favorable aspect of the use of metric units for land surveying will be the uniformity of records, as well as the elimination of conflicting evidence from the past. No one suggests that all old land records be converted to metric units. Only when an old record is used for a resurvey, transfer of ownership, or subdivision will it be necessary to convert the values of length, height, or area to their metric equivalents.

Land surveying in urban areas is subject to zoning bylaws and subdivision regulations. These codes and standards have been developed through the years and are based on integral values such as 2 rod roads, 50 ft streets, 1 chain (66 ft) street rights-of-way, and 10 ft easements. When metric units are introduced, the planners must be sure that the variables in zoning regulations are clearly defined. The amended regulations should recognize 10, 12, or 15 m roads, 20, 22, 25 m streets, 2, 3, or 5 m easements, and so on. "Hard" conversion should be encouraged, and dual dimensioning discouraged—preferably, avoided (Figure 5.2).

Also, in urban areas the concept of rectangular city lots belongs to an earlier era. Curves and cul-de-sacs dominate the new developments. Lot sizes in integral values of meters will be exceptions. The number of decimal places to be shown on plots is a matter of judgment and the associated accuracy of the survey. If the parcel of land is small, such as a city lot, the area should be shown in square meters. The value of the land may determine the number of decimal places. For larger parcels the area should be shown in hectares, the value of the land again being a factor in setting the number of decimal places. Areas of public lands such as national parks or forests may be shown in square kilometers. These three metric units of area—square meter, hectare, and square kilometer—will replace the three English units—square foot, acre, and square mile. Sections and townships should be continued as descriptors of property but more for geographic location or local political subdivision than for definition of area.

With modern instruments the surveyor can determine areas with such accuracy that the qualifying (or quantifying) "more or less," as in the description of a farm as "160 acres more or less," may be dropped. Land use, land management, and land tax groups insist on this higher accuracy, and everyone will benefit. Conversion to metric units will also facilitate the establishment of a modern land data system or, more specifically, a national cadastre.

PROGNOSIS

For surveying and mapping it should be evident that the change to SI units and notation can be made without any great technical difficulty. Surveyors of all branches are skilled in making measurements. Automated systems for transforming survey measurements into a format suitable for computer-controlled plotters reduce this choice of units to a single program step or a console switch. The critical aspect relates to acceptance, not so much by the surveying and mapping professions themselves, as by their clients—the users of their services and products.

Architects, engineers, scientists, and educators generally recognize the merits

LEGAL DESCRIPTION

From the Northeast corner of Section 11, Township 00 South, Range 00 East, 00000 County, Florida, run S 89°12'36"W, along the North line of said Section 11, for 279.54 feet (85.204 meters); thence run S 00241'42"E, for 150.00 feet (45.72 meters) to the POINT OF BEGINNING; thence continue to run S 00°41'42"E, for 472.50 feet (144.018 meters); thence run S 89°12'36"W, parallel with the North line of said Section 11, for 458.23 feet (139.669 meters); thence run N 00°41'42"W, for 472.50 feet (144.018 meters); thence run N 89°12'36"E parallel with the North line of said Section 11, for 458.53 feet (139.669 meters) to the POINT OF BEGINNING; containing 4.970 acres (2.012 hectares).

LEGAL DESCRIPTION

From the Northeast corner of Section 11, Township 00 South, Range 00 East, 00000 County, Florida, run S 89°12'36"W, along the North line of said Section 11, for 85.204 meters; thence run S 00°41'42"E, for 45.72 meters to the POINT OF BEGINNING; thence continue to run S 00°41'42"E, for 144.018 meters; thence run S 89°12'36"W, parallel with the North line of said Section 11, for 139.669 meters; thence run N 00°41'42"W, for 144.018 meters; thence run N 89°12'36"E, parallel with the North line of said Section 11, for 139.669 meters to the POINT OF BEGINNING; containing 2.012 hectares.

Figure 5.2 First-step and final land survey conversions, from the Florida Society of Professional Land Surveyors.

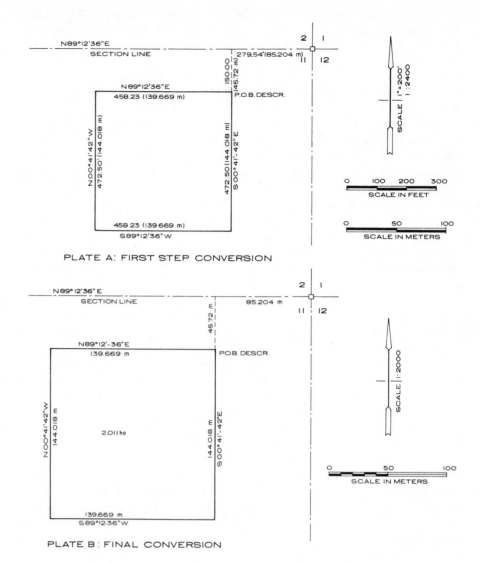

PLATE A: FIRST STEP CONVERSION

PLATE B: FINAL CONVERSION

of the SI system. Lack of recognition, which contributes to lack of acceptance, is more common in other groups. Therefore the professional "measurers" should lengthen and broaden their foresights to extend their confidence in SI to others. Even the philosophy of the familiar advertisement might succeed: "Try it! You'll like it!"

DIMENSIONAL COORDINATION IN BUILDING

HANS J. MILTON, FRAIA

Technical Consultant, Center for Building Technology
National Bureau of Standards
U.S. Department of Commerce

Dimensional coordination is not new to American architects. The original development of the concept is attributed to American industrialist Albert Farwell Bemis. His efforts to improve methods of assembling unrelated materials and components may be traced back to the early 1920s. Bemis outlined the basic principles of a comprehensive system of dimensional coordination for the building industry, based on the 4 in module as a functional unit of size. The term "modular coordination" was adopted for use of the basic module and preferred dimensions in design, production, and construction.

In 1934 the National Bureau of Standards of the U.S. Department of Commerce assumed promotion of these concepts. In 1939 the American Standards Association (now ANSI) organized Project A62, a cooperative study of dimensional coordination. Between 1945 and 1971 a series of standards was issued concerning dimensional coordination.

During this period valuable work was done in dimensional coordination by other groups as well. The Modular Building Standards Association was organized in 1957 by the American Institute of Architects, Associated General Contractors of America, National Association of Home Builders, and the Producers' Council, Inc. Cooperating groups included the Building Research Advisory Board (BRAB), National Academy of Sciences-National Research Council. Development of a manual entitled *Modular Practice* was funded by the Ford Foundation, and the book was published by John Wiley & Sons in 1962. Activity in this area by the National Forest Products Association included the 1962 Unicom Method of House Construction, and the Brick Institute of America (formerly SCPI) developed modular masonry units that met the ANSI standards in this field. Many building products were modified as a result of this widespread effort.

The responsibility for this subject area was then transferred to the American Society for Testing and Materials (ASTM) Committee E-6, Performance of Building Constructions. Subcommittee E-6.62, Coordination of Dimensions for Building Materials and Systems, has the basic responsibility for standards in this field, including the development of metric standards.

On the international scene the post-World War II reconstruction in Europe caused dimensional coordination principles to be widely accepted. The 100 mm basic module for construction had been adopted by 10 countries by 1954. In that year formation of the European Productivity Agency (EPA) strengthened work in

DEVELOPMENT IN THE UNITED STATES

INTERNATIONAL DEVELOPMENTS

modular coordination on an international scale. In 1956 and 1961 two reports dealing with modular coordination in building were published, indicating general agreement on several issues. By 1961 the majority of European countries had adopted the 100 mm module.

On the basis of these agreements, the International Organization for Standardization (ISO) was able to issue draft recommendations proposing this module as the international basic module for use in metric countries. Its adoption spread through eastern Europe, including the Soviet Union, as well as Central and South America and other major nations, such as India and Japan. When Britain and other English speaking nations converted to SI, they introduced dimensional coordination and the use of the 100 mm module in conjunction with the change in the building industry. Since 1973, ISO has issued a range of international standards on modular coordination in building, superseding earlier recommendations. The work in ISO comes under Technical Committee (TC) 59, Building Construction, and its Subcommittee 1, Dimensional Coordination.

The United States can take advantage of the experience gained by other countries that have recently converted to SI units, as well as its own past experiences in applying dimensional coordination concepts to American building needs. The American Institute of Architects' Metric Conversion/Dimensional Coordination Task Force, working with the American National Metric Council and the Center for Building Technology of the National Bureau of Standards, U.S. Department of Commerce, has recommended adoption of dimensional coordination for design and construction to benefit from metric conversion.

DIMENSIONAL OR MODULAR COORDINATION

Some confusion has arisen from the indiscriminate use of the terms "dimensional coordination" and "modular coordination."

Dimensional coordination has been defined (ISO Standard 1791–1973) as follows: "a convention on related sizes for the coordinating dimensions of building components and the buildings incorporating them, for their design, manufacture, and assembly." This definition is followed by a note, explaining that the purposes of dimensional coordination are to "permit the assembly of components on site without cutting or fitting," and "permit the interchangeability of different components."

Modular coordination has been defined as follows: "dimensional coordination employing the basic module or a multimodule." This definition is supplemented by a note, explaining that the purposes of modular coordination are to "reduce the variety of component sizes produced," and "allow the building designer greater flexibility in the arrangement of components."

According to these definitions, modular coordination is a particular form of dimensional coordination, based on the internationally agreed basic module of 100 mm. For all practical purposes these terms should be regarded as interchangeable in the United States, but in the early stages of the conversion to SI it may be well to preface references to the coordination of dimensions with the word "metric" to clearly establish the reference as relating to the basic 100 mm module, rather than the superseded unit of 4 in.

MODULES AND PREFERRED DIMENSIONS

Dimensional (modular) coordination is based on the use of a generally agreed upon and accepted fundamental unit of size—or basic module—and a set of selected multiples and submultiples as theoretically preferred dimensions in building design, production, and construction.

ELEMENTS OF DIMENSIONAL COORDINATION

The essential concepts or elements constituting the basis of dimensional coordination described below are illustrated in Figures 6.1 to 6.12.

100 mm

Figure 6.1 The *basic module* for the construction industry is 100 mm. This is an internationally accepted value. The basic module should apply to building components as well as entire buildings.

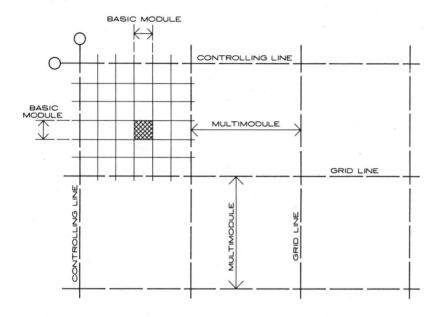

BASIC MODULE

CONTROLLING LINE

BASIC MODULE

MULTIMODULE

GRID LINE

CONTROLLING LINE

MULTIMODULE

GRID LINE

Figure 6.2 *Multimodules,* if carefully selected, can coordinate with the controlling dimensions for a building and limit component sizes to a minimum.

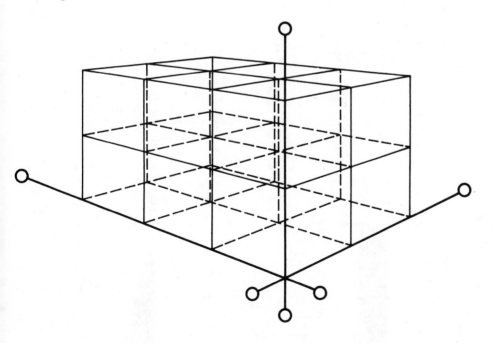

Figure 6.3 In a *dimensional reference system* the reference space grid is made up of the horizontal and vertical planes used to define the locations of points, lines, or surfaces in space.

BASIC MODULAR GRID
(100 mm x 100 mm)

PLANNING GRID

n = SELECTED
WHOLE NUMBER

Figure 6.4 Grids for use with dimensional coordination.

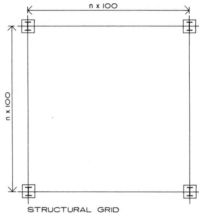

STRUCTURAL GRID

TARTAN GRID: 1:2 RATIO OF
BAND WIDTHS

Figure 6.5 Zones and usable spaces.

Zones are the spaces between controlling planes. They may be occupied but not always filled by one or more components. Finishes should be contained within the zone, although on occasions they may be placed outside as long as this does not inhibit the use of other coordinated components.

The space between zones can be referred to as an activity space. This is the space in which human or mechanical activities take place. In turn it may contain components such as partitions or stairs.

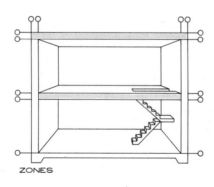

ZONES

ACTIVITY SPACES

Figure 6.6 *Neutral zones* are nonmodular interruptions of a modular reference grid to accommodate intermediate building elements, such as walls or floors, or parts of a building placed at an angle with a separate grid for each portion.

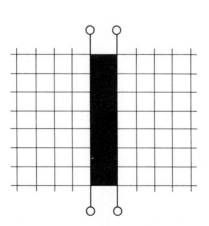

PARALLEL REFERENCE PLANES

OBLIQUE REFERENCE PLANES

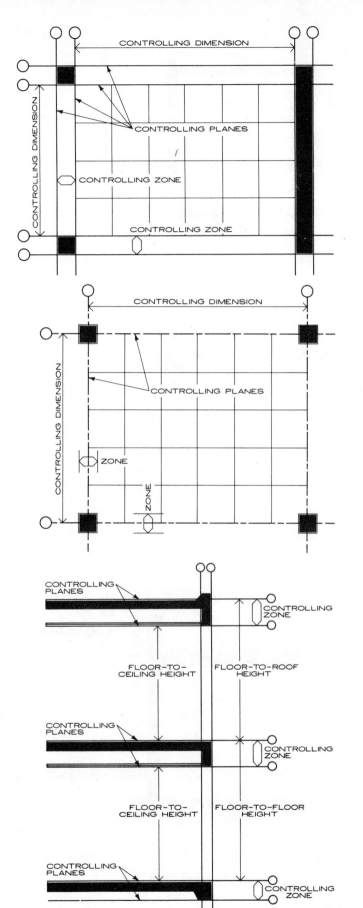

Figure 6.7 Boundary controlling planes.

Figure 6.8 Axial controlling planes.

Figure 6.9 Vertical controlling dimensions.

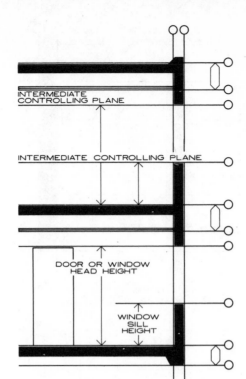

Figure 6.10 Intermediate controlling planes.

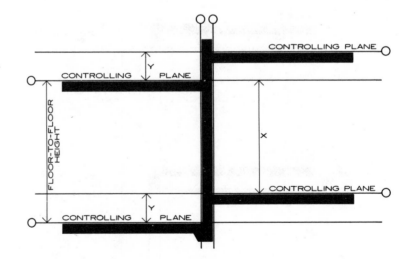

Figure 6.11 Change of level for floors and roofs.

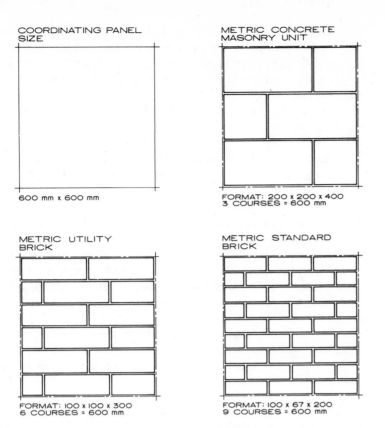

COORDINATING PANEL SIZE

600 mm x 600 mm

METRIC CONCRETE MASONRY UNIT

FORMAT: 200 x 200 x 400
3 COURSES = 600 mm

METRIC UTILITY BRICK

FORMAT: 100 x 100 x 300
6 COURSES = 600 mm

METRIC STANDARD BRICK

FORMAT: 100 x 67 x 200
9 COURSES = 600 mm

Figure 6.12 Metric brick and block sizes in relation to a 600 mm × 600 mm coordinating masonry panel size.

SPACE REFERENCE SYSTEMS (GRIDS)

Dimensional coordination requires the use of a space reference system to define locations (points, lines, or planes) in space. The general reference system is a three-dimensional grid (shown as two-dimensional grids in drawings) whose intervals should be based on established dimensional preferences.

USER NEEDS: FUNCTIONAL AND ACTIVITY SPACES

Before design begins, specifications are required for all activity spaces associated with the specific use of the building, as well as fixtures and equipment. The design interpretation of activity space can be two- or three-dimensional. Building spaces can be regarded as "voids," which generally permit some freedom in the selection of preferred dimensions.

CONTROLLING DIMENSIONS IN BUILDING DESIGN

The application of dimensional coordination in building design involves the use of horizontal and vertical controlling dimensions between the major reference planes for structural elements, which may be either axial or face-to-face dimensions. Enclosing elements, or "solids," are assigned controlling zones, such as for floors, roofs, structural walls, or columns. Controlling lines normally coincide with the space reference system. To permit maximum flexibility and interchangeability of building components, controlling dimensions should bear a direct relationship to the coordinating sizes of building products.

COORDINATING DIMENSIONS FOR BUILDING PRODUCTS AND ASSEMBLIES

Dimensional coordination includes a system of coordinating dimensions for building components and assemblies, including an allowance for joints and tolerances.

WORK SIZES, RULES OF FIT, JOINTS

Comprehensive dimensional coordination requires the definition of manufacturing sizes—or work sizes—and permissible deviations, to ensure acceptable "actual sizes" in relation to coordinating sizes at the place of manufacture.

LAYING OUT AND POSITIONING COMPONENTS IN CONSTRUCTION

To ensure the physical application of dimensional coordination in practice, rules and guidelines are required for accuracy in laying out and positioning components and elements in construction.

CONVENTIONS, SYMBOLS, AND DEFINITIONS FOR DRAWINGS

Dimensional coordination is accompanied by a set of conventions and symbols for the representation of dimensionally coordinated building projects in drawings and other construction documents. These conventions and symbols need to be generally understood and carefully observed to prevent misunderstanding and misinterpretation.

A number of these concepts and their practical application in a metric building environment are discussed below.

METRIC MODULES

Dimensional or modular coordination is based on application of the internationally agreed upon 100 mm basic module and selected derived dimensional units, multimodules, and submodules.

BASIC MODULES

The *basic module* of 100 mm replaces the customary module of 4 in. The module is large enough to rationalize possible ranges of component sizes and small enough to provide an adequate variety of design dimensions for buildings of various types. Any multiple of the basic metric module is immediately visible in the dimension; for example, 3200 mm represents 32 modular units, whereas 32 modules in customary dimensions are concealed as 10'8".

MULTIMODULES

Multimodules are whole multiples of the basic module. They are used for structural and planning grids and for determining ranges of sizes for building elements and components. With careful selection of multimodules, component sizes can be limited to a minimum.

Horizontal Multimodules. Preferred horizontal multimodules for construction are 300, 600, 1200, 3000, and 6000 mm. Additional multimodules for special uses are 900 and 1500 mm, and in small buildings built with masonry units a horizontal multimodule of 200 mm may also be used. The large 6000 mm multimodule provides a useful systems module for the overall coordination of buildings, especially as it is a whole multiple of the following multimodules: 200, 300, 400, 500, 600, 1000, 1200, 1500, 2000, and 3000 mm.

Vertical Multimodules. Preferred vertical multimodules are 200, 300, and 600 mm. For vertical dimensions up to 3000 mm, increments of the basic 100 mm module may be used in special circumstances.

SUBMODULES

The preferred *submodule* is 50 mm; the second preference is 25 mm. Sizes based on submodules should be used only where it is technically or economically impracticable to use modular or multimodular sizes.

NONMODULAR DIMENSIONS

Nonmodular dimensions occur in practice and need to be accommodated in any system of dimensional coordination, but they should never be used as planning modules. Quite a few component dimensions will be nonmodular, especially thickness.

For nonmodular dimensions up to 600 mm, multiples of 50 mm are acceptable, and up to 300 mm additional multiples of 25 mm may be used. For dimensions smaller than 100 mm, inframodular sizes based on 50, 25, 20, and 10 mm are recommended, in that order, leading to the following values: 10, 20, 25, 30, 40, 50, 60, 70, 75, 80, and 90 mm.

DIMENSIONAL REFERENCE SYSTEMS (GRIDS)

Grids have been a feature in the development of dimensional coordination; in fact, the term "modular coordination" was first used to describe a geometric reference system in which the basic module was the fundamental reference for the consecutive spacing of lines or planes in each coordinate direction.

Reference grids provide a constant space reference system from the inception to the completion of a project. Grids assist designers in the coordination of building dimensions and the expression of how the coordination between structure, elements, and systems is to be achieved. They convey instructions for the manufacture or purchase of suitable components, and they provide the positional reference for the precise location of components and elements. In construction, grid lines in plan and section assist in laying out the building and its elements.

In dimensional coordination the rigidity of a modular grid has been replaced by a more liberal system of controlling lines and planes, which normally coincide with the basic modular or a multimodular grid. The grid becomes a tool for the better detailing of decisions, rather than a straitjacket. To clarify the concepts, the principal terms have been defined.

The *basic modular grid* is a grid with consecutive parallel lines spaced 100 mm apart horizontally and vertically. This grid has the greatest merit in large scale drawings (1:1 to 1:20), where it clarifies component location and interrelationships.

BASIC MODULAR GRID

The *multimodular grid* is used for determining the layout of a building and the location of the main structural features. The grid interval is normally chosen from preferred horizontal and/or vertical multimodules, and the spacing between grid lines may differ in different coordinate planes. Multimodular grids are most useful in planning (planning grids) and structural positioning (structural grids), and are recommended for drawings with scale ratios of 1:50 to 1:200. Sometimes, more than one grid may be used and offset from the other as a displaced grid.

MULTIMODULAR GRID

In certain circumstances a *tartan* grid may be used as a position coordination system for building elements and to organize materials and space in a systematic way. A typical tartan grid has alternate bands of 100 mm and 200 mm in plan.

SPECIAL GRIDS

Controlling planes are selected planes in the reference system which reference elements of construction, such as a floor plane or ceiling plane. In plans, sections, or elevations, controlling planes are shown as controlling lines. Dimensions between controlling planes are known as controlling dimensions. Controlling lines, indicated by a small circle, are at the end of the dimension line.

CONTROLLING PLANES, LINES, AND DIMENSIONS

In dimensional coordination a distinction is made between usable (functional) space and nonusable space by means of controlling zones. The zones occur between controlling lines and include elements such as walls, floors, or ceiling-to-floor spaces. A nonmodular zone, which interrupts the reference grid, is called a neutral zone.

CONTROLLING ZONES

Controlling dimensions in building are dominant dimensions which determine the principal geometric relationships and, therefore, influence the sizes of many building elements, assemblies, or components. They are "ideal" dimensions and should not be confused with work sizes. Horizontal and vertical controlling dimensions should be selected by the designer in relation to functional and/or user requirements for the particular building type.

CONTROLLING DIMENSIONS IN BUILDING

Horizontal controlling dimensions either occur as distances between *boundary* controlling planes of vertical zones, or as distances between *axial* controlling planes, such as centerlines of structural elements. The same preferences are used for both systems, illustrated in Figures 6.7 and 6.8.

Preferred horizontal controlling dimensions should be selected from the following appropriate multimodules:

HORIZONTAL CONTROLLING DIMENSIONS (BOUNDARY OR AXIAL)

Up to 3600 mm: 300 mm
Up to 9600 mm: 600 mm
Above 9600 mm: 1200 mm

Table 6.1 Horizontal Controlling Dimensions (mm)

Horizontal Controlling Dimension	Multiples of Multimodules					Most Preferred Values
	300	600	1200	3000	6000	
300	x					
600	x	x				x
900	x					
1 200	x	x	x			x
1 500	x					
1 800	x	x				x
2 100	x					
2 400	x	x	x			x
2 700	x					
3 000	x	x		x		x
3 300	x					
3 600	x	x	x			x
4 200		x				
4 800		x	x			x
5 400		x				
6 000		x	x	x	x	x
6 600		x				
7 200		x	x			x
7 800		x				
8 400		x	x			x
9 000		x		x		x
9 600		x	x			x
10 800			x			
12 000			x	x	x	x
13 200			x			
14 400			x			
15 000				x		
15 600			x			
16 800			x			
18 000			x	x	x	x
19 200			x			
20 400			x			
21 000				x		
21 600			x			
22 800			x			
24 000			x	x	x	x
25 200			x			
26 400			x			
27 000				x		
27 600			x			
28 800			x			
30 000			x	x	x	x

For large structures the first preference is 6000 mm; the second, 3000 mm. See Table 6.1 for the rationale of selecting horizontal controlling dimensions up to 30 000 mm (30 m).

SECTIONAL CONTROLLING DIMENSIONS

For dimensions up to 600 mm, multiples of 100 mm are preferred; above 600 mm, multiples of 300 mm are the first preference, and multiples of 200 mm the second. In actuality these dimensions are often nonmodular neutral zones.

VERTICAL CONTROLLING DIMENSIONS

Distances between *controlling planes,* such as floor-to-floor height, floor-to-roof height, floor-to-ceiling height, change of level between floors and roofs, or heights of controlling zones for floors and roof, are vertical controlling dimensions. (See Figures 6.9 and 6.11.)

Floor-to-Floor and Floor-to-Roof Planes. Between 2300 and 3000 mm the 100 mm module should be used; from 3000 to 4800 mm the first preference is for the 300 mm multimodule, and the second preference for the 200 mm multimodule. Above 4800 mm the 600 mm multimodule is preferred.

Floor-to-Ceiling Height. Between 2100 and 2800 mm the 100 mm module should be used. From 2800 to 3600 mm the first preference is for the 300 mm multimodule. Above 3600 mm the first preference is for 600 mm; the second preference, for 300 mm. Above 4800 mm no preference is listed because other factors may determine the economical or functional dimension.

Controlling Zones for Floors and Roofs. Up to 600 mm the 100 mm module should be used. Between 600 and 1800 mm the 300 mm multimodule is preferred; second preference is for the 200 mm multimodule. Above 1800 mm use of the 600 mm multimodule is recommended. These dimensions may be nonmodular.

Changes in Level of Floors and Roofs. Up to 2400 mm, 300 or 200 mm multimodules may be used, with preference given to 300 mm. Above 2400 mm, 600 mm multimodules should be used. Change of level is illustrated in Figure 6.11.

Intermediate controlling dimensions are taken from the floor plane to door and window heads or window sills. Selected multiples of the 100 mm module are used. Typical intermediate controlling dimensions are illustrated in Figure 6.10.

Doorset and window head heights may be any multiple of 100 mm above 2000 mm, with the following preferences: 2100, 2200, or 2400 mm.

For *window sill heights* preferred dimensions are 600, 800, 900, or 1200 mm. Second preferences are as follows:

> For low sills: 200, 300, or 400 mm
> For normal sills: 700 or 1000 mm
> For high sills: 1500, 1600, or 1800 mm

Note   The sills and heads of windows should be set to a modular coordinating size. For multimodules 600, 300, or 200 mm is preferred, in that order. Sill heights should be checked with desk or counter heights (700 to 1000 mm), where appropriate.

INTERMEDIATE CONTROLLING DIMENSIONS

Preferred sizes for building components and assemblies are an integral part of a dimensioning system. These coordinating dimensions define the theoretical space occupied by a component or assembly, including all necessary allowances for tolerances and joints. The coordinating dimensions can also be the distances between the theoretical centerlines of joints or, in the case of overlapping components, the distances representing effective cover.

Should manufacturers and designers agree to use a preferred set of metric sizes for components and assemblies, greater flexibility of selection, greater interchangeability, and less wasteful construction may be achieved using a small range of products. Although special sizes may be required in special cases, the advantages of preferred dimensions will serve to keep such special circumstances to the minimum. Preferred dimensions are grouped according to size:

PREFERRED SIZES FOR BUILDING COMPONENTS AND ASSEMBLIES

Small components:	under 500 mm
Medium-size components and assemblies:	under 1500 mm
Heavy or large-size components and assemblies	between 900 and 3600 mm
Very large components and assemblies:	over 3500 mm

Table 6.2 Preferred Sizes for Building Components and Assemblies

Category	Typical Examples of Components and Assemblies	Dimensional Preference (mm) First	Second	
A. Small components (under 500 mm)	Bricks, blocks, tiles, paving units	100	25	
		200	50	
		300	75	
		400	150	
			250	
B. Medium-size components and assemblies (under 1500 mm)	Sheets, panels, partition units, doorsets, windows, slabs	600	500	
		800	700	
		900	1 000	
		1 200	1 400	
			See Note a.	
C. Large-size components and assemblies (up to 3600 mm)	Precast floor units, precast wall units, panels, door assemblies, window assemblies, precast stairs, precast ducts	1 800	($n \times 300$)	($n \times 200$)
		2 400	1 500	1 600
		3 000	2 100	2 000
		3 600	2 700	2 200
			3 300	2 600
				2 800
				3 200
				3 400
			See Note b.	
D. Very large components and assemblies (over 3600 mm)	Prefabricated building elements, precast floor and roof sections	4 800	($n \times 600$)	($n \times 1500$)
		6 000	4 200	4 500
		7 200	6 600	7 500
		8 400	7 800	10 500
		9 600	9 000	
		10 800	10 200	
		12 000	11 400	
			See Note c.	

[a]For the purposes of rationalization, those multiples of 100 mm, above 1000 mm, which are prime numbers (e.g., 1100, 1300, 1700, 1900, 2300, 2900) constitute a lower order of preference and should be considered only when special requirements exist.

[b]Alternative second preferences are shown; for vertical dimensions the use of multiples of 200 mm may sometimes be more appropriate than the use of multiples of 300 mm, particularly in conjunction with masonry materials.

[c]Alternative second preferences are shown; for some projects it will be more appropriate to size large components or assemblies in multiples of 1500 mm.

Table 6.2 shows a systematic approach to the development of preferred sizes for building components and assemblies. Preferred dimensions are ranked as first preference and second preference. First preferences provide the fewest possible number of sizes in each group of products. Preferred product sizes here are suggestions only. Actual sizes will be determined by various actions, including those of manufacturers and others.

SUGGESTED PREFERRED SIZES FOR BUILDING UNITS, COMPONENTS, AND ASSEMBLIES

This information has been included to assist designers to appreciate the practical application of preferred metric sizes to various building products. The information is tentative only, and may be complemented or contradicted by subsequent metric American National Standards.

PRODUCTS FOR USE IN THE VERTICAL PLANE—MASONRY PANELS

The dimensions of prebuilt or site-built masonry panels are listed in Table 6.3 in order of preference. The first preference of 600 mm × 600 mm has been designated as the *coordinating panel* size for masonry panels and walls, because it integrates the formats of most masonry brick and block units.

Table 6.3 Masonry Panels

Table 6.3 Masonry Panels

Vertical Dimension (mm)	Horizontal Dimension[a] (mm)		
	$n \times 600$	$n \times 300$	$n \times 200$
$n \times 600$	1	2	3
$n \times 200$	2	3	3
$n \times 100$	3	3	—

[a]Where n is a whole number.

Suggested preferred horizontal and vertical dimensions for precast panels are as follows:

PRECAST PANELS

First preference:	$n \times 600$ mm
Second preference:	$n \times 300$ mm
Third preference:	$n \times 100$ mm

where n is a whole number.

Suggested dimensions for modular masonry units, showing the format size, which includes a 10 mm joint, are tabulated in Table 6.4 in order of preference.

MODULAR MASONRY UNITS

Table 6.4 Modular Masonry Units

Height (mm)	Width (mm)	Length (mm)		
		200^a	300^a	400
50	100	—	2	—
67	100	1	2	—
	150	—	2	—
75	100	2	2	—
80	100	2	2	—
	150	2	2	—
100	100	1	1	1
	150	2	2	—
	200	1	2	1
133	100	2	2	—
150	100	2	2	2
200	100	1	2	1
	150	2	2	2
	200	1	2	1
	300	2	2	2
300	300	—	1	—

[a]Supplementary lengths of 100 mm and 150 may be needed to maintain bond patterns. These units may either be custom-made or cut on site.

Nonmodular masonry units should be sized to coordinate, as far as practicable, with the preferred masonry panel sizes tabulated above. The basic size should be computed from the format size, which includes an allowance for 10 mm joints. Where fractions of a millimeter are required to achieve a preferred coordinating size (as, e.g., with three courses to 200 mm, or three courses to 400 mm), the basic size should be rounded to the nearest millimeter, and the marginal adjustment effected in the joints (Table 6.5).

NONMODULAR MASONRY UNITS

Table 6.5 Coordinating Heights for Modular Masonry Units with 10 mm Joint

Format Size (mm)	Coursing (mm)	Basic Size (mm)	Makeup in Joints
50	2 courses to 100	40	—
67	3 courses to 200	57	−1 mm in 3 courses
75	4 courses to 300	65	—
80	5 courses to 400	70	—
100	100	90	—
133	3 courses to 400	123	+1 mm in 3 courses
150	2 courses to 300	140	—
200	200	190	—
300	300	290	—

RIGID FLAT SHEET MATERIALS AND BOARDS

Rigid flat sheet material include boards, panels, and planks manufactured from plywood, hardboard, particle board, pressed fiber, fiber cement, gypsum, and laminated materials.

Suggested preferred dimensions are shown in Table 6.6.

Table 6.6 Preferred Dimensions for Panels and Planks

Type	Preference	Width (mm)	Length (mm)
Panels, boards	First	1200	2400
	Second	600	2400
			3000
		1200	1200
			1800
			3000
			3600
	Third	1200	2100
			2700
Planks	First	400	2400
	Second	400	3000
			3600

CORRUGATED AND PROFILED SHEET MATERIALS

Cover. Effective cover for various roll formed or pressed cladding materials is taken from centerline to centerline of side laps. Preferred dimensions for effective cover are $n \times 100$ mm, where n is a whole number between 3 and 10.

Length. Suggested preferred lengths, between 1800 and 9000 mm, are as follows:

First preference: $n \times 600$ mm
Second preference: $n \times 300$ mm

For large orders, increments of 100 mm may be specified.

PRODUCTS FOR USE IN THE HORIZONTAL PLANE

Ceiling Panels. The following dimensions, in millimeters, are recommended for ceiling panels:

First preference: 1200×600, 600×600, 600×300, 300×300
Second preference: 1500×600, 900×600, 900×300

Resilient Flooring. The following dimensions, in millimeters, are recommended for the sizing of resilient floor tiles: 300×300, 400×400.

Sheeting—Width. The following widths are recommended for resilient floor sheeting: 1200, 1800, 2700, 3600 mm.

Note The width of carpet is not covered by these recommendations.

Paving Slabs. The following dimensions, in millimeters, are recommended for the sizing of paving slabs (including appropriate joint allowances):

First preference: 600 × 600, 600 × 300, 300 × 300
Second preference: 900 × 600, 400 × 400

The following dimensions, in millimeters, are recommended for the sizing of wall and floor tiles (including joint allowances):

First preference (modular sizes): 100 × 100, 200 × 100
Second preference (submodular sizes): 100 × 50, 50 × 50, 150 × 150

WALL AND FLOOR TILES

Nonmodular Sizes. Nonmodular sizes should be chosen in such a way that groups of tiles will coincide with a coordinating panel size of either 200 × 200, 300 × 300, 600 × 600 mm.

Note For example, a 150 × 75 tile would fit a 300 × 300 panel, and a 120 × 120 tile would fit a 600 × 600 panel.

Pattern Mosaic Tiles. Pattern mosaic tiles are generally prelocated on sheets. Preferred sheet sizes are as follows:

First preference: 300 × 300
Second preference: 400 × 400

Note Where practicable, patterns should be so arranged that further subdivision of sheets into 100 or 200 mm sections is possible.

Spacing of Studs and Other Framing Members. Where framing members support rigid, flat, or other lining materials, as in the case of studs or ceiling joists, the following center-to-center spacings are recommended:

First preference: 600 mm
Second preference: 400 mm
Third preference: 300 mm

COORDINATING DIMENSIONS FOR CONCEALED MEMBERS

Spacing of Suspended Ceiling Runners. The spacing of exposed or concealed suspended ceiling runners is directly related to the coordinating sizes of the ceiling panels that are supported. The following center-to-center spacings are preferred: 1200, 600, 300 mm.

Nonbearing partitions should be sized to suit preferred floor-to-ceiling dimensions, with suitable allowances for positioning clearances and fixing requirements.

Suggested preferred widths of nonbearing partitions are as follows:

First preference: 1200 mm
Second preference: 900, 1500 mm

COORDINATING DIMENSIONS OF COMPONENTS AND ASSEMBLIES NONBEARING PARTITIONS

Other preferences may be determined by functional requirements or by special user needs in a building. Such other sizes should preferably by in widths of n × 100 mm, where n is a whole number.

GENERAL PURPOSE DOORSETS (EXTERNAL AND INTERNAL)

General purpose doorsets include framed single-leaf and double-leaf doors to buildings and accessible spaces within buildings. Suggested doorset dimensions are stated as coordinating dimensions for the door and frame assembly, thus allowing the doorset to be positioned and fixed within an opening of preferred dimensions (Table 6.7).

Table 6.7 Preferred Door Sizes[a]

Height (mm)	Width (mm)					
	Single-leaf			Double-leaf		
	800	900	1000	1200	1500	1800
2100	2	1	2	1	1	1
2200	2	2	1	2	2	1
2400	2	1	1	2	2	1

[a]If special doorsets are required for functional reasons, they should preferably be sized to the heights indicated above; the widths should be based on $n \times 100$ mm, where n is a whole number.

WINDOWS (ALL TYPES)

Suggested window dimensions are stated as coordinating dimensions for the entire window and frame, thus allowing the assembly to be positioned and fixed within openings of preferred dimensions.

First preferences for window openings are multiples of 600 mm horizontally and vertically, as these preferences agree with the preferred dimensions of masonry and precast panels and other building elements.

Second preferences should be selected to agree with the coordinating sizes of components that surround the window; for example, multiples of 400 mm and 200 mm horizontally and 200 mm vertically involve a minimum of cutting of masonry units.

Table 6.8 shows suggested preferred window sizes for openings with coordinating dimensions, ranging from heights of 600 to 2400 mm and widths of 600 to 3000 mm. Smaller heights for highlight windows and narrower widths for strip windows should be selected from multiples of 100 mm, such as 300, 400, or 500 mm.

Table 6.8 Preferred Sizes for Windows

Height (mm)	Width(mm)									
	600	800	1000	1200	1400	1600	1800	2000	2400	3000
600	1	2	2	1	2	2	1	2	1	1
800	2	3	3	2	3	3	2	3	2	2
1000	2	3	3	2	3	3	2	3	2	2
1200	1	2	2	1	2	2	1	2	1	1
1400	2	3	3	2	3	3	2	3	2	2
1600	2	3	3	2	3	3	2	3	2	2
1800	1	2	2	1	2	2	1	2	1	1
2000	2	3	3	2	3	3	2	3	2	2
2200	2	3	3	2	3	3	2	3	2	2
2400	1	2	2	1	2	2	1	2	1	1

Note Where other sizes are needed for functional or other reasons, it is recommended that coordinating dimensions be selected that are multiples of 100 mm and, where possible, multiples of 600 or 200 mm in at least one direction.

The coordinating dimensions for a square or rectangular skylight are taken as the dimensions of the inner face of the skylight frame, which coordinate with the overall dimensions of the projecting curb. The following dimensions, in millimeters, are recommended:

Square Skylights	Rectangular Skylights
600 × 600	600 × 900
900 × 900	600 × 1200
1200 × 1200	

Note Other sizes, designed to suit specific functional requirements of a project, should be sized so that the coordinating dimensions in each direction are as follows:

First preference: multiples of 200 mm
Second preference: multiples of 100 mm

Dimensional coordination is a helpful device for computerized design. Drawings will be easier if each component fits within a coordinated system. Wider use of standard details will be possible, and interchangeability of components will permit closer cost control or substitution of one material for another in short supply. Built-in furniture or equipment will require less on-site fitting. Mathematical calculations and cost estimates will also be simplified.

Dimensional coordination will probably make it possible to reduce the number of standard size components, which in turn will result in a more efficient labor force and simplified materials handling and inventory control. These benefits should lead to improved delivery schedules and quality control.

Quantity takeoff and estimating will be easier. Building layout will be simplified. Reduction of cutting and fitting on the job will probably be the source of the greatest cost saving.

Dimensional coordination will make it easier to remodel buildings or add to them. Maintenance and repair, including replacement of building components, will also be simplified.

ADVANTAGES OF DIMENSIONAL COORDINATION

The potential advantages and disadvantages of dimensional coordination may be summarized in the following way:

SUMMARY OF PROS AND CONS

Simplification of:
Design and project documentation
Estimating and costing of building projects
Layout out on site and construction or assembly procedures
Ordering of materials and site organization
Manufacture of standard building products and assemblies
Distribution and transportation of building products
Maintenance of dimensionally coordinated buildings

PROS

Reduction of:
Unnecessary variety of building products
Manufacturers' and distributors' inventories
Nonproductive labor and materials wasted on the building site (less cutting, trimming, and fitting)
Requirements for skilled on-site labor

Promotion of:
Computer-aided design and documentation
Use of standard details
Prefabrication of building components in preferred dimensions
Specialization in erection techniques using preferred components

Improvement of:
Liaison between design professions and contractor
Product performance (better allocation of research and development)
Building flexibility

CONS   All groups involved in the building design, production, and construction process will have to be reeducated.

There is sure to be some resentment of and resistance to the change on the part of those who see it as unnecessary regimentation.

Random solutions are penalized; and, in general, dimensional coordination is not applicable to nonrectilinear or free-form buildings.

In order to produce preferred products, manufacturing investment requires an assured market, especially from the public sector.

Dimensionally coordinated construction requires greater on-site accuracy than is traditionally used in conventional building projects.

7

ARCHITECTURAL
AND ENGINEERING DRAWING

RUDOLPH DREYER, AIA

*Chairman, AIA Metric Conversion/Dimensional
Coordination Task Force*

This chapter, giving the current information relating to metric drawing practice, is derived from parts of the national standards published in Canada, Australia, and Great Britain, and where possible conforms to the criteria of the International Standards Organization (ISO). The material presented is intended as a guide to architects, engineers, designers, and draftsmen throughout the transitional period of metric conversion. It does not represent the final word on these subjects, as there may be some changes when the Metric American National Standards are published.

The recommended standard metric sheet sizes to be adopted for all drawing and written material are the International Standard Organization "A" (ISO) A series. The standard metric drawing sheet is the A0 sheet (1189 × 841 mm), which has an area of exactly one square meter and a ratio of sides of $\sqrt{2}:1$. Smaller sizes are obtained by halving the long dimension, and larger sizes by doubling the short dimensions. This makes possible simple reduction or enlargement, and sheets are easily folded for filing or mailing. Provision is made for the use of a supplementary B1 size sheet in instances where a larger sheet than A1 is required, and where the A0 size drawing sheet cannot be conveniently accommodated on present drawing boards or in filing cabinets. The relationship between drawing sheet sizes is illustrated in Figure 7.1, and the sizes are listed in Table 7.1.

Every drawing sheet should have border lines, a binding margin, a title block, and an information panel and may also contain a sheet grid reference system and camera alignment marks for microfilming.

Every drawing sheet should have an all-round border with a substantially wider left side margin for binding. Without such a border, there is a risk of information being lost if the printing paper slips or is carelessly trimmed, or the print is damaged in use.

The ISO-A series drawing sheets are particularly well suited to reduction onto 35 mm microfilm. Their aspect ratio is $\sqrt{2}:1$ throughout the range, which is also the aspect ratio of the microfilm frame. A selection of print sizes on A series standard sensitized sheets can be obtained by employing uniformly related reduction and enlargement ratios. For example, a plan produced at 1:100 on an A2 sheet can be reproduced as 1:50 on A1 or 1:200 on A3 size.

Where required, camera alignment marks should be provided in the form of an outline arrowhead pointing outward and should be placed outside the drawing frame.

METRIC DRAWING SHEETS

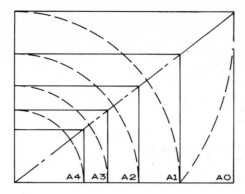

Figure 7.1 The relationship between metric drawing sheets.

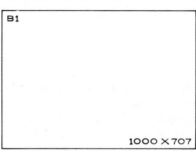

SUPPLEMENTARY B1 SIZE SHEET

B1

1000 × 707

The original size of a drawing prepared for microfilming should be denoted; this can be done by indicating the drawing frame dimensions. These may be shown outside the drawing frame near a corner. In addition, a graduated line 300 mm long representing the scale of the drawing should be shown in a suitable location, for use when a microfilm printout to a different sheet size is required.

The sheet size designation number should be indicated on the drawing, preferably in the right-hand bottom corner of the drawing frame, where it may be included in the title block.

A north point should be shown adjacent to the title panel on every location plan. Whenever practicable, all plans for a particular project should be drawn with the same orientation on the drawing sheet, with the north point facing the top.

Where a plan occupies more than one sheet, a key diagram may be included to graphically relate the particular block to the overall design. This key, with the appropriate part hatched or blacked in, should be located in or adjacent to the information panel on each relevant drawing sheet.

Table 7.1 Drawing Sheet Dimensions[a]

Drawing Sheet Size Designation	Sheet-Size	Nominal Width of Margins and Borders			Net Size of Drawing Area
		Top and Bottom	Binding Margin	Right-Hand Border	
A0	1189 × 841	20	40	16	1133 × 801
A1	841 × 594	14	28	12	801 × 566
A2	594 × 420	10	20	8	566 × 400
A3	420 × 297	7	20	6	394 × 283
A4[a]	297 × 210	7	20	6	283 × 184
B1	1000 × 707	14	28	12	960 × 679

[a]The filing edge on A4 size sheets is the long edge. A4 size sheets should be reserved for schedules and standard details.

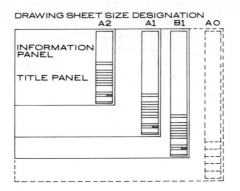

Figure 7.2 Vertical arrangements of information and tile panels on drawing sheets.

Drawings may be classified according to the order of building construction, with small-scale general drawings first, followed by detail drawings and schedules. Drawings within these categories should then be numbered sequentially.

When design and working drawings are produced in accordance with a system of preferred dimensions, the use of a reference grid will facilitate and speed up the drawing process.

For detail drawings (1:1 to 1:20) the use of a 10 mm grid is recommended; for working drawings (1:50 to 1:200) a 6 mm grid is frequently useful.

A reference grid underlay can be used. Alternatively, a reproducing or non-reproducing reference grid may be printed on the back of the drawing sheet.

When prints are folded, to facilitate reference the title panel should be in either the vertical or the horizontal format, located in the position shown in Figures 7.2 and 7.3. It should include the following information as applicable:

1 Job title (usually consisting of name of project, name of owner, and site address).
2 Subject of drawing.
3 Scale or scales of drawings.
4 Date of drawing.
5 Job number.
6 Drawing number and revision suffix.
7 Drawing reference, when a classification system has been adopted.
8 Names of architects, engineers, and consultants, together with addresses and telephone numbers.
9 Architects' and/or engineers' seal.
10 Dates and initials of individuals making the drawing, or tracing.
11 United States metric symbol (the use of the U.S. metric symbol on metric drawings will facilitate their identification during the transitional period of metric conversion).

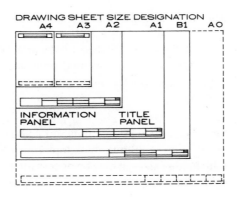

Figure 7.3 Horizontal arrangement of information and title panels on drawing sheets.

The title panel may be preprinted on the drawing sheet or on adhesive plastic film to avoid repetitive work.

All notes and general information should be located in an information panel, which should be combined with the title panel to form a block in a vertical or horizontal arrangement located in the bottom right corner (Figures 7.2 and 7.3). The panel may contain the following information:

1 Revision details (each of which is indexed to the revision suffix, dated, and initialed).
2 Notes (general or specific, which are better consolidated under this heading than loosely placed on the drawing).
3 Key to symbols and abbreviations. (The application of these by rubber stamp or transfer will save labor and also facilitate standardization.)
4 North point (on plans).

LINEAR DIMENSIONS ON DRAWINGS

Dimensions in meters or millimeters should be expressed on drawings as follows:

1 All dimensions in meters—expressed as numbers to three decimal places, for example, 10.800 (ten point eight meters).
2 All dimensions in millimeters—expressed as a whole numbers (no decimal point), for example, 10 800 (ten thousand eight hundred millimeters).

In the above cases the unit symbol m or mm need not be used as long as these three rules are followed:

1 Whole numbers indicate millimeters.
2 Decimalized numbers to three places to the right of the decimal point indicate meters (i.e., 0.100).
3 All other values must be followed by the appropriate unit symbols if the dimensions expressed do not conform to the above rules. For example, it may be necessary to express dimensions less than 1 mm (e.g., 0.008 mm), or in surveys of very large areas it may be desirable to express dimensions in minimum units of a meter (e.g., 7500 m, 125 725 m, 102.7 m).

When symbols are not given on a drawing or when there is a possibility of confusion, the drawings should be labeled "All dimensions are in meters" or "All dimensions are in millimeters." The mixing of units on the same drawing should be avoided.

Dimensions given in written documents or specifications must always be followed by the unit or symbol.

DECIMAL NOTATION

The decimal point (marker) should be used as follows:

1 In the United States, the decimal point, or period is recommended, but not the comma or decimal point inserted at mid height.
2 In numbers less than unity, a zero must precede the decimal point, that is, 0.23.

UNIT NOTATION

When expressing sizes, units should be consistent and not mixed, e.g., 1500 mm × 400 mm × 30 mm thick (not 1.5 m × 400 mm × 30 mm). Occasionally, as with lumber sizes, it may be necessary to mix units, i.e., 100 mm × 75 mm × 10 m long. An exception is made, however, when certain equations must contain

Table 7.2 Comparison of Drawing Scales

Scales for Use with Metric Drawings	Replaced Scales for Use with U.S. Customary Units	
	Scale Ratio	Ratio in Mixed Units
1:5	1:4	3″ = 1′ 0″
1:10	(1:8	1½″ = 1′ 0″
	1:12	1″ = 1′ 0″
1:20	(1:16	3/4″ = 1′ 0″
	1:24	1/2″ = 1′ 0″
1:50	1:48	1/4″ = 1′ 0″
1:100	1:96	1/8″ = 1′ 0″
1:200	1:192	1/16″ = 1′ 0″
1:500	(1:384	1/32″ = 1′ 0″
	(1:480	1″ = 40′ 0″
	(1:600	1″ = 50′ 0″
1:1000	(1:960	1″ = 80′ 0″
	(1:1200	1″ = 100′ 0″
1:2000	1:2400	1″ = 200′ 0″
1:5000	(1:4800	1″ = 400′ 0″
	(1:6000	1″ = 500′ 0″
1:10 000	(1:10 560	6″ = 1 mi
	(1:12 000	1″ = 1000′ 0″
1:25 000	(1:21 120	3″ = 1 mi
	(1:24 000	1″ = 2000′ 0″
1:50 000	1:63 360	1″ = 1 mi
1:100 000	1:126 720	2″ = 1 mi

similar units for calculation purposes. In these circumstances the figures may be written as 0.100 × 0.075 × 10.000 (if all in meters) or 100 × 75 × 10 000 (if all in millimeters).

Metric unit symbols should be used as shown in Chapters 2–4. The symbol, for example, m, mm, or kg, is the same for singular and plural values (1 kg, 10 kg), and no full stops or other punctuation marks should be used after the symbol unless it occurs at the end of a sentence. The slash as a separator between numerator and denominator should be used as it is in the customary system, that is, 3 kg/m^3 (3 kilograms per cubic meter).

The unit should be written in full if there is doubt about the meaning of a symbol. For example, the internationally recognized symbol l for the unit liter can be confused with the number 1, and therefore has been changed to capital L to avoid any confusion. Also, during the transition period the unit symbol for the metric ton should be avoided in situations where it may be confused with the customary ton, and the unit metric ton or megagram should be written in full.

When symbols are raised to various powers, it is only the symbol which is involved, not the number attached to it. Thus 3 m^3 equals 3 (m)^3 and not 3 m × 3 m × 3 m (i.e., the value is 3 cubic meters, not 27 cubic meters).

During the changeover period, difficulty may be experienced with some office machinery and computers in current use when reproducing the squaring and cubing indices m^2 or mm^2, and m^3 or mm^3. In such cases the abbreviations sq' and cu' may be substituted temporarily (sq m and cu m), but the use of these should be limited to the United States as they may not be understood internationally.

Hyphenating a unit (milli-meters) is wrong. Even hyphenation to avoid over-

METRIC SYMBOLS

running a margin should be avoided; write "millimeters," not "milli- (next line) meters."

A single space should separate figures from symbols: 10 m, not 10m.

SCALES The change to the metric system will require an understanding of a range of new scales with ratios similar to the foot-inch units, but not quite the same. Over the past decades such familiar scale (ratio) expressions as $\frac{1}{16}'' = 1'0''$, $\frac{1}{8}'' = 1'0''$, and $\frac{1}{4}'' = 1'0''$ have developed as idioms for the actual scale ratios of 1:192, 1:96 and 1:48, respectively (Table 7.2).

The simplicity of the metric system is demonstrated by the ease with which the metric scale can be manipulated in developing metric ratios. Almost all drawings can be done with one metric scale, using the decimal subdivisions of the scale ratios of 1:1 and 1:100 as indicated in the examples in Figure 7.4.

The scale selected for a particular drawing should be determined by considering the following:

1 The type of information to be communicated.

2 The need to adequately and accurately convey specific information.

3 The need for economy of time and effort in drawing production.

(Recommended drawing scales as shown in Tables 7.3 and 7.4.)

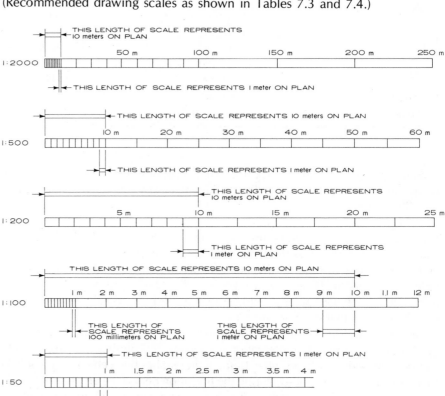

Figure 7.4 Metric lengths to scale.

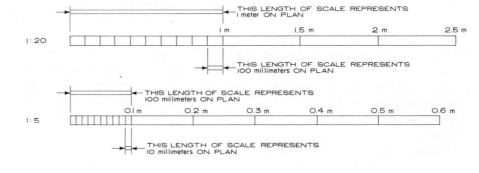

Table 7.3 Recommended Scales for Use on Various Architectural and Engineering Drawings[a]

Scale Ratios	Architectural and Building Practice	Engineering Drawing Practice	Surveying and Mapping
Enlargement ratios			
10:1		x	
5:1		x	
2:1		x	
Full size	x	x	
Reduction ratios			
1:2	x	x	
1:5	x	x	
1:10	x	x	
1:20	x	x	
1:25		x	
1:50	x	x	x
1:100	x	x	x
1:200	x	x	x
1:250		x	x
1:500	x	x	x
1:1 000	x	x	x
1:2 000	x	x	x
1:2 500	x	x	x
1:5 000		x	x
1:10 000		x	x
1:25 000		x	x
1:50 000		x	x
1:100 000		x	x
1:250 000			x
1:500 000			x
1:1 000 000			x

[a]When interdisciplinary projects are involved, compatible scale ratios should be chosen.

Dimensions on drawings should be used to indicate the distance between planes or surfaces. Only those dimensions essential for carrying out the work should be shown; duplication of dimensions should be avoided.

Expression of dimensions as metric units should follow the rules indicated in Chapters 2, 3, and 6.

Dimensions of components and assemblies are written in millimeters (mm): for example, 123 mm, 2472 mm. If the dimensions are written in the following sequence: length, width, height, and the figures are separated simply by a multiplication sign, the symbol is given only after last figure: e.g., 89 × 38 mm wood stud. If the dimensions are written in any other sequence, each dimension should be followed by the symbol, which should in turn be followed by the identifying word, for example, 612 mm deep × 229 mm wide, 900 mm long × 1200 high × 100 mm wide. When quoting tolerances, the appropriate symbol should be given only at the end of the expression: 70 ± 2°C, 1200 ± 3 mm.

Dimension figures should be written immediately above and parallel with the dimension lines to which they relate. (See Figure 7.5 for conventions for lines on drawings.) Their position on the dimension line should be toward the center of the space. Running dimension figures, however, should be placed toward the arrowhead end of the dimension line, or at right angles to the dimension line at the arrowhead.

LETTERING DIMENSIONS ON DRAWINGS

Table 7.4 Preferred Scales for Building Drawings[a]

Drawing	Recommended Scale	Use
Design Drawings		
Sketch plans	1:200 1:100 1:50	To show the overall design of the building
Production Drawings		
1. Location Drawings		
Block plan	1:2000 1:1000 1:500	To locate the site within the general district
Site plan	1:500 1:200	To locate building work, including services and site works, on the site
General location drawings	1:200 1:100 1:50	To indicate the juxaposition of rooms and spaces, and to locate the position of components and assemblies
Special area location drawings	1:50 1:20	To show the detailed location of components and assemblies in complex areas
2. Construction detail drawings		
Construction details	1:20 1:10 1:5 1:2 1:1	To show the interface of two or more components or assemblies for construction purposes
3. Component and assembly drawings		
Range drawings	1:100 1:50 1:20	To show in schedule form the range of specific components and assemblies to be used in the project
Component and assembly details	1:10 1:5 1:2 1:1	To show precise information regarding components and assemblies for workshop manufacture

[a]Indication of scales: The drawing scale should be stated in the title panel of each drawing sheet. When two or more scales are used in the same sheet, the particular scales should be clearly indicated.

The scale of drawing should be indicated by one of the following methods:

(a) A scale shown on the drawing, for example,

```
                    0      20           40           60      80 m
|___|___|___|___|___|_____|_____|_____|_____|
20  15  10   5
```

(b) A ratio prefixed by the word "Scale," for example, "Scale 1:100."
(c) "Scale: Not to scale" (NTS).

COORDINATING DIMENSION LINE

WORK DIMENSION LINE
(Actual and Manufacturing Dimensions)

WORK DIMENSION LINE
(Alternate)

RUNNING COORDINATING DIMENSION LINE

RUNNING WORK DIMENSION LINE
(Actual and Manufacturing Dimensions)

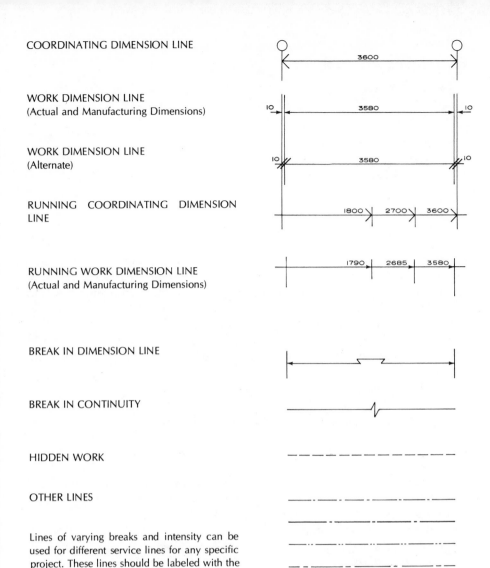

Figure 7.5 Conventions for lines on drawings.

BREAK IN DIMENSION LINE

BREAK IN CONTINUITY

HIDDEN WORK

OTHER LINES

Lines of varying breaks and intensity can be used for different service lines for any specific project. These lines should be labeled with the respective service or its abbreviation.

Dimension figures should be written to be viewed only from the bottom or right-hand edges of the sheet.

When parts of a drawing are not drawn to scale, or when breaklines do not make this obvious, the dimension figures should be followed by the abbreviation NTS (not to scale).

Running dimensions may be stated as x, y, and z coordinates from a common datum to form a reference grid. Only the positive axes of x, y, and z should be used. Care should be taken that the datum is beyond the space occupied by the building project and can be physically established.

Controlling dimensions in dimensional coordination are shown with open arrows (45°) and a small circle at the end of the controlling line. Boundary controlling lines are shown as solid lines; axial controlling lines are shown as broken lines. For work dimensions use closed arrows or slash lines.

The drawing process consists essentially of the identification and description of the various components of a building, and their relationships to one another to form the total building. Most recommended procedures make use of a "relationship hierarchy," which classifies information in a hierarchical order, thus en-

DRAWING PRACTICE FOR DIMENSIONAL COORDINATION

REFERENCING OF DRAWINGS

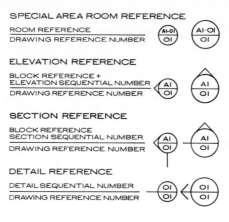

Figure 7.6 Conventions for cross referencing of drawings.

abling one to extract data in the form desired, ranging from general overall layouts to specific details. Inherent within such a hierarchy is the need for referencing. Various techniques of referencing are recommended according to the application (see Figure 7.6). These make use of codes or symbols, either alphabetical, numerical, alphanumerical, or graphic.

A code should be allocated to each specific project to identify the year of commencement and the drawing sequence within the overall program, for example:

> Last two digits of year
> Sequential project number......79 001

Where necessary, an additional code may be used to identify each project according to building type: schools, hospitals, etc.

A sequential alphabetical code is given to individual blocks within each project. A block may refer to a separate building or to a convenient subdivision of a large building to permit document production on suitable drawing sheet sizes: Block A, Block B, and so on.

Each floor of a multistory building should be numbered sequentially, starting from the lowest level. This code may be used independently or in conjunction with a particular floor function or designation title:

> Level 05: Street level
> Level 01: Basement 1

Each room or space in a building should be numbered sequentially for each level. The allocated number for a specific room may be combined with a floor level code and block code to form a room or space code. This code may be used independently or in conjunction with a particular room function or designation title:

> Block A
> Level 1   A1:01
> Room 1   CLASSROOM

Vertical circulation spaces within a building may be given an appropriate identification code for the type of space and sequential number for the particular space:

> Stairs: S1, S2, S3, etc.

Cross referencing of components and assemblies to schedules should be indicated on drawings by the rectangular schedule symbol, the upper segment containing an appropriate identification code for the component and assembly, and the lower segment containing the sequential number for the particular item. Examples:

Door Assembly
Door Sequence Number for Each Block

D
01

Window Assembly
Window Sequence Number for Each Block

W
01

Partition Assembly
Partition Sequence Number for Each Block

P
01

Structural assemblies (e.g., columns, beams, and slabs) may also be cross referenced to schedules, with this symbol:

Steel Column Assembly
Steel Column Sequence Number

SC
01

Note All schedules must clearly indicate the specific areas to which they apply, namely, block number, floor level number, and so on.

A circle should be used as a symbol for cross-referencing drawings. The upper segment of the circle should contain the specific item classification code, and the lower segment the drawing number or sheet reference (Figure 7.5). Arrows should be used where necessary to identify the location and direction of the specific item.

Areas on location drawings which require additional information should be cross-referenced to special area drawings by the use of the circle symbol. The upper segment of the circle should contain the room number or area code, and the lower segment the specific special area drawing number or sheet reference.

Location drawings may be coded to identify specific elevations and cross referenced to elevational drawings by the use of the circle symbol. The upper segment of the circle should contain the block code and the sequential elevation number for the particular block, and the lower segment of the circle the elevation drawing number or sheet reference.

Location drawings should be coded to identify specific positions where detailed construction information is required, and cross referenced to construction or assembly detail drawings by the use of the circle symbol. The upper segment of the circle should contain a sequential detail number, and the lower segment the specific detail drawing number or sheet reference.

Levels record the distance above or below a defined datum; either standard datum (mean sealevel) or a selected datum for the particular project. Levels related to any datum other than standard datum are referred to as reference levels (RL).

A reference datum should be established for each project in order to define the reduced levels of the building project. This job datum should be readily located on site and clearly indicated on all drawings. The datum adopted for a project should ensure that all reference levels are positive numbers.

All levels should be expressed in meters to three decimal places or to an accuracy of 0.005 m. Levels of contours and specific points should be indicated by the appropriate recommended symbols. When there is a possibility that levels may be confused with other figures on a drawing, the use of prefixes is recommended, for examples, RL or FFL (finished floor level) or FCL (finished ceiling

LEVELS ON DRAWINGS (ELEVATIONS)

Table 7.5 Expression of Slope

Ratio y/x	Angle	Angle (rad)	Percentage (%)
Shallow slopes			
1:100	0° 34′	0.0100	1
1:67	0° 52′	0.0150	1.5
1:57	1°	0.0175	1.75
1:50	1° 09′	0.0200	2
1:40	1° 26′	0.0250	2.5
1:33	1° 43′	0.0300	3
1:29	2°	0.0349	3.5
1:25	2° 17′	0.0399	4
1:20	2° 52′	0.0499	5
1:19	3°	0.0524	5.25
Slight slopes			
1:17	3° 26′	0.0599	6
1:15	3° 48′	0.0664	6.7
1:14.3	4°	0.0698	7
1:12	4° 46′	0.0832	8.3
1:11.4	5°	0.0873	8.75
1:10	5° 43′	0.0998	10
1:9.5	6°	0.1047	10.5
1:8	7° 07′	0.1245	12.5
1:7.1	8°	0.1396	14
1:6.7	8° 32′	0.1490	15
1:6	9° 28′	0.1652	16.7
1:5.7	10°	0.1745	17.6
1:5	11° 19′	0.1975	20
1:4.5	12° 30′	0.2182	22.2
1:4	14° 02′	0.2450	25
Medium slopes			
1:3.7	15°	0.2618	25.8
1:3.3	16° 42′	0.2915	30
1:3	18° 26′	0.3217	33.3
1:2.75	20°	0.3491	36.4
1:2.5	21° 48′	0.3805	40
1:2.4	22° 30′	0.3927	41.4
1:2.15	25°	0.4363	46.6
1:2	26° 34′	0.4537	50
1:1.73	30°	0.5236	57.5
1:1.67	30° 58′	0.5405	60
1:1.5	33° 42′	0.5880	67
1:1.33	36° 52′	0.6434	75
1:1.2	40°	0.6981	84
1:1	45°	0.7854	100
Steep slopes			
1.19:1	50°	0.8727	119
1.43:1	55°	0.9599	143
1.5:1	56° 19′	0.9827	150
1.73:1	60°	1.0472	173
2:1	63° 26′	1.1071	200
2.15:1	65°	1.1345	215
2.5:1	68° 12′	1.1903	250
2.75:1	70°	1.2217	275
3:1	71° 34′	1.2491	300
3.73:1	75°	1.3090	373
4:1	75° 58′	1.3253	400
5:1	78° 42′	1.3735	500
5.67:1	80°	1.3963	567
6:1	80° 32′	1.4056	600
11.43:1	85°	1.4835	1143
∞	90°	1.5708	∞

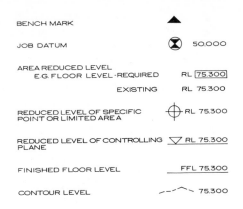

BENCH MARK	▲
JOB DATUM	⊗ 50.000
AREA REDUCED LEVEL E.G. FLOOR LEVEL - REQUIRED	RL 75.300
EXISTING	RL 75.300
REDUCED LEVEL OF SPECIFIC POINT OR LIMITED AREA	⊕ RL 75.300
REDUCED LEVEL OF CONTROLLING PLANE	▽ RL 75.300
FINISHED FLOOR LEVEL	FFL 75.300
CONTOUR LEVEL	75.300

Figure 7.7 Conventions for levels on drawings.

level). The level of a horizontal plane or surface with defined boundaries should be shown with the figures enclosed in a rectangular box, drawn adjacent to the area name or code. In elevation and section, levels should be expressed in the same manner as in plan, with the figures placed immediately above and parallel to the reference line. Figures expressing levels may be related to specific reference lines by arrowheads to facilitate identification (Figure 7.7).

In the past many different expressions have been used for slope, such as angle in degrees and minutes; ratio, expressed as a "1 in" or "1 to" pitch in inches per feet or feet per mile; and gradient as a percentage. The use of millimeters and, to some extent, meters in building drawings greatly favors the adoption of a nondimensional ratio as an expression of slope. This can be related directly to preferred metric dimensions, which do not apply to the expression of slope in degrees or, indeed, the SI unit radian. For instance, a slope of 1:2 indicates a vertical/horizontal ratio of 100:200 or 50:100 much more directly than the angular equivalent of 26°34′ or 0.4628 rad (Table 7.5).

In expressing slope as a ratio, the vertical component should always be shown first, that is, y/x. For slopes of less than 45° the vertical component should always be shown as unity; for example, a ratio of 1:5 indicates a rise of 1 mm for every 5 mm of horizontal dimension, or of 100 mm for every 500 mm, or of 1 m for every 5 m, and so on. For slopes greater than 45° the horizontal component should always be 1 for ease of verification; for example, a ratio of 5:1 expresses a rise of 5 mm for a horizontal dimension of 1 mm, or 500 mm for each 100 mm, and so on.

The past practice of expressing slope by a defined ratio in mixed units, such as 1 in in 4 ft or 10 ft/mi, should be discouraged in converting to metric units. Expressions such as millimeters per meter (mm/m) or meters per kilometer (m/km) should be avoided.

SLOPE AS RATIO

ANTHROPOMETRIC DATA

NIELS DIFFRIENT
and
ALVIN R. TILLEY

Henry Dreyfuss Associates

Ancient architecture, which was measured with human parts—the finger, the palm, the foot, and the cubit (one foot plus two palms)—may be said to have had human scale. In Egypt a larger unit, the "royal" cubit (about 15% greater), was used to give its sacred architecture more imposing dimensions. The Renaissance builders concentrated on geometric patterns at the apparent expense of human relationships. When the Roman numeral system was replaced by simple Arabic notation, including the Hindu zero, the number system dominated. The industrial era favored the use of numbers over proportions. But in today's more democratic climate we try to design to accommodate all people. Human factor specialists have given us the measurements of men, women, and children—large, average, and small. We are again becoming aware of human scale.

During the upheaval of the French Revolution, in 1799 the old measures gave way to the meter, which was based on one ten-millionth of an arc of the earth's meridian from pole to equator and is now defined in terms of radiation from a light source—hardly a human scale!

The French architect Le Corbusier made a valiant effort with his "modulor" to establish within the metric system a set of measurements based on human proportions, at the same time complying with the laws of growth. He said that 10, 20, 30, 40, 50 centimeters or 1, 2, 3, 4, 5 meters were total strangers to the dimensions of our body. He preferred the golden rule of the Greeks and the Fibonacci series of numbers (4, 6, 10, 16, 26, 42, etc.), making a progression of foot, solar plexus, head, and fingers of a raised hand. Unfortunately, by taking a 6-foot (1.83 m) Englishman for a standard and using the "golden section," he introduced fractional numbers which, even when rounded, produced some architectural inconsistencies.

When the Romans divided the foot into 12 thumb breadths, a duodecimal system was begun which had the advantage of being divisible evenly by 2, 3, 4, 6 as compared with the decimal sytem, which is evenly divided only by 2 and 5. The binary system of today's computer era is divisible by 2 only, being based on switch operations (on or off). The ancient Chaldeans also made use of the duodecimal arrangement. The circle was divided into 360 degrees, the year into 360 days, the day into 24 hours, the hour into 60 minutes, and the minute into 60 seconds. All are divided evenly by 2, 3, 4, 6, 12 (hence the 12 signs of the zodiac). When the inch was divided into 16 parts, however, the seeds of destruction were sown for the foot-inch system. Now only the Americans, among English-speaking people, are confronted with engineering tools and components based on the fractional system $\frac{1}{32}$, $\frac{1}{16}$, $\frac{1}{8}$, $\frac{1}{4}$, etc. In an effort to obtain more precision than $\frac{1}{64}$ in, engineers introduced the decimal inch, but fractions do not decimalize easily ($\frac{1}{64}$ in = 0.015625). Now we are in the midst of metric conversion: the conversion process may be painful, but the sooner we think metric, the sooner we will have peace of mind.

HUMAN MEASUREMENT

Human factors data are often taken in centimeters. Since the millimeter will be the standard unit of linear measurement, however, centimeters will not be used in the building construction industry. By using millimeters as a standard, the decimal point is avoided. The scale of drawings will of necessity change (English scales of $1, \frac{1}{2}, \frac{1}{4}, \frac{1}{8}$, become decimal metric scales $1:1, 1:2, 1:5, 1:10$, which are acceptable).

Foot-inch proportions are not necessary for human factors, as we have learned that one person's foot is not another's. But by accommodating the human being, we automatically gain proportions which are right for comfort, safety, and environment.

The goal of architecture should be to accommodate people at an appropriate human scale regardless of size, age, sex, race, or mobility. The study of anthropometry, and that of safety factors, are emerging fields from which to draw useful data to reinforce this purpose.

Human measurements, which have been difficult to collect and collate, must be generalized from inadequate and entangled data. The anthropometric charts at the end of this chapter are intended to condense, simplify, and complete data that will apply to and enlarge on the architect's sphere of interest.

USING THE ANTHROPOMETRIC DRAWINGS

The anthropometric drawings (Figures 8.1 to 8.7) show three values for each measurement: the top figure is for the large person or 97.5 percentile; the middle figure, for the average person or 50 percentile; and the lower figure, for the small person or 2.5 percentile. The chosen extreme percentiles thus include 95%. The remaining 5% includes some who learn to adapt, while others, not adequately represented, are excluded to keep designs for the majority from becoming too complex and expensive. Space and access charts are designed to accept the 97.5 percentile large man and will accept all adults save a few giants. The 97.5 percentile should, therefore, be used to determine space envelopes; the 2.5 percentile, to determine maximum hand- or foot-reach areas, "kinetospheres"; and the 50 percentile, to establish control and display heights. To accommodate both men and women, it is useful at times to add a dimension of the large man to the corresponding dimension of the small woman and divide by 2 to obtain data for the average adult. This is the way height standards evolve. Youth data are combined for both sexes. Although girls and boys do not grow at the same rate at corresponding ages, differences are small when compared with size variations.

Pivot point and link systems make it easy to construct articulating templates and manikins. Links are simplified bones. The spine is shown as a single link; since it can flex, pivot points may be added. All human joints are not simple pivots, though it is convenient to assume them so. Some, like the shoulder, move in complicated patterns. The reaches shown are easy and comfortable, but it is possible to extend reach by bending and rotating the trunk and extending the shoulder. Stooping to reach low is better than stretching to reach high. The dynamic body may need 10% more space than the static posture allows. Shoes have been included in all measurements, but allowance may be required for heavy clothing. Sight lines and angles of vision given in one place or another apply to all persons.

The metric system of measurement in millimeters has been included in all drawings. Rounding to 5 mm is within the tolerance of most human measurements.

DISABILITY AND SAFETY CONSIDERATIONS

Disabilities must be reckoned with: 3.5% of men and 0.2% of women are color blind, 4.5% of adults are hard of hearing, over 30% wear glasses, 15 to

20% are handicapped, and 1% are illiterate. The number of left-handed people is increasing to over 10% of the population.

Safety information, although difficult to find, must not be overlooked. The maximum safe temperature of metal handles is 50°C (122°F) and of nonmetallic handles is 62°C (144°F); the maximum air temperature for warm-air hand dryers is 60°C (140°F); water temperatures over 46°C (115+°F) are destructive to human tissue. The environmental comfort temperature range is 17 to 24°C (63 to 75°F). Weights that can be lifted without discomfort or excessive strain range up to 23 kg (50+ lb) for 90% of men and 16 kg (35+ lb) for women, but are limited to 9 kg (20 lb) if carried by one hand for long distances. Push and pull forces for such things as moving carts are 260 N (58 lbf) and 235 N (53 lbf) initially but drop to 130 N (29 lbf) and 140 N (32 lbf) if sustained. Noise above the following values can cause permanent deafness: 90 decibels (dB) for 8 h, 95 for 4, 100 for 2, 105 for 1, and 110 for 0.5.

ANTHROPOMETRIC DATA—ADULTS

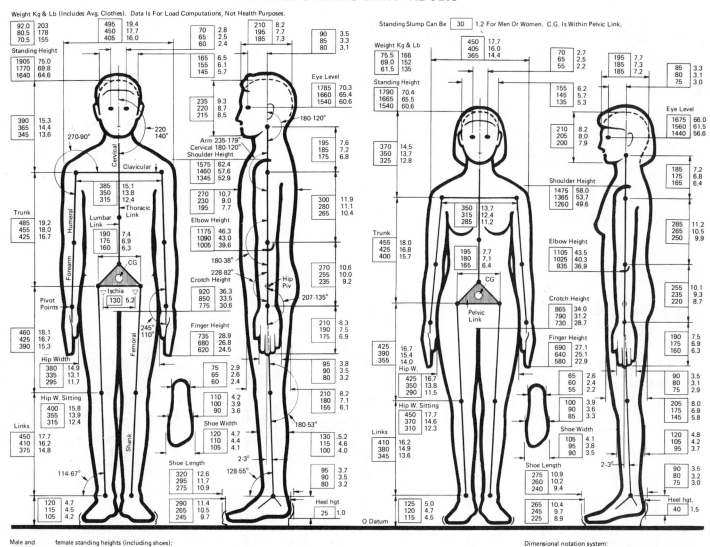

Niels Diffrient, Alvin R. Tilley; Henry Dreyfuss Associates; New York, New York

Figure 8.1

ANTHROPOMETRIC DATA—CHILDREN

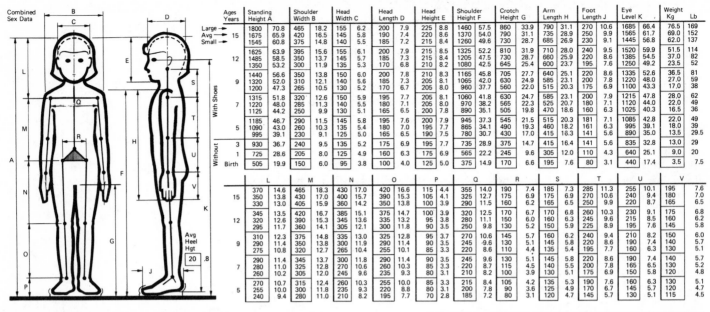

Ages Years	Standing Height A		Shoulder Width B		Head Width C		Head Length D		Head Height E		Shoulder Height F		Crotch Height G		Arm Length H		Foot Length J		Eye Level K		Weight Kg	Lb
15	1800	70.8	465	18.2	155	6.2	200	7.9	225	8.8	1460	57.5	860	33.9	790	31.1	270	10.6	1685	66.4	76.5	169
	1675	65.9	420	16.5	145	5.8	190	7.4	220	8.6	1370	54.0	790	31.1	735	28.9	250	9.9	1565	61.7	69.0	152
	1545	60.8	375	14.8	140	5.5	185	7.2	215	8.4	1260	49.6	730	28.7	685	26.9	230	9.1	1445	56.8	62.0	137
12	1625	63.9	395	15.6	155	6.1	200	7.9	215	8.5	1325	52.2	810	31.9	710	28.0	240	9.5	1520	59.9	51.5	114
	1485	58.5	350	13.7	145	5.7	185	7.3	215	8.4	1205	47.5	730	28.7	660	25.9	220	8.6	1385	54.5	37.0	82
	1350	53.2	300	11.9	135	5.3	170	6.8	210	8.2	1080	42.5	645	25.4	600	23.7	195	7.6	1250	49.2	23.5	52
9	1440	56.6	350	13.8	150	6.0	200	7.8	210	8.3	1165	45.8	705	27.7	640	25.1	220	8.6	1335	52.6	36.5	81
	1320	52.0	310	12.1	140	5.6	185	7.3	205	8.1	1065	42.0	630	24.9	585	23.1	200	7.8	1220	48.0	27.0	59
	1200	47.3	265	10.5	130	5.2	170	6.7	205	8.0	960	37.7	560	22.0	515	20.3	175	6.9	1100	43.3	17.0	38
7	1315	51.8	320	12.6	150	5.9	195	7.7	205	8.1	1060	41.8	630	24.7	585	23.1	200	7.9	1215	47.8	28.0	62
	1220	48.0	285	11.3	140	5.5	180	7.1	205	8.0	970	38.2	565	22.3	525	20.7	180	7.1	1120	44.0	22.0	49
	1125	44.2	250	9.9	130	5.1	165	6.5	200	7.8	890	35.1	505	19.8	470	18.6	160	6.3	1025	40.3	16.5	36
5	1185	46.7	290	11.5	145	5.8	195	7.6	200	7.9	945	37.3	545	21.5	515	20.3	181	7.1	1085	42.8	22.0	49
	1090	43.0	260	10.3	135	5.4	180	7.0	195	7.7	865	34.1	490	19.3	460	18.2	161	6.3	995	39.1	18.0	39
	995	39.1	230	9.1	125	5.0	165	6.5	190	7.5	780	30.7	430	17.0	415	16.3	141	5.6	890	35.0	13.5	29.5
3	930	36.7	240	9.5	135	5.2	175	6.9	195	7.7	735	28.9	375	14.7	415	16.4	141	5.6	835	32.8	13.0	29
1	725	28.6	205	8.0	125	4.9	160	6.3	175	6.9	565	22.2	245	9.6	305	12.0	110	4.3	640	25.1	9.0	20
Birth	505	19.9	150	6.0	95	3.8	100	4.0	125	5.0	375	14.9	170	6.6	195	7.6	80	3.1	440	17.4	3.5	7.5

Ages	L		M		N		O		P		Q		R		S		T		U		V	
15	370	14.6	465	18.3	430	17.0	420	16.6	115	4.4	355	14.0	190	7.4	185	7.3	285	11.3	255	10.1	195	7.6
	350	13.8	430	17.0	400	15.7	390	15.3	105	4.1	325	12.7	175	6.9	175	6.9	270	10.6	240	9.4	180	7.0
	330	13.0	405	15.9	360	14.2	350	13.8	100	3.9	290	11.5	160	6.2	165	6.5	250	9.9	220	8.7	165	6.5
12	345	13.5	420	16.7	385	15.1	375	14.7	100	3.9	320	12.5	170	6.7	170	6.8	260	10.3	230	9.1	175	6.8
	320	12.6	390	15.3	345	13.6	335	13.2	95	3.8	280	11.1	150	6.0	160	6.3	245	9.6	215	8.5	160	6.2
	295	11.7	360	14.1	305	12.1	300	11.8	90	3.5	250	9.8	130	5.2	150	5.9	225	8.9	195	7.6	145	5.8
9	310	12.3	375	14.8	335	13.0	325	12.8	95	3.7	270	10.6	145	5.7	160	6.3	240	9.4	210	8.2	150	6.0
	290	11.4	350	13.8	300	11.9	290	11.4	90	3.5	245	-9.6	130	5.1	145	5.8	220	8.6	190	7.4	140	5.7
	275	10.8	320	12.7	265	10.4	255	10.1	85	3.3	220	8.6	110	4.4	135	5.4	195	7.7	160	6.3	130	5.1
7	290	11.4	345	13.7	300	11.8	290	11.4	90	3.5	245	9.6	130	5.1	145	5.8	220	8.6	190	7.4	140	5.7
	280	11.0	325	12.8	270	10.6	260	10.3	85	3.3	220	8.7	115	4.5	140	5.5	200	7.8	165	6.5	130	5.2
	260	10.2	305	12.0	245	9.6	235	9.3	80	3.1	210	8.2	100	3.9	130	5.1	175	6.9	150	5.8	120	4.8
5	270	10.7	315	12.4	260	10.3	255	10.0	85	3.3	215	8.4	105	4.2	135	5.3	190	7.6	160	6.3	130	5.1
	255	10.0	300	11.8	235	9.3	220	8.8	80	3.1	200	7.8	90	3.6	125	4.9	170	6.7	145	5.7	120	4.7
	240	9.4	280	11.0	210	8.2	195	7.7	70	2.8	185	7.2	80	3.1	120	4.7	145	5.7	130	5.1	115	4.5

Large → Avg → Small
With Shoes / Without
Avg Heel Hgt 20 .8

	Ages	High Reach A		Low Reach B		Reach Distance C		High Reach D		Reach Radius E		Eye Level F	
HS	15	2085	82.0	815	32.0	735	29.0	1440	56.7	660	25.9	1215	47.8
		1915	75.3	730	28.7	685	27.0	1375	54.1	610	24.1	1160	45.6
		1765	69.4	665	26.2	635	25.1	1315	51.7	570	22.4	1100	43.3
Jr. HS	12	1860	73.2	705	27.6	665	26.2	1320	52.0	600	23.6	1100	43.3
		1705	67.1	630	24.7	620	24.3	1250	49.2	555	21.9	1040	41.0
		1545	60.9	560	22.1	565	22.3	1185	46.6	510	20.1	990	38.9
4th.	9	1645	64.8	605	23.8	600	23.6	1175	46.3	540	21.2	975	38.4
		1510	59.4	555	21.8	550	21.7	1120	44.0	495	19.5	925	36.5
		1345	53.0	510	20.0	485	19.1	1040	40.9	435	17.1	880	34.6
2nd.	7	1505	59.3	545	21.5	550	21.7	1080	42.6	500	19.6	890	35.0
		1370	53.9	510	20.1	495	19.5	1015	40.0	445	17.5	850	33.5
		1245	49.0	485	19.0	445	17.5	960	37.7	395	15.6	815	32.0
KDG	5	1330	52.3	500	19.7	480	19.0	970	38.1	430	16.9	815	32.1
		1210	47.7	465	18.3	435	17.1	915	36.1	385	15.2	770	30.4
		1085	42.7	425	16.7	390	15.3	865	34.1	345	13.6	720	28.4

Starting School Grades

Up To Ages	Hat Shelf Height G		Lavatory Height H		Work Top J		Work Depth K		Table Height L		Seat Length M	
15	1675	66.0	760	30.0	915	36.0	460	18.0	650	25.5	370	14.6
12	1485	58.5	685	27.0	795	31.3	420	16.5	590	23.3	340	13.3
9	1320	52.0	635	25.0	695	27.3	380	15.0	525	20.7	300	11.8
7	1220	48.0	585	23.0	635	25.0	355	14.0	480	18.9	275	10.8
5	1090	43.0	485	19.0	570	22.5	330	13.0	445	17.5	250	9.9

Ages	Seat Height N		Seat To Backrest O		Min Backrest Height P		Armrest Spacing Q		Seat Width R		Basic Table Width S	
15	405	15.9	150	6.0	175	6.8	445	17.5	380	15.0	760	30.0
12	370	14.6	145	5.7	160	6.2	420	16.5	370	14.5	710	28.0
9	325	12.8	135	5.4	140	5.6	355	14.0	330	13.0	610	24.0
7	290	11.4	130	5.1	130	5.1	330	13.0	305	12.0	610	24.0
5	265	10.4	120	4.8	125	5.0	305	12.0	280	11.0	535	21.0

Chalk Board Height
Comfortable High Reach
Hat Shelves At Head Height Rule Also Applies To Adults
Clothes Pole Or Hook Strip
Reach Distance
Work Counter
Lav Rim
Chalk Rail
100 4
15°

High Shelf
50 2
205 8
Eye Level
Functional Grips
40°
0–20°

WC Ages	Hgt	
14+	355	14
9–14	305	12
2–9	255	10

Min Armrest
150 6
50 2
Min 280 11
Greater For Storage

Standing heights (including shoes)—typical example:
1800	70.8	large 15 year youth = 97.5 percentile	combined sex data U.S. youths
1675	65.9	average 15 year youth = 50 percentile	
1545	60.8	small 15 year youth = 2.5 percentile	

NOTE: Metric dimensions shown may be affected by later U.S. Metric Standards.

Dimensional notation system:
1000	39.3	Numbers appearing in boxes are measurements in millimeters. Numbers outside boxes are measurements in inches.
100	3.9	
25.4	1.0	

Niels Diffrient, Alvin R. Tilley; Henry Dreyfuss Associates; New York, New York

Figure 8.2

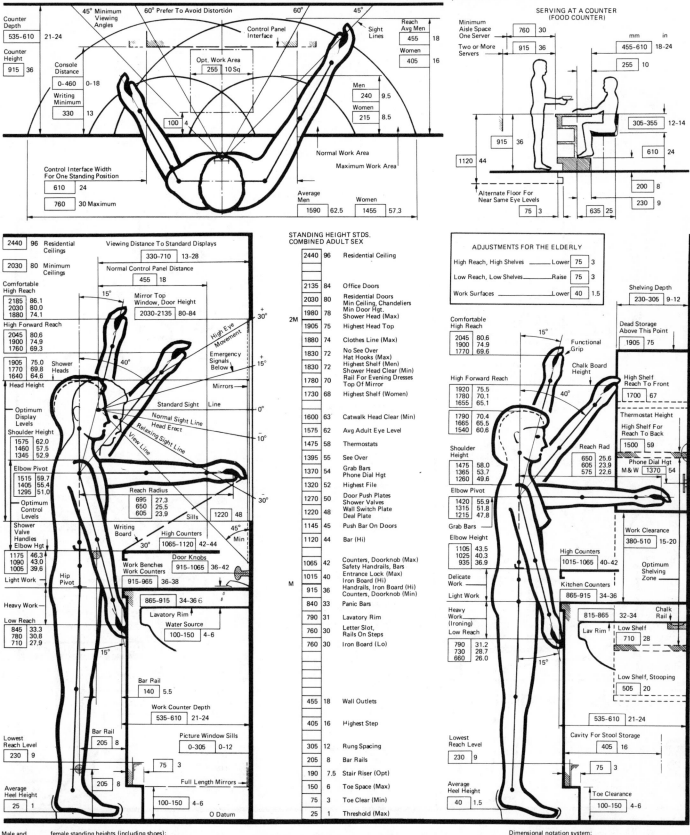

Figure 8.3

Niels Diffrient, Alvin R. Tilley; Henry Dreyfuss Associates; New York, New York

NOTE: Metric dimensions shown may be affected by later U.S. Metric Standards.

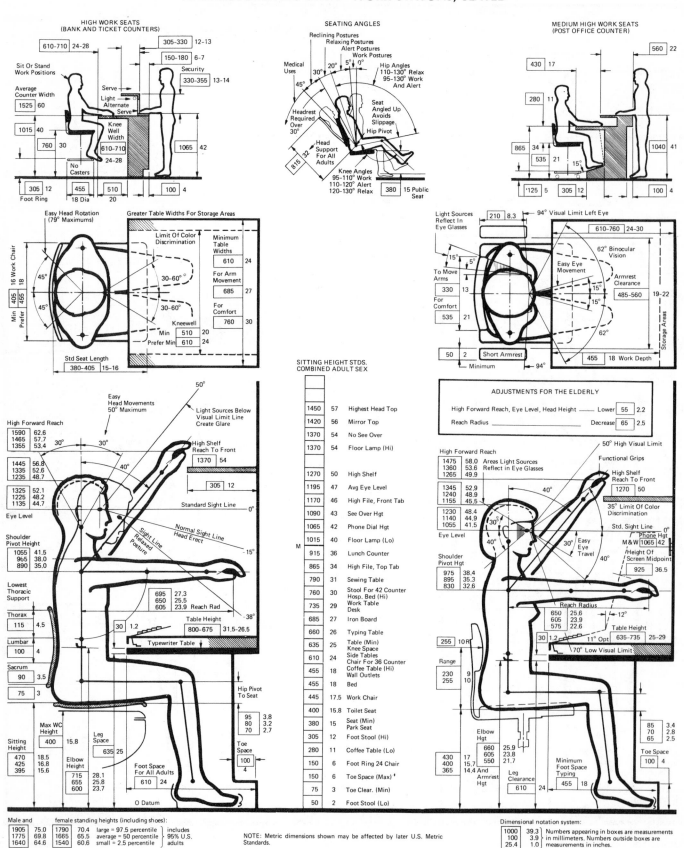

Niels Diffrient, Alvin R. Tilley; Henry Dreyfuss Associates; New York, New York

NOTE: Metric dimensions shown may be affected by later U.S. Metric Standards.

Figure 8.4

ANTHROPOMETRIC DATA—SPACE USAGE

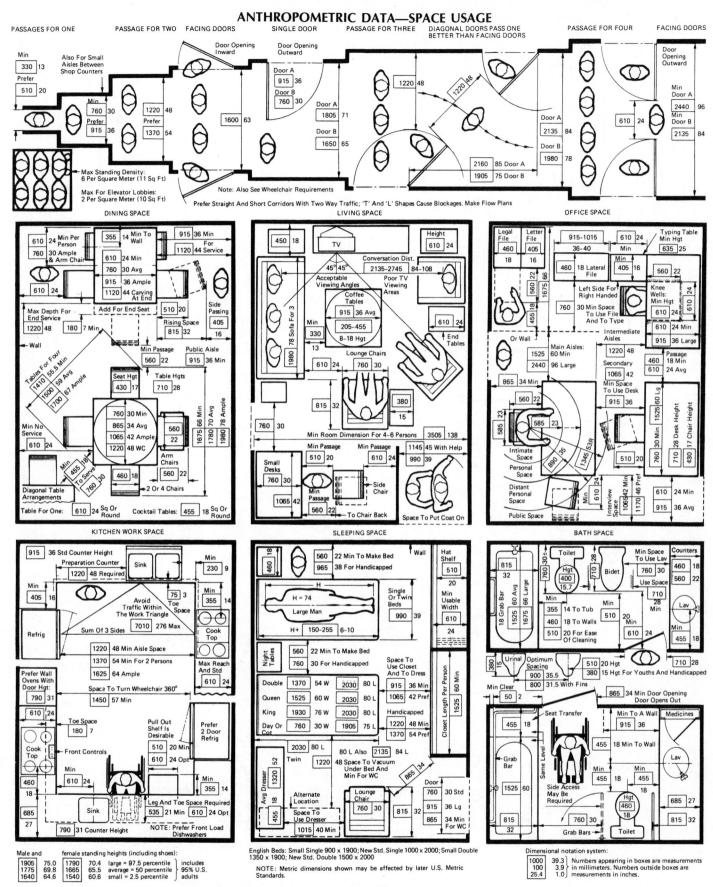

Niels Diffrient, Alvin R. Tilley; Henry Dreyfuss Associates; New York, New York

Figure 8.5

Anthropometric Data 81

ANTHROPOMETRIC DATA—ACCESSIBILITY

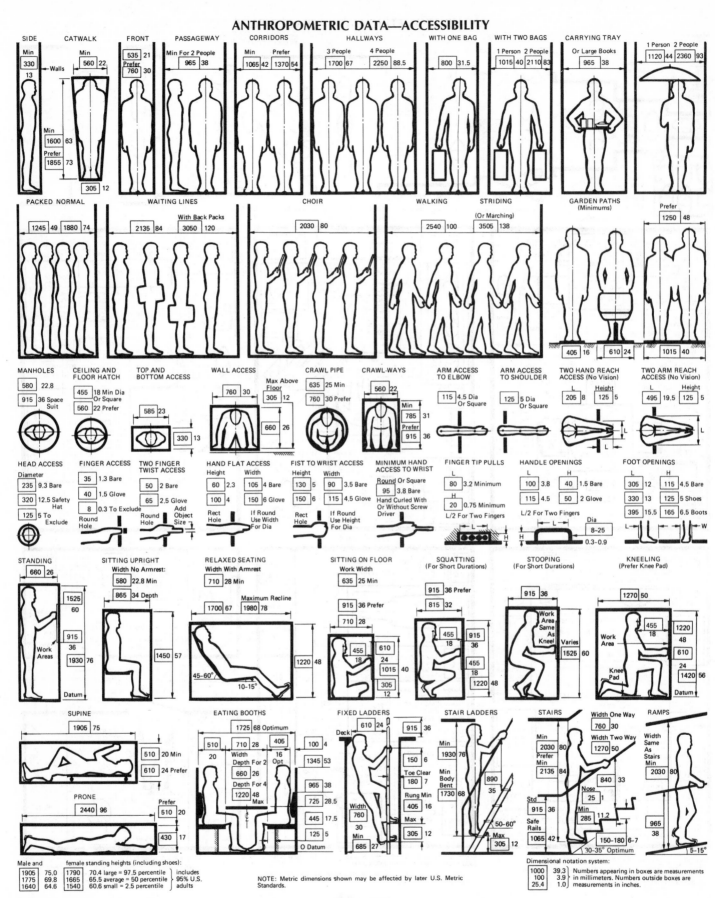

Niels Diffrient, Alvin R. Tilley; Henry Dreyfuss Associates; New York, New York

NOTE: Metric dimensions shown may be affected by later U.S. Metric Standards.

Figure 8.6

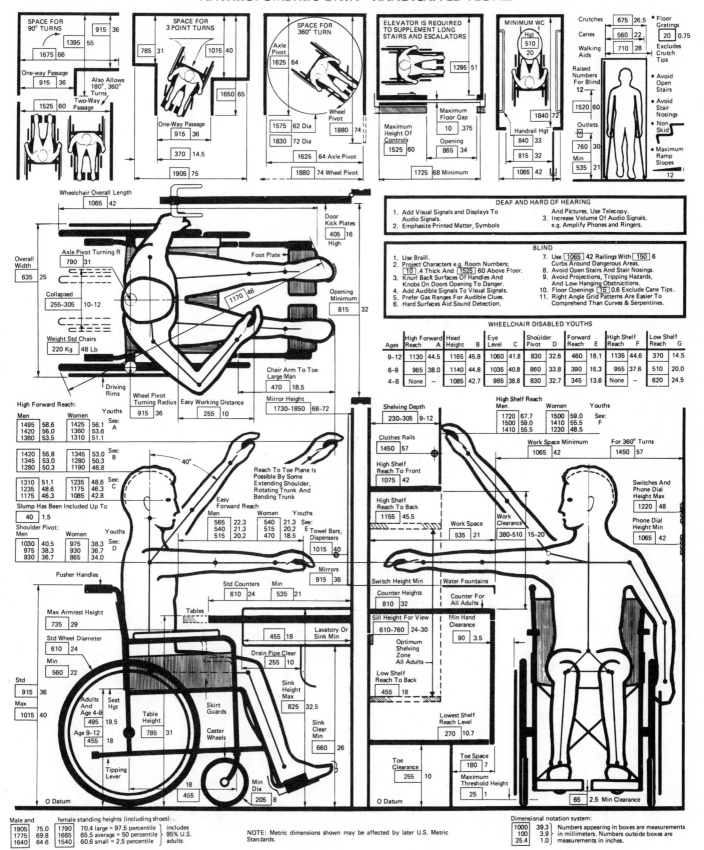

SPACE FOR 90° TURNS
915 | 36
1395 | 55
1675 | 66

One-way Passage
915 | 36

Two-Way Passage
1525 | 60
Also Allows 180°, 360° Turns

SPACE FOR 3 POINT TURNS
785 | 31
1015 | 40
1650 | 65

One-Way Passage
915 | 36
370 | 14.5
1905 | 75

SPACE FOR 360° TURN
Axle Pivot 1625 | 64
Wheel Pivot 1880 | 74

Wheel Pivot
1575 | 62 Dia
1830 | 72 Dia
1625 | 64 Axle Pivot
1880 | 74 Wheel Pivot

ELEVATOR IS REQUIRED TO SUPPLEMENT LONG STAIRS AND ESCALATORS
1295 | 51
Maximum Height Of Controls 1525 | 60
Maximum Floor Gap 10 | .375
Opening 865 | 34
1725 | 68 Minimum

MINIMUM WC
Hgt 510 | 20
1840 | 72
Handrail Hgt 840 | 33
815 | 32
1065 | 42

Crutches 675 | 26.5
Canes 560 | 22
Walking Aids 710 | 28
Raised Numbers For Blind 12
1520 | 60
Outlets 760 | 30
Min 535 | 21

- Floor Gratings 20 | 0.75
- Excludes Crutch Tips
- Avoid Open Stairs
- Avoid Stair Nosings
- Non Skid
- Maximum Ramp Slopes 12

Wheelchair Overall Length 1065 | 42
Overall Width 635 | 25
Axle Pivot Turning R 790 | 31
Collapsed 255-305 | 10-12
Weight Std Chairs 220 Kg | 48 Lb
Door Kick Plates 405 | 16 High
Foot Plate 1170 | 46
Opening Minimum 815 | 32
Driving Rims
Wheel Pivot Turning Radius 915 | 36
Easy Working Distance 255 | 10
Chair Arm To Toe Large Man 470 | 18.5
Mirror Height 1730-1850 | 68-72

DEAF AND HARD OF HEARING
1. Add Visual Signals and Displays To Audio Signals.
2. Emphasize Printed Matter, Symbols And Pictures. Use Telecopy.
3. Increase Volume Of Audio Signals. e.g. Amplify Phones and Ringers.

BLIND
1. Use Braill.
2. Project Characters e.g. Room Numbers; 10 | .4 Thick And 1525 | 60 Above Floor.
3. Knurl Back Surfaces Of Handles And Knobs On Doors Opening To Danger.
4. Add Audible Signals To Visual Signals.
5. Prefer Gas Ranges For Audible Clues.
6. Hard Surfaces Aid Sound Detection.
7. Use 1065 | 42 Railings With 150 | 6 Curbs Around Dangerous Areas.
8. Avoid Open Stairs And Stair Nosings.
9. Avoid Projections, Tripping Hazards, And Low Hanging Obstructions.
10. Floor Openings 15 | 0.6 Exclude Cane Tips.
11. Right Angle Grid Patterns Are Easier To Comprehend Than Curves & Serpentines.

WHEELCHAIR DISABLED YOUTHS

Ages	High Forward Reach A		Head Height B		Eye Level C		Shoulder Pivot D		Forward Reach E		High Shelf Reach F		Low Shelf Reach G	
9-12	1130	44.5	1165	45.8	1060	41.8	830	32.6	460	18.1	1135	44.6	370	14.5
6-9	965	38.0	1140	44.8	1035	40.8	860	33.8	390	15.3	955	37.6	510	20.0
4-6	None	—	1085	42.7	985	38.8	830	32.7	345	13.6	None	—	620	24.5

High Forward Reach:

Men		Women		Youths See: A
1495	58.6	1425	56.1	
1420	56.0	1360	53.6	
1360	53.5	1310	51.1	

Men		Women		See: B
1420	55.8	1345	53.0	
1345	53.0	1280	50.3	
1280	50.3	1190	46.8	

Men		Women		See: C
1310	51.1	1235	48.6	
1235	48.6	1175	46.3	
1175	46.3	1085	42.8	

Slump Has Been Included Up To 40 | 1.5

Shoulder Pivot:

Men		Women		Youths See: D
1030	40.5	975	38.3	
975	38.3	930	36.7	
930	36.7	865	34.0	

40°

Reach To Toe Plane Is Possible By Some Extending Shoulder, Rotating Trunk And Bending Trunk

Easy Forward Reach

Men		Women		Youths See: E
565	22.3	540	21.3	
540	21.3	515	20.2	
515	20.2	470	18.5	

Towel Bars, Dispensers 1015 | 40
Mirrors 915 | 36

Shelving Depth 230-305 | 9-12
Clothes Rails 1450 | 57
High Shelf Reach To Front 1075 | 42
High Shelf Reach To Back 1155 | 45.5
Work Space 535 | 21

High Shelf Reach

Men		Women		Youths See: F
1720	67.7	1500	59.0	
1500	59.0	1410	55.5	
1410	55.5	1230	48.5	

Work Space Minimum 1065 | 42
For 360° Turns 1450 | 57
Work Clearance 380-510 | 15-20
Switches And Phone Dial Height Max 1220 | 48
Phone Dial Height Min 1065 | 42

Pusher Handles
Max Armrest Height 735 | 29
Std Wheel Diameter 610 | 24
Min 560 | 22
Std 915 | 36
Max 1015 | 40
Adults And Age 4-9 495 | 19.5
Age 9-12 455 | 18
Seat Hgt
Table Height 785 | 31
Skirt Guards
Caster Wheels
Tipping Lever
18
Min Dia 455
205 | 8
O Datum

Tables
Std Counters 610 | 24
Min 535 | 21
455 | 18
Lavatory Or Sink Min
Drain Pipe Clear 255 | 10
Sink Height Max 825 | 32.5
Sink Clear Min 660 | 26

Switch Height Min
Counter Heights 810 | 32
Sill Height For View 610-760 | 24-30
Optimum Shelving Zone All Adults
Low Shelf Reach To Back 455 | 18
Lowest Shelf Reach Level 270 | 10.7
Toe Clearance 255 | 10
O Datum

Water Fountains
Counter For All Adults
Min Hand Clearance 90 | 3.5
Toe Space 180 | 7
Maximum Threshold Height 25 | 1
65 | 2.5 Min Clearance

Male and female standing heights (including shoes):
1905 | 75.0 | 1790 | 70.4 large = 97.5 percentile | includes
1775 | 69.8 | 1665 | 65.5 average = 50 percentile | 95% U.S.
1640 | 64.6 | 1540 | 60.6 small = 2.5 percentile | adults

NOTE: Metric dimensions shown may be affected by later U.S. Metric Standards.

Dimensional notation system:
1000 | 39.3 | Numbers appearing in boxes are measurements
100 | 3.9 | in millimeters. Numbers outside boxes are
25.4 | 1.0 | measurements in inches.

Niels Diffrient, Alvin R. Tilley; Henry Dreyfuss Associates; New York, New York

Figure 8.7

THE EFFECT OF METRICATION ON BUILDING CODES AND STANDARDS

CHARLES T. MAHAFFEY

Senior Building Standards Specialist
Center for Building Technology
National Bureau of Standards

BUILDING CODES

Building codes are technical regulations that establish reasonable levels of public health and safety in regard to the design and construction of buildings. If the building process is thought of as being naturally divisible into a design phase and construction phase, building codes represent the interface between them. This means that before any design concept or building product can be used in the physical construction of a building, it must pass through a building code review. From a marketing viewpoint, building codes thus become a sounding board for determining the acceptability of building products, components, systems, and designs. Generally speaking, nothing gets into the built environment unless it passes through this building code scrutiny.

During (and after) the U.S. metrication effort, building codes will continue to occupy this same key position or role.

BUILDING STANDARDS

Building standards represent the technical backbone of building codes. The term "standards" is intended to represent agreements that are technical descriptions or models of things used in the building process. These agreements include the following: definitions and symbols, building classifications, product/material specifications, test methods, design loads and geophysical maps, and codes of practice—even *model* building codes. Anything of this nature on which an agreement can be reached can be considered a standard. Compliance with standards is usually considered to be voluntary unless they are made part of legal regulations or contracts.

The extent of this agreement is regularly used to determine the stature or character of the standard. A standard representing an agreement among representatives of a *national* cross section of those affected by the subject of the standard is known as a *national* standard. One that represents an agreement within a certain *area* of the country may be known as a *regional* standard. One that may represent a national agreement but only among members of a *segment* of the construction industry is usually referred to as an *industry* standard. Some industry standards may achieve national status by virtue of their countrywide acceptance.

In order for a standard to achieve national status, it is not always necessary for

This chapter is a contribution of the National Bureau of Standards; not subject to copyright.

its developers to be a national consensus group. But involvement in the drafting process of a group representing all nationally affected interests naturally assumes wider acceptance. In the end it is the breadth of this acceptance that truly establishes the local, regional, national, or international character of any standard.

INTERDEPENDENCE OF CODES AND STANDARDS

Building standards form an important part of all building codes. Throughout such codes there are numerous references to standards. When standards are included in regulations, compliance becomes mandatory. In some instances the technical contents of the standard often have a direct bearing on code requirements themselves. Thus any changes in the standards governing, for example, wire rope diameters will certainly be scrutinized for an effect on elevator regulations. Any changes in the standards governing the thicknesses of fireproofing materials will prompt a review of existing building regulations.

Thus the metrication of building standards is going to have a very direct effect on the technical contents of metric building codes. Generally speaking, the metrication of building standards, particularly those governing code requirements, must precede the metrication of building codes.

Unlike the situation in other metricating English-speaking countries (United Kingdom, South Africa, Australia, New Zealand, Canada), there are many originating sources of codes and standards in the United States. In the United Kingdom (U.K.) there is one national institution, the British Standards Institute (BSI), that produces *all* U.K. standards. In contrast over 100 U.S. institutions produce standards used primarily in construction. In the United Kingdom there are only three code-promulgating districts (Scotland, the city of London, and the rest of Great Britain). In the United States there are thousands of relatively independent code-promulgating jurisdictions. Obviously, the problem of developing and coordinating a metric changeover plan could be expected to be much simpler in the United Kingdom than in the United States.

RELEVANCE OF DIMENSIONAL COORDINATION

While it may be too early to assess the cost/benefit value of the British dimensional coordination effort on its own merits (and not just as a way of facilitating a metric conversion), it is interesting to note that Canada, Australia, South Africa, and New Zealand all have studied the British program and all have opted to tie a national program of dimensional coordination to their metrication efforts. There is a strong trend developing in this direction in the United States in current discussions within the American National Metric Council (ANMC). If this trend continues, the U.S. building industry will also choose to implement a national program of dimensional coordination as its way of "getting something out of going metric."

If the decision is made to tie dimensional coordination to metrication, decisions on many fundamental codes and standards revisions will be required early in the conversion program. In some cases, where codes originate dimensional requirements, decisions on such code changes must lead. In other cases, changes in reference standards (such as dimensional lumber) will have to occur before code decisions can be reached. Obviously, before any dimensional changes in codes or reference standards can be initiated, national agreements—standards—will have to be established, not only regarding the SI units to be used in construction, but also concerning the principles behind the application of dimensional coordination.

As an example of a dimensional change originating in codes, consider the familiar 22 in unit of exit width. Translated into metric, 22 in is equal to 558.8 mm. This awkward number should be rounded to some new dimension. Applying the principles of dimensional coordination may require some serious rethinking of the whole area. Rounding 558.8 mm to 600 mm fits a first preference 300 mm multimodule, but 600 mm translates into $23\frac{5}{8}$ in, while 500 mm, a second preference number, is only 19$\frac{11}{16}$ in. Proponents of dimensional coordination will point out that not only does it make good sense to use corridor widths that relate to dimensionally coordinated space layouts of buildings, but also, if the many claimed construction productivity advantages are to be realized, *all* building spaces (and the components that fill them) will have to be dimensionally coordinated. Proponents of a simple rounding—say to 550 or 560 mm (21$\frac{5}{8}$ or 22$\frac{3}{64}$ in, respectively)—might claim that this 22-in unit of exit width is so well accepted that it would be foolish to make a drastic change just for slavish devotion to a design principle. Others might say that the 22-in unit was established a long time ago when people were generally smaller and that the increase to 600 mm would be reasonable. A decision in this matter will not be simple to reach. Obviously, because it affects the dimensions of doors, windows, stairs, and so on (besides corridors), many segments of the industry must be involved in this decision. A way of precluding unilateral actions in matters of such industrywide impact will have to be devised and implemented.

In such code subject areas as elevators, the American National Standard Committee A17 (sponsored by the American Society of Mechanical Engineers and operating under ANSI procedures) may find much useful information in the current activities of Subcommittee 12 of Technical Committee (TC) 59, Building Construction, of the International Organization for Standardization (ISO). This very active international standards committee is hard at work devising many applications of dimensional coordination in SI units to the whole field of elevators. Certainly, all of the dimensions, quantities, and values presently contained in the A17 document will have to change to new SI equivalents. The dimensional coordination work being done in TC 59 could provide guidance in arriving at a new metric A17 American National Standard.

Since industry discussions already have started on this subject of dimensional coordination, promulgators of codes and standards are faced with making some basic decisions in the near future. Obviously, they should be involved in these discussions, but how, when, and where they can be represented most effectively remains to be decided.

SOME ASPECTS OF PLANNING AND COORDINATION

This planning-coordination problem in the United States will be formidable. All of the measurement-sensitive building codes and standards must be subjected to a careful scrutiny, new metric values advanced, and agreements reached on reasonable new values. Since the change to the new values will often result in physical size changes of some standard components, with the attendant possibility of new and different metric code requirements, much careful planning will be required. In addition, all of this activity must be carried out on some kind of scheduled basis.

Developing and scheduling a plan for the conversion process in the codes and standards sector will need to take into account the necessity of putting together an organizational structure capable of cooperatively (a) identifying the problems to be faced not only in the codes and standards area, but also in the industry as a whole; (b) establishing priorities among these problems; and (c) timing, coordinating, and monitoring appropriate responses among codes and standards sources.

SELECTION OF SI UNITS

Highest on the list of problem priorities was the establishment of a national standard describing the SI units to be used in the building industry. The many questions involved both with the units themselves and with the conventions regarding their use have been answered in ANSI/ASTM E-621-78, *Standard Practice for the Use of Metric (SI) units in Building Design and Construction*. Little attention can be paid to the actual application of the metric units until it is known what SI working units the building community will select. Although it would appear that the ANMC route is the most appropriate forum, since all segments of the building industry (and other industries) are represented there, ways must be found for developing a codes and standards "position" and of ensuring that this position is understood and given adequate consideration by others. More than just a few discussion meetings will be required. Drafts of recommended SI working units have to be developed and studied, along with the units adopted in other countries. The units recommended by ISO must be given careful consideration, for this one-time opportunity to establish an international technical language for the building industry should not be wasted by either a precipitate or a "muddle through" effort. (See Chapters 2, 3, and 4.)

DIMENSIONAL COORDINATION

Neither the principles of dimensional coordination nor the corresponding erection techniques, of themselves, will have much bearing on the safety aspects of a building. However, the application of these principles to familiar products could cause a reevaluation of old permissible uses. Using these principles to arrive at new sizes of dimension lumber, for instance, could result in thinner and/or narrower lumber sections. This, in turn, could affect existing span tables for headers, joists, and rafters. Similarly, if the thickness of gypsum board is reduced, this reduction plus any that may be connected with dimension lumber may be cause to reevaluate the fire ratings or sound transmission characteristics of constructions involving combinations of such materials. In all cases those responsible for the promulgation of safety standards need to be aware of product and/or system safety performance changes that may result from new metric-sized product standards. (See Chapter 6.)

REGULATORY COORDINATION

Even after agreements have been reached regarding the complex technical problems connected with the selection and appropriate application of SI units and preferred dimensions, coordinating the timing of their introduction into the nation's regulatory system will be a particularly difficult problem. Consider this problem just as it relates to the *model* building and plumbing codes and to special regulatory-type standards like A17 (elevator) or C1 (the American National Standard Electrical Code). Those responsible for the promulgation of these independently produced documents (each group having a distinct generating constituency) will have to participate in the development of agreements not only on the uniform bases and techniques for making the necessary metric and dimensional coordination changes, but also on the staging of the revised editions required and the establishment of coordinated publishing dates. If more than one edition seems to be required, should the first revised edition contain both metric and customary units or should only metric appear? Should rounding of the metric values be attempted in the first stage, or should all such changes be made after the promulgation dates of preferred dimension standards? Could not some old and arbitrary dimensional differences among some of these model documents be cooperatively resolved during this size conversion process?

While there are many more examples of these kinds of problems facing the regulatory sector, the purpose in stating some of them is not to present a hopeless picture but rather to illustrate the pressing need for a new era of communication among the principals involved. Although the number and nature of these problems may appear overwhelming, the ease with which they will be solved will depend on the conversion teams the principals establish among themselves and with other industry teams. The key problem area seems to lie not in dealing with the new units themselves, but in timing and coordinating the introduction of these units into the regulatory system.

INTERNATIONAL PROGRESS

If, as seems likely, the United States also decides on a national program of dimensional coordination as an integral part of metric conversion, the use of 100 mm and its multiples will then become worldwide practice. When the United States completes its conversion, not only will the whole world be using the common metric measurement base provided by SI but, in addition, the metric building world will then have a common dimensioning system for buildings and building components. As a result some American component manufacturers will find that their new *standard* line of metric products can be marketed throughout the world. This will be a unique situation, an opportunity that never existed before, and one that begs for exploitation.

If this situation does develop, some may feel that, instead of offering an opportunity for American firms to start exporting their products, all that will happen will be that foreign firms will now be able to enter the U.S. marketplace. While this may be true, it should be understood that this was always a practical possibility for some of them. It quite often made economic sense for a manufacturer in a foreign country to make a *special* inch-based product for the American market because of the latter's wealth and size. It never made economic sense, however, for an American manufacturer to turn away from the huge American market and make a *special* metric product for a much smaller foreign market. But in the developing worldwide, metric/dimensional coordination situation, *standard* American metric components will have an unprecedented opportunity to find their way into the international marketplace.

Besides the dimensional coordination factor, three other important current international activities are setting the stage for an era of increased trade in building products and know-how as a result of the worldwide movement to SI. In 1975 at a meeting in Helsinki entitled "Conference of Security and Cooperation in Europe," the heads of 35 of the top industrialized nations of the world signed a unique agreement. The final act of the agreement pledged governmental support for activities aimed at reducing obstacles to trade caused by technical regulations, national standards, and certification to standards requirements. President Ford signed this agreement for the United States. The agreement, popularly known as the Helsinki Agreement, is unique because this was the first time that national standards were singled out for international attention as obstacles to trade in a political document of this nature.

The significance of this Helsinki Agreement has not gone unnoticed by the many international organizations involved in the technical aspects of standards and product evaluations. These organizations are already beginning the implementation of the agreement.

The standards harmonization theme of the Helsinki Agreement is central to the international activities associated with the standards code currently being developed by the General Agreement of Tariffs and Trade (GATT). Currently GATT is circulating a proposed methodology for developing national standards so as to ensure their international compatibility. As might be expected, this methodology is cumbersome but could be made to work. It is interesting to note that the GATT negotiators suggest an increased use of performance standards and recommend the use of international standards, particularly test methods, wherever possible.

One important metric-related international standards activity is occurring in the United Nations' Economic Commission for Europe (UN/ECE) and is aimed at the international harmonization of national building regulations. Thirty-four nations, including the Nordic countries, all of Europe, and the Soviet-bloc countries, are involved in the UN/ECE project. The United States and Canada are voting members of the UN/ECE and are represented in this activity. This project is based on the international development and national application of a methodology for employing the performance concept in building regulations. It is centered around the use of the International Organization of Standardization (ISO) for the development of standardized methodology for writing regulations in performance terms and includes the development of the internationally standardized test methods required. The governmental bodies in UN/ECE are also promoting the development of an internationally acceptable product evaluation/

INTERNATIONAL HARMONIZATION OF BUILDING REGULATIONS

certification system to go with the performance-based regulations. They are also asking ISO to develop fundamental standards, such as methods for describing worldwide climatological and seismic conditions.

Although it is the stated intention of the 34 participating nations to rewrite their building regulations using the ISO-developed performance methodology and test methods, it is recognized that each of the nations will internally establish its own acceptance levels. International harmonization (rather than uniformity) of these *acceptance* values is the primary goal of this project, through the uniform use of international standard test methods in determining compliance with national performance requirements. It is in this sense that this UN/ECE-ISO project is referred to as the "harmonization" of national building regulations.

In the direction shown by the converging forces behind the Helsinki Agreement and the GATT standards code, the worldwide movement to dimensional coordination, and this UN/ECE-ISO building code and standards project, we see for the first time in modern history all of the world's collection of building codes and standards able to move towards harmonization as a result of the worldwide adoption of the common technical communication base—SI.

10

GUIDELINES FOR METRIC TRAINING AND THE TRANSITIONAL PERIOD

HANS J. MILTON, FRAIA

Technical Consultant, Center for Building Technology
National Bureau of Standards
U.S. Department of Commerce

TRAINING AND FAMILIARIZATION

There are many differing opinions as to the desirability, value, or necessary extent of a formal metric education program for the construction community. Precedent indicates, however, that a brief, well-conceived, suitably timed, task-oriented metric education program will ultimately save money by removing individual resistance to or fear of the change to SI, and by providing a common basis for the application of metric units.

It must be remembered that the change to SI will be gradual and may not affect many people for quite some time. In the construction community those involved in the preparation of metric standards, codes, and technical data will become involved some time before those engaged in design and documentation. Both groups will work in metric long before people working in building production or construction. Moreover, people's needs for training and orientation will vary considerably according to the type of work they do. A consulting engineer, for example, will require a different kind of reeducation program from that of an architect, whose needs will again be quite different from those of a building tradesman or laborer.

Every organization should therefore establish a policy on training as early as possible in the metrication process to ease the transition to a metric working environment. The policy should clearly establish the objectives of the metric education program in relation to the obligations and responsibilities of individuals, groups, and the organization as a whole.

Within a single organization there will often be the need for a number of different metric training programs to respond to specific work experience. For example, a large design/construction organization may require training programs aimed at the following staff categories.

EXECUTIVES AND SENIOR MANAGEMENT

A general program will be needed to create metric awareness, with discussions centering on the management procedures and policies necessary to ensure a smooth and cost-effective change to metric measurement.

PROFESSIONAL STAFF

This group will require a specific series of programs designed to deal with all aspects of metrication and dimensional coordination relating to the efficient

---

performance of metric tasks. Because this group operates at a conceptual level and is concerned with the use of a wide variety of SI units, a detailed explanation of new concepts will be necessary. A task-oriented program with actual metric exercises on pilot projects should precede actual involvement in metric work. The program should be supported by accurate technical literature and reference material.

TECHNICAL SUPPORT AND DRAFTING STAFF

This group will require a job-related education program to familiarize its members with SI units and to give them some conceptual explanation of the system and some practical experience by means of exercises in metric technical work.

ADMINISTRATIVE AND CLERICAL STAFF

A brief, basic program is all that is needed to give this group essential information enabling it to work effectively in a metric technical environment. The group should have access to a well-written guide to the rules governing metric use, type, style, and punctuation.

ON-SITE CONSTRUCTION PERSONNEL

A specific task-oriented training program should be provided for this group just before commencement of metric work, concentrating on those areas of measurement that are directly related to the performance of its members' tasks. Exercises in familiarization, such as on-site measurement and setting out or positioning items in line with a metric drawing, ought to be included. A basic pocket book or guide, summarizing the main training information in simple terms, should be issued at the end of the program.

SCOPE OF METRIC TRAINING PROGRAMS

For the purpose of preparing a training program for personnel engaged in building design, production, or construction activities, the following list itemizes information that could be incorporated selectively into the different training programs outlined.

General Information
Responsibility for conversion activities
Timing of the change and vital dates (for the industry and the organization)
Organizational metric policy
Need for personal involvement to overcome problems and to identify opportunities (metric suggestion scheme)
The basis of SI—the "modern metric system": coherence, decimal nature, only one unit for each quantity, international (worldwide) system and symbols

The Modern Metric System—SI
Metric measurement—units and prefixes
Basic and derived units and their relationships
SI units and non-SI units
Use of SI units and rules and recommendations for presentation
Thinking in metric: examples

Application of SI
Exercises, calculations, and worked examples
Conversion of customary values, rounding, and rationalization

Coordination of Dimensions in Building
Basic principles
Application of preferred dimensions and preferred product sizes
Accuracy and on-site control

Presentation
Notation in metric drawings and specifications
Drawings and scale ratios
Rationalized documentation

Cost Estimating
Metric units and unit rates
Metric cost schedules
Sizes of building materials and estimating practices

Laying Out
Use of metric measuring equipment
Linear measurement, angular measurement, and levels
Horizontal and vertical laying out

Legal and Contractual Aspects
Contract clauses for the transitional period
Special conditions or arrangements, for example, substitutions
Building regulations
Metric building standards, specifications, and codes of practice

Building Products (Manufacture, Distribution, Sales)
Metric dimensions of key products
Metric properties and performance characteristics
Tolerances and fits
Substitution of products

METRIC FAMILIARIZATION: MENTAL IMAGES AND RECOGNITION POINTS

In the solution of both simple and complex problems, people rely on "mental models" of the world around them. These models—or mental images—provide the basis for comparing and assessing, for estimating, and for abstraction. Many mental images have measurement approximations connected with them. In the change to SI, people need to become familiar with new mental images in metric reference units, without having to constantly revert to the time-consuming and error-prone process of direct conversion.

It will take a while to acquire a "feel" for metric units, such as millimeters and meters, when the mental data bank is in inches, feet, and yards. The quickest way to make metric units meaningful is to generate "metric recognition points" by direct measurement or comparison, and to supplement them by actual work on "metric examples" in measurement and calculations. Rulers and other measuring devices are indispensable tools in making the transition to metric, and no training program should be without correctly marked rulers, tapes, and scales to relate estimated to actual values.

The metric data bank will be supplemented over a period of time and will be extended at about the same rate at which the customary reference points are no longer used.

In any metric training program, one of the quickest and most meaningful ways of developing mental images is to establish personal recognition points, based on human sizes and functions. For example, a person's body mass (weight) in kilograms can be established very quickly, and then provides a useful reference value to relate the mass of objects.

Human dimensions change far less than mass (weight) and are important reference points in the judgment of dimensions in the metric world, particularly in a highly measurement-sensitive industry, such as construction. The width of a man's hand is approximately 100 mm, and the span from outstretched thumb to middle finger 200 mm. Typically, a 1.85 m (1850 mm) tall man will have an upward reach of 2400 mm, a shoulder height of 1600 mm, and a forward reach of 800 mm. Each person can develop personal recognition points to make the metric environment more meaningful; for example, during the metric training program measurements can be made and entered into a metric body dimensions reference sheet. Such reference values, once established, are unlikely to be forgotten.

ADAPTATION OF MATERIALS AND COMPONENTS DURING THE TRANSITION

The basic "metric problem" clearly is *how* to effect the least disruptive and most economical transition to a metric building environment. To play their part in the transition, designers will have to prepare metric documents in good faith that metric components will be available when needed in construction. In turn, manufacturers are expected to produce metric products in time for their incorporation into a rapidly growing number of metric projects without the burden of having to maintain dual or slow-moving inventories. Such synchronization will not be easy, for reasons ranging from a lack of communication, through inadequate coordination, to a reluctance to change. Generally, a lack of action will be masked by the excuse that "the time for a change is not appropriate for economic reasons." But without a commitment to the change by all parties, a vicious circle could evolve which will increase costs for all concerned. The most likely losers in a building environment with unbalanced demand and supply are the client, who has to pay for inefficiencies in one way or another, and the contractor, who has to deal with a hybrid situation.

ADAPTATION STRATEGIES IN DESIGN AND CONSTRUCTION

Precedent has shown that metric design and construction *can* proceed, even before manufacturers have available a comprehensive range of building materials and components in rationalized and preferred metric sizes. Although only a few of the building products currently in use in the construction community convert directly to acceptable metric sizes, in many instances it will be possible to develop "new" products in preferred metric sizes over the next few years. Such products can then be sold in both market segments: under "nominal" descriptions in the declining market for customary items, and in "actual" preferred dimensions in the growing and, ultimately, exclusively metric market. Similarly, other properties, such as strength grades, can be assigned in preferred metric values where new grades are developed.

However, the solution to the metric transition in the building industry lies in the very nature of construction itself. In most buildings and structures there is a preponderance of "fluid dimensions" for work carried out in concrete, bricks, or blocks, whose dimensions can be adjusted to accept any range of preferred component and assembly sizes. Some building components themselves have always been readily adaptable to design or construction dimensions, either because of their small size or because of the techniques of jointing and fitting. Such components can be integrated without too much trouble into building projects designed in preferred metric dimensions, even though initially they may not have been manufactured in rationalized metric sizes. Many other components and assemblies are normally purpose-made rather than standardized, especially in large or highly repetitive projects. These items can be produced in preferred metric sizes just as easily as in customary sizes; in fact, with circumspect decision-making and insistence on preferred metric dimensions, the designer can frequently achieve greater standardization of purpose-made items to obtain the benefits of maximum repetition of a minimum number of sizes.

With proper planning the construction of metric buildings in preferred dimensions with components in preferred sizes will involve fewer complications and greater savings than the use of uncoordinated sizes in the customary system. However, until there is an ample supply of metric products, the need for adaptive action in design and/or construction will not be totally eliminated. To avoid long delays and to minimize the need for last-minute substitutions, early

Table 10.1 Materials and Components for Metric Building in the Transitional Period—Suggested Adaptation in Design and Construction for Various Product Categories[a]

Category	Complexity of Adpatation	Typical Examples of Materials and Components	Adaptive Action in Design	Adaptive Action in Construction
		A. Dimensional Coordination not required		
A.1	No change in materials—no problems foreseen	Formless or plastic materials: water, paint, mastics, tar; sand, cement, lime, dry mortar mix, loose-fill insulation; read-mixed concrete, pre-mixed masonry mortar	Specify in metric units. Develop necessary site guidelines.	Weigh or measure in metric quantities. Use metric data on coverage, mix ratios, etc.
A.2	Customary sizes usable—interim "soft conversion"	Structural steel sections, reinforcing bars, pipes, tubes, hardware, fixtures, fittings	Specify metric equivalents or show permissible substitutions. Select preferred "free" dimensions such as length or centerlines.	Order or cut to metric length; set out to coordinated centerlines.
		B. Minor Site Adjustments to Coordinate with Preferred Dimensions		
B.1	Modification in one direction to fit in with preferred dimensions	a. Adjustment by trimming: lumber studs and joists, laminates, roofing, gutters b. Adjustment by lapping: shingles, tar felt, underlay, sheathing, waterproof membranes c. Adjustment by change in joint width: bricks, blocks, ceramic tiles	Specify preferred metric dimensions to expedite the transition. Indicate construction adjustments in drawings or instructions.	Lay out project in preferred building dimensions and adjust products accordingly.
		C. Dimensional Coordination Required		
C.1	Purpose-made items—no difficulties foreseen	Precast panels and slabs, door assemblies, window assemblies, fabricated metalwork, built-in units	Specify rationalized metric sizes.	Order or fabricate components in rationalized metric sizes.
C.2	Reshaping of customary dimensions possible	Glazing, plywood, gypsum wallboard, sheathing, lath, rigid insulation materials	Investigate supply in rationalized metric sizes and specify.	Order rationalized metric sizes. Cut off site or on site.
C.3	Reshaping of customary dimensions difficult, costly, or impossible	Windows, doors, metal partitions, metal roof decking, fluorescent fixture, metal cladding panels, stainless steel sections and sinks, large ceramic panels, distribution boards and panels, fixed appliances and cabinets, lockers	Preorder preferred sizes before job commencement. Discuss trial batches with manufacturers. Use adaptive design and detailing.	Adapt during the interim period until preferred metric sizes emerge. Construct suitable openings or spaces for noncoordinated components and assemblies.

[a] The list may be expanded or modified to suit particular market conditions.

and careful planning of metric material orders is essential. Table 10.1 indicates the various types of adaptive action in design and construction that may be taken to integrate different categories of dimensionally sensitive building products into metric projects. A general distinction has been made between items *not requiring* dimensional coordination and those *requiring* it. Short-term problems caused by the nonavailability of genuine metric sizes can nearly always be overcome by a clear and early appreciation of the various adaptation possibilities in relation to geometric requirements. After all, the construction community has a long legacy of adaptive ingenuity in its work, as nonavailability of particular items is not an unusual occurrence.

The design sector can simplify the transition by employing restraint in the selection of building materials and components. The variety of products often can be reduced, and the specification of special nonmetric items avoided altogether. Reduced variety will ensure longer production runs, better inventories and availability, and fewer instances where adaptation or substitution is needed, thus providing greater efficiency throughout the industry. The change to metric production is likely to create economic conditions which will prevent designers from arbitrarily rejecting standardized metric sizes, especially if such products are functionally and aesthetically acceptable. This could be a very positive outcome of the change to metric measurement.

COORDINATION WITH EXISTING BUILDINGS

The fact that the existing building environment represents a vast legacy of nonmetric design and construction is frequently advanced as a potentially significant problem associated with the change to metric sizes, but a closer look at the issues involved in the maintenance and rehabilitation of traditional building assets in a metric building world will put these problems into perspective. Valuable lessons can be learned from current maintenance and renovation of existing and historic structures.

To place specific issues in perspective, and to correct distorted views of the "metric interface problems" likely to be encountered, three categories of building maintenance and modification have been considered:

Routine maintenance and repair in existing buildings or structures.

Major renovation, alteration, or complete rehabilitation of existing buildings or structures.

Identical horizontal or vertical extensions of, and additions to, existing buildings or structures.

ROUTINE MAINTENANCE AND REPAIR OF EXISTING NONMETRIC BUILDINGS

Most of the routine maintenance in existing buildings is concentrated on the preservation of surface finishes, and the maintenance of fixtures, fittings, appliances, and other mechanical equipment to keep them in proper working condition. Generally, surface finishes will constitute no problem after the change to metric measurement where caulking, patching, painting, or wallpapering is involved, although these items constitute the largest portion of the maintenance account. Some minor difficulties may arise with surface laminates; however, approximately 90% of all laminated material is cut to size to suit job requirements, and it will still be possible to cut to size from metric sheets. Pattern matching is entirely dependent upon the supplies available in the marketplace—it is almost impossible at present to obtain laminates whose patterns match those of 10 or 20 years ago.

Repair work in existing buildings is normally occasioned by general wear and tear, breakdown of mechanical parts, accidental damage, and damage resulting from building movement or natural hazards. No problems will be encountered when repair work necessitates full replacement of items that are cut from larger sheets, panels, or rolls, such as glass, laminates, or carpet, and then fitted. Some difficulties may arise in situations where metric products in preferred dimensions have replaced traditional items that were 1.6% larger. While this difference in size can generally be accommodated in the joint if only one or two items are replaced, such size difference may be functionally or aesthetically unacceptable when a large number of items are involved. Blocks and bricks in preferred metric dimensions, although slightly smaller, can generally be fitted with a larger joint. Wall, floor, or ceiling tiles require more ingenious adaptive strategies when no products in customary sizes can be obtained from a dealer in replacement items.

It may be necessary to transfer ceiling tiles from a concealed or minor use area to a highly visible area that has damaged tiles, and then effect any adjustments in the minor area. Broken ceramic tiles could create slightly greater problems, and may require the cutting and fitting of metric replacement tiles if no replacement tiles in customary sizes can be obtained. Floor tiles, whether ceramic or plastic, will require similar adaptation.

It is important to recognize, however, that these replacement strategies are not unusual in the building repair and renovation industry, because many instances arise now where it is impossible to match products or patterns that were initially installed a good many years ago. One obvious answer for more recent buildings, or nonmetric buildings now under construction, is to create a small store of possible replacement items in customary sizes for any repair contingencies, especially of products such as tiles, which are installed in a situation of dimensional fit.

As far as standard sections in metal or lumber are concerned, it is unlikely that they would be "pieced into position" in small pieces; rather, they would be replaced as a finite length. For example, where a baseboard was damaged and was to be replaced, it would be common practice to take a length from a corner to a corner, or from a corner to a doorframe. The use and fitting of marginally different profiles is a common occurrence now, and does not cause much trouble to the repair contractor. Where an exact match is required for historical or prestige purposes, a replacement item would normally be custom made.

Some people have advanced difficulties with the maintenance of customary fixtures, fittings, and equipment as a "potential problem area" in the metric building world and associated some wild estimates of increased cost with their hypotheses. The experience of other countries that have made the change to metric provides much more realistic guidance. On closer examination the issues associated with the maintenance and repair of mechanical items and the replacement of defective components will not create new or unique situations, but will resemble those that are adequately dealt with by maintenance staff and engineers now.

If a suitable fastener cannot be obtained, another fastener can always be adapted, or a new thread cut. Spare parts dealers will still stock spare parts according to demand, so that a good many parts in customary sizes should remain available well into a fully metric engineering environment. Fluorescent lamps, where the bulk of production is sold in the replacement market, will continue to be available for use in customary fittings for many years to come. Any new, fully metric tubes produced in preferred dimensions will be shorter and are bound to be marketed with a cheap adaptor or converter for use in customary housings. Changes in electrical wiring have been made on a number of occasions in the past, and will probably be made again; they have never prevented electricians from joining, splicing, or adapting electrical circuits.

In relation to plumbing systems, similar considerations apply. Most plumbing fixtures are in "neutral dimensions," based on anthropometric considerations, and there is no reason to expect unnecessary metric modifications. The working parts in toilets are likely to be changed only when better designs emerge. It is expected that manufacturers who produce pipes in rationalized metric sizes will simultaneously market connectors, to enable such pipes to be joined to existing fittings or pipes, where this is required. As connecting pieces are required in the normal course of making a connection or junction, the only difference will be the choice of a customary-to-metric connector, rather than a customary-to-customary connector. Copper and lead pipes can be flared and dressed to deal with variations in size at the connection. There is a possibility that some current pipe sizes will remain in the metric building world, so that the only consideration will be the choice of appropriate taps or dies to enable a threaded connection to be made.

Most importantly, the change to a metric building environment does *not* mean that nonmetric tools and accessories should be discarded in the building maintenance and repair industry; there will be many instances where customary drills, taps, dies, wrenches, sockets, and so on will be needed to carry out a maintenance or repair job.

MAJOR RENOVATIONS, ALTERATIONS, AND REHABILITATION

Major renovations, alterations, and rehabilitation are taken to mean extensive modifications to an existing building or structure, generally retaining only the structural frame and replacing all or most of the surfacing materials, components, assemblies, service systems, and equipment.

With the exception of the replacement of doors and windows in existing walls, the activities involved in major renovation of traditional buildings in a metric building world will follow the same course now in use. Work will need to be based on actual on-site measurements, rather than original contract drawings (should such still exist), and construction activities will follow the measure-and-fit pattern.

It is well to remember that the building renovation industry has always shown a great deal of ingenuity in dealing with the problems of matching and/or replacement, and that there is no reason to suspect that this will not continue. The replacement of entire doorsets (doors plus frames) and windowsets (window assembly, including all cover strips, casings, stops, sills, and flashings, where appropriate) generally will be accomplished with custom-made assemblies. Where standard-size windows have been used, it may be possible to adapt slightly smaller metric windows manufactured to preferred dimensions, but custom-made replacement windows may prove less costly. Where a change in framing material is involved, it will invariably be necessary to custom-fabricate replacement windows.

While a range of standard door sizes has been recognized for some time in the U.S. building community, stock doors generally require some adaptation in a renovation or replacement situation. Where the opening size can be controlled, it is desirable to use metric doorsets in preferred dimensions, as this may facilitate any future replacements.

Although standard windows and doors have been widely used in the past, such standards vary from region to region, and from building type to building type, so that the adaptation of existing stock items is frequently necessary in current replacement situations. Thus the metric change imposes little or no additional burden. With respect to doors, the existing major preferences, such as the 2 ft 8 in × 6 ft 8 in door (which always varies a little from this designated size), may continue to be produced and stocked for quite some time to service the replacement market.

Where the replacement of framing lumber is required, customary lumber sizes will show substantial differences in actual size according to the age of the structure. The use of framing lumber in metric dimensions will not impose any significant complications.

While partition units in preferred metric sizes are likely to be smaller than those manufactured in customary dimensions—the difference between 8 ft and 2400 mm is 1½ in or 38 mm—most partition units or systems are shorter than their functional length to allow for adjustment to variations in floor-to-ceiling height. With marginal changes to coverstrips and baseboards, metric partition units will fit customary room heights.

When extensive internal renovation of buildings is undertaken and partitions are used for the subdivision of space, these are normally custom-made to suit functional or location requirements, so that a metric environment will not complicate matters.

A distinction is made between an extension to an existing structure or building, involving a continuity of existing design and construction, and an addition to an existing structure or building, which may differ in shape and/or materials used.

In building extensions it is generally necessary to closely match the external and internal surface treatment and detailing; therefore the vertical or horizontal extension of customary buildings or structures predominantly becomes an exercise in applying a "metric veneer" to customary design, with metric materials and components adapted as required.

The vertical extension can be adjusted more easily to marginal changes in product sizes, since the floor plane also provides a dividing line. Where external columns and precast panels are involved in the extension, existing sections and profiles should be followed, but specified to the nearest metric equivalent in millimeters. Similarly, windows for such vertical extensions will be required to fit into existing horizontal spaces, but may be adjusted slightly to take advantage of preferred metric vertical dimensions if an economic benefit can be proved. Internal vertical dimensions can be adjusted to preferred metric values without undue visual disturbance, yet this will ensure vertical compatibility of metric products. All vertical connecting shafts, ducts, stairwells, and service systems should be matched for continuity, especially elevator shafts. Pipes and ducts in vertical extensions may be in preferred metric dimensions, with adaptors or connecting pieces to take up any differences in size, provided that functional requirements are not impaired. In short, the vertical extension does not create insurmountable problems for the designer.

The horizontal extension of existing buildings or structures involves considerations of continuity similar to those encountered in the vertical extension, although horizontal dimensions are more flexible. While vertical dimensions and heights will generally be required to continue at their existing levels, thus providing the overriding design restraint. It may sometimes be possible to change the floor level in a horizontal extension marginally to take advantage of preferred metric products in the vertical plane, by introducing a shallow ramp in connecting links. Considerations for the connection of services are similar to those for vertical services, although a horizontal extension generally imposes fewer restraints on plumbing systems.

Horizontal and vertical additions to buildings provide much greater freedom for the designer than do extensions, as the principal considerations relate to the junction of the structure, materials, and services, which is no different from the circumstances encountered in any addition made in customary measurement. It is the designer's responsibility to ensure proper weatherproofing and structural continuity, where required, and there are innumerable ways to properly articulate the junction. Compared with an extension of an existing building, an addition can be treated as a discrete metric project, with certain customary-metric interface considerations.

Although the issue of legal implications arising from the change to metric measurement in building design, production, and construction has been raised in some of the countries that have preceded the United States in making the change, there have not been any instances of legal action arising out of causes partially or substantially attributable to metrication.

The implications of a design error caused by new and unfamiliar units are related to the design process and not the measurement system.

A change in regulatory requirements caused by metrication is unlikely to have a retroactive effect on existing buildings, because in nearly all instances a metric minimum will fall slightly below a customary minimum, and a metric maximum will be slightly above a customary maximum. Any changes in regulations solely

EXTENSIONS TO EXISTING BUILDINGS

ADDITIONS TO EXISTING BUILDINGS

LEGAL IMPLICATIONS OF THE CHANGE TO SI

attributable to new technology must not be confused with marginal changes and rounding or rationalization caused by metrication.

CONTRACTUAL IMPLICATIONS OF THE CHANGE TO SI

As the change to metric measurement gathers momentum in the construction community, metric-sized materials and components will become more readily available, and customary-sized ones less so, most of them eventually disappearing altogether.

While designers are expected to thoroughly investigate metric material sizes and their availability, contractors will find that certain items ordered for delivery on short notice cannot be obtained in the measurement or characteristics specified in the building contract. Equally, this transitional problem will be encountered in nonmetric projects, where certain traditional materials or equipment sizes will have been replaced by metric sizes.

Contract documents should clearly point out the effect of metric conversion or projects carried out during the transitional period. A condition of contract should require the contractor to give reasonable notice of items difficult to obtain as a result of the change to metric, thus enabling the designer to consider alternatives. A distinction needs to be made between items which are unavailable because of a shortage of supply, and items which are not yet available as anticipated in preferred metric sizes or characteristics.

The contract should provide for an adequate adjustment of contract sums—upward or downward—when substitution is necessary to meet an unforeseeable supply situation. In no case should a contractor make substitutions without the approval of the designer, because such substitution of different size or quality may well have design implications that the architect or engineer will need to consider. The designer's subsequent instructions, whether they merely authorize substitution of materials in the only size or quality available, or also involve redesign, constitute a variation to the contract.

Despite the existence of an early warning system, delays may be incurred as a result of nonavailability of specified items. This may lead to an extension of the contract period in unusual cases.

RESOLUTION OF PROBLEM AREAS

There is no simple answer to all contractual contingencies, and precedent in other countries has shown that substitutions caused by a lack of effort either to obtain the items specified or to place orders in good time will occur just as often as genuine nonavailability. It is also possible that mistakes in the building drawings and specifications for a metric building project will require changes or substitution at the construction stage.

11

THE METRICATION PROCESS

THOMAS CLARK TUFTS, AIA

*Chairman, Construction Industries Coordinating Committee
American National Metric Council*

and

A. CHARLES DANNER, Jr.

*Private Sector Coordinator
U.S. Metric Board*

The United States has reached a point in its national history where it is no easy task to make substantial alterations to the status quo. To change our measurement system from one so firmly established in the language and idiom of the people is a project of immense proportions, demanding, at the very least, sound organization, comprehensive planning, and flexible, skillful management of a dynamic set of circumstances. In fact, conversion to the International System of Units (SI) in the United States demands a new, almost revolutionary approach to the management of change in a democracy.

By the mid-1960s there was a strong surge in the scientific and technical community in the United States toward an increased use of the metric system. The American Society for Testing and Materials (ASTM) established a metric committee which led to the publication in 1964 of the *ASTM Metric Practice Guide*, which later became ASTM E 380-76 *Standard for Metric Practice*. Many technical, professional, and trade associations established similar committees.

In August 1968 Public Law 90-472, which authorized a U.S. metric study by the Department of Commerce, was signed by President Johnson. The purposes of the study were to (1) determine the impact on the United States of the increasing worldwide use of the metric system; (2) consider both the desirability and the practicability of increasing the use of metric weights and measures in this country; (3) study the feasibility of international use of standards based on the customary system; (4) examine the implications of the metric trend for international trade, national security, and other areas of foreign relations; and (5) identify the practical difficulties that might be encountered should the metric system be used more widely in this country, and evaluate the costs and benefits of courses of action which the United States might realistically take.

At about this time the American National Standards Institute (ANSI) established its Metric Advisory Committee. During the next 3 years in-depth study was carried out, directed by the National Bureau of Standards under the leadership of Dr. Daniel de Simone. Serving in an advisory capacity to that study was the

---

Portions of this chapter were derived from "Metrication: What Needs to be Done" © 1978 American National Metric Council.

Metric Study Advisory Panel, chaired by Dr. Louis F. Polk, later to become Chairman of the U.S. Metric Board.

In July 1971 a report of the study, entitled "A Metric America: A Decision Whose Time Has Come," was sent to Congress. The major recommendations of the Secretary of Commerce were that the United States change to the international metric system deliberately and carefully, that this be done through a coordinated national program, and that Congress assign the responsibility for guiding the change to a central coordinating body responsive to all of our society.

Following the release of this report a number of metric bills were introduced in Congress. For one reason or another, however, no such bill was enacted into law until December 1975, when President Ford signed Public Law 94-168, the Metric Conversion Act. The law declared a national policy of coordinating voluntary conversion and authorized the U.S. Metric Board. As is the nature of the deliberative process in Congress, which responds over time to a number of influences, Public Law 94-168 did not follow exactly the recommendations of the U.S. Metric Study Report. It did, however, authorize the U.S. Metric Board as *the* central coordinating body.

FORMATION OF THE AMERICAN NATIONAL METRIC COUNCIL (ANMC)

In the meantime, with the issuance of the 1971 U.S. report, "A Metric America," there was considerable interest on the part of commerce and industry in establishing a focal point and forum to debate issues surrounding the growing use of metric measurement in the United States. In response to this interest, ANSI called a special conference in September 1972. This conference was attended by a broad spectrum of the leading figures in industry, science, and education. The consensus of the conference was that ANSI should sponsor an organization which would provide the needed services, and thus the concept of the American National Metric Council (ANMC) was born. In December 1972 the ANSI Board of Directors authorized the expenditure of $25,000 to initiate ANMC, with the understanding that it would thereafter be separately funded.

The American National Metric Council became operational as a branch of ANSI early in 1973, developed its charter, and selected a Board of Directors, which held its first meeting in May of the same year. Dr. Malcolm O'Hagan, later to be first Executive Director of the U.S. Metric Board, was employed as Executive Director, and the newly founded Council began a major campaign for charter subscribers. The campaign was a success, and ANMC has been growing ever since. In July 1976, ANMC incorporated as a separate organization and formally cut its corporate ties with ANSI.

In spite of years of delay culminating in President Carter's appointment of the U.S. Metric Board, ANMC has been carrying on and is continuing to manage the task of planning and coordinating the private sector's conversion to the metric system. Through the involvement of over 300 trade, professional, labor, consumer, and government organizations and over 400 major corporations, the change to metric is being managed in an organized, cost-effective manner. Representatives from the various companies and organizations are participants on ANMC's coordinating and sector committees, which are charged with planning and coordinating conversion in and among the different sectors of the U.S. economy. The organizational chart in Figure 11.1 depicts the current committee organization of ANMC.

THE CONSTRUCTION INDUSTRIES COORDINATING COMMITTEE (CICC):SECTOR AND SUBSECTOR COMMITTEES

Before the Metric Conversion Act of 1975 was enacted by Congress, the Construction Industries Coordinating Committee (CICC) met to define its policies and strategies and to organize to effectively discharge its role. Sectors were identified. Lists of professional and trade associations were matched with the respective sectors, and contact was made with each organization to determine the status of its metric conversion policies or level of metric awareness within its

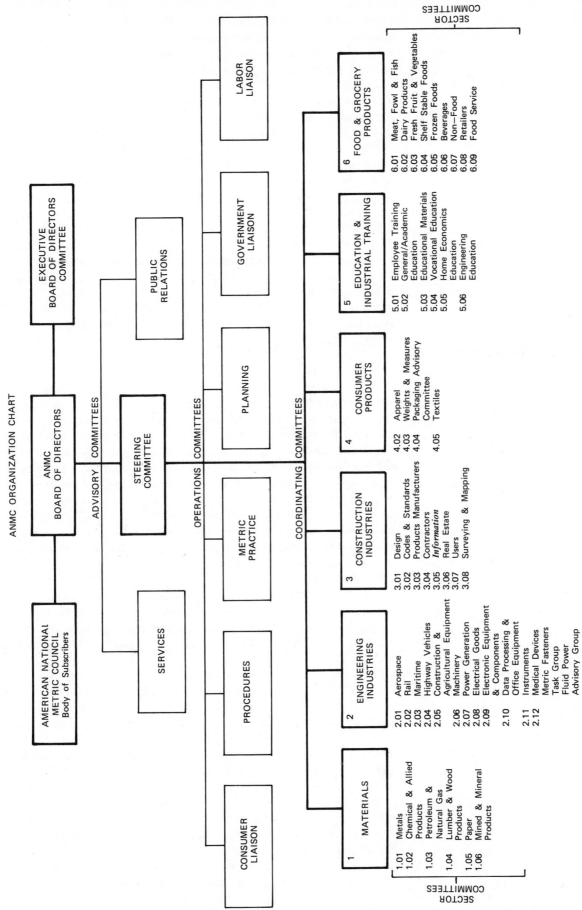

Figure 11.1 American National Metric Council organization chart.

current activities. Each association was also invited to appoint representatives to a sector committee, or committees, of its choice. The sector committees met and organized, and each elected a chairperson who would also serve on the coordinating committee. Subsectors of the sector committees were also identified and organized in a similar manner. An organizational necessity was the establishment of a secretariat for each sector and subsector to provide the necessary backup to each committee in the form of staff, accommodations for meetings, and facilities for the preparation and mailing of rosters, meeting notices, and minutes. For example, until 1978, the secretariat for the Design Sector was the Center for Building Technology of the National Bureau of Standards, while the American Institute of Architects acts as secretariat for the Architects Subsector of the Design Sector, as well as sponsor of the related Metric Conversion/ Dimensional Coordination Task Force.

Because the organization of the sectors and subsectors has relied heavily on representation from existing professional and trade associations, they have become a ready source of volunteers to serve on committees, and are expected to be the primary communications channel between the committees and the broad-based membership of the associations. Use of their publications, newsletters, and conferences to disseminate metric information is likely to be the most successful approach to informing the industries' public and gaining acceptance of the planning process.

The construction industry is still largely domestic, and international considerations as yet play a small role in the average member's day-to-day work activities. But these international considerations are expanding annually, in relation to design, codes and standards, and product manufacturing, and are reaching a new intensity with the current metric conversion of Canadian construction. The standards and product-manufacturing communities will be forced to meet Canadian needs and will begin to bring pressure on U.S. domestic industry to eliminate hardships encountered when dual standards and products have to be maintained. The "Who goes first?" syndrome has been pointed out as a dilemma by many observers of metric conversion. Designers will not design in metric when there are neither metric codes, products, nor technical material. Standards are not developed until needed, codes are not saleable until regulatory agencies require them, manufacturers will not produce until there is a market for their products, and obviously builders will not work in metric until the lead sectors described have resolved to make a coordinated effort. Because being either too early or too late in the market could be economically disastrous, we are not likely to see many individual companies adopt a metric conversion policy without recognized industrywide commitment. Therefore planning and managing the events which would lead to this commitment becomes the goal and purpose of ANMC-CICC.

In this light the voluntary nature of the Metric Conversion Act becomes desirable, for the steps toward industrywide commitment are to develop a comprehensive plan, or conversion schedule, publicize the plan widely, and have it approved by consensus. An agreed upon time schedule would then eliminate the "Who goes first?" problem, and conversion could proceed in an orderly manner. In this way the salutary effects of a mandated time schedule would be achieved, but conversion would still be voluntary, to the extent that each industry or company could make its individual decisions based on the market and economic factors pertaining to its own circumstances. Many manufacturers may decide to produce customary-dimensioned products for the maintenance and renovation market and forego the new construction market initially. Others will change to metric sizes and develop adaptors to enable them to work in either renovation or new construction markets. The only penalties to be incurred will be the penalties of the marketplace for poor business decisions, not the penalties of the law.

PLANNING AND SCHEDULING IN A VOLUNTARY CLIMATE

In order for committees to develop the necessary recommended conversion schedules on which to base an industrywide consensus, an appropriate planning methodology was needed. Network analysis was chosen because it is recognized as the formal basis for a number of the best planning techniques, particularly in the construction industry.

The logic network has simplicity as one of its primary and fundamental advantages. By closely simulating the human thought process in planning, it enables planners to impose order and symmetry on what would otherwise be an overwhelming accumulation of detail.

Each of the seven construction sectors was given the task of development of a Sector Conversion Plan (SCP) based on the logic network. To develop a logic network, each sector first identified and described the myriad tasks to be performed for conversion of that sector of the economy. Figure 11.2 shows how the task identification process culminates in the development of a flow chart or logic network that graphically describes the tasks and their sequential relationship to one another.

Logic networks are particularly helpful in displaying the order in which tasks are to be performed and in identifying the tasks which may be performed simultaneously, given existing resources. They then become the basis for a more comprehensive, long-term plan which goes beyond the objectives and specifies the tasks required for complete or partial sector conversion to metric usage. The completed plan also identifies those responsible for performing the tasks and includes a schedule for their accomplishment.

In the construction sectors each task on the individual networks will be thoroughly analyzed in terms of the validity of its inclusion, the order in which it occurs, and the estimated length of time for its accomplishment.

It is important to stress the reiterative nature of the process. Forecasting is only an initial, imprecise means of establishing baselines and targets. The sectors will continue throughout the life of the conversion plan to update and refine information with the goal of providing the most accurate time estimates possible. From the estimated time durations assigned to each task, a plan showing "SI Day" (start implementation) and "M Day" (after which bids for construction projects are taken in metric) with estimated time durations for each, may be produced.

To describe the concepts of SI Day and M Day, one must envision three plateau or phases of metric activity. The first, or "pre-SI Day," phase is characterized by the accomplishment of tasks which may proceed without either a national or an industrywide commitment to actually implement the use of the metric system. Tasks such as organization, planning, identifying units, and drafting metric practice guides constitute pre-SI Day or phase I activity.

Phase II is characterized by tasks that can be accomplished only *after* a national or industry commitment to adopt SI (e.g., U.S. Metric Board approves CICC conversion plan). This commitment is called SI Day. Many tasks which necessarily precede the use of metric measurement could not reasonably be expected to proceed without such an acknowledged commitment.

Phase III or M Day will be the date that a particular sector actually begins working in SI. M Day will necessarily be different for the Design Sector than for the Contractors Sector, but SI Day will be common to the entire industry. By estimating the time interval between SI Day and M Day in months or years for each sector, an industry M Day can be derived which is an elasped time, rather than a specific date such as 1979 or 1995. As soon as a date is set for actual SI Day, the committee can then convert estimated durations to actual calendar dates.

The assignment of actual calendar dates to each sector plan will make it possible to develop an overall master conversion plan for the entire industry.

Figure 11.8 illustrates a first draft of an industrywide logic network which identifies the sector conversion tasks common to the whole construction industry. By adding the estimated time durations for the 23 tasks necessary to accomplish the conversion of the construction industry to the metric system, a master conversion schedule (Figure 11.9) with start and finish calendar dates may be developed. It must be pointed out that assignment of dates will necessarily follow extensive consultation with all affected parties within the sector, with other related sectors, and with the U.S. Metric Board. The draft industry plan will then be published for comment and submitted to the U.S. Metric Board for review.

To date, Pre-SI Day tasks have proceeded in all sectors of the industry, representing an impressive degree of metric activity and progress.

A significant milestone was the adoption of the document, *Standard Practice for the Use of Metric (SI) Units in Building Design and Construction,* by the American Society for Testing and Materials (ASTM) as Standard E621-78 (see Chapter 3). Other milestone activities include the identification of 1800 critical standards contained in the existing model building codes and the efforts to set priorities among these for eventual conversion; the adoption of 100 mm as the basic design module for the industry; and numerous decisions on the product sizes in SI units (e.g., metric panel size 1200 mm × 2400 mm).

The activities listed above follow exactly the course of the pre-SI Day tasks listed on the draft CICC logic network (Figure 11.3). The next and last pre-SI Day task to be accomplished is the decision of the Users Sector to contract for a metric building. The enormity of the planning required for this task can be fully realized only by enumerating the people, organizations, places, companies, and things that will be affected. Metrication will, of course, ultimately touch everyone in the country and could be considered the largest voluntarily planned event that has ever been undertaken.

A COORDINATED APPROACH

The value of well-coordinated plans for all public and private sectors of the economy is obvious, yet it must be recognized that voluntarily prepared plans will have certain undesirable characteristics. Plans from some sectors will be later in development than others; some will be constantly changing and, in certain situations, will be chaotic; and the degree of commitment will necessarily vary from sector to sector. These are the occupational hazards of a voluntary approach in a dynamic environment which we must work to minimize. Indeed, to do so is a major contribution of the ANMC to metrication in the United States.

It must also be understood that the freedom inherent in our system causes a wide diversity of thought and action which may not necessarily contribute to the successful completion of the task. Some individuals will do an excellent job; others will not. We must understand our system and use its strengths to accomplish our task.

With this in mind the ANMC planning methodology must be well understood and carefully disseminated in a patient, persistent, cooperative effort to realize the full advantages of SI.

It is important that planning start by being as simple as possible, for it will inevitably become more sophisticated and complex as it evolves.

The tasks and organization of individual companies do not fall within the planning scope of ANMC. Sector plans, however, are naturally affected by the progress of individual companies.

An added advantage for ANMC-CICC is access for study to the plans and methodologies of the Commonwealth countries, beginning with the United Kingdom and culminating with Canada. These international precedents provide many valuable opportunities for shortcuts, but are not necessarily relevant to all aspects of building design, production, and construction in the United States. Although none of these countries is of the size and complexity of the United

States, each has built its programs and methodologies on those of its predecessor, with the result that each new format has become increasingly refined and sophisticated. Chronology and geography make the Canadian experience most relevant to ours. Our study of the preceding countries and the adaptation of their principles to the needs of U.S. industry will also help ANMC adapt its planning format to the specific requirements of our own industry.

A graphic explanation of the actual planning process is shown in Figure 11.10, which identifies the major elements, the preparers, the reviewers, and the approvers. All planning documents are prepared on an annual basis. The Management Events Calendar and the Long-Range Plan were prepared by the ANMC staff and may be obtained from the ANMC offices in Washington, D.C. A summary of the schedule of preparation, review, and distribution of plans is given in Figure 11.11.

All of the planning described above can be achieved within the ANMC-CICC and sector committee structure. Through broad publicity of their activities, logic, and schedule, a consensus for implementation can be achieved. Once such a consensus affirms a metric conversion schedule, the schedule will be presented to the U.S. Metric Board with the request that the plan be approved and a calendar schedule approved as national policy. Both an SI Day and an M Day will then be established as target dates. Throughout the entire process the ANMC-CICC structure will continue to monitor progress and to provide a forum for settling conflicts and revising schedules if necessary.

Conversion to SI by the last—and largest—industrial nation should be viewed in the same light as any other challenge to the American pioneering spirit, and should lead to the kind of constructive innovation that has characterized the best in this country's history.

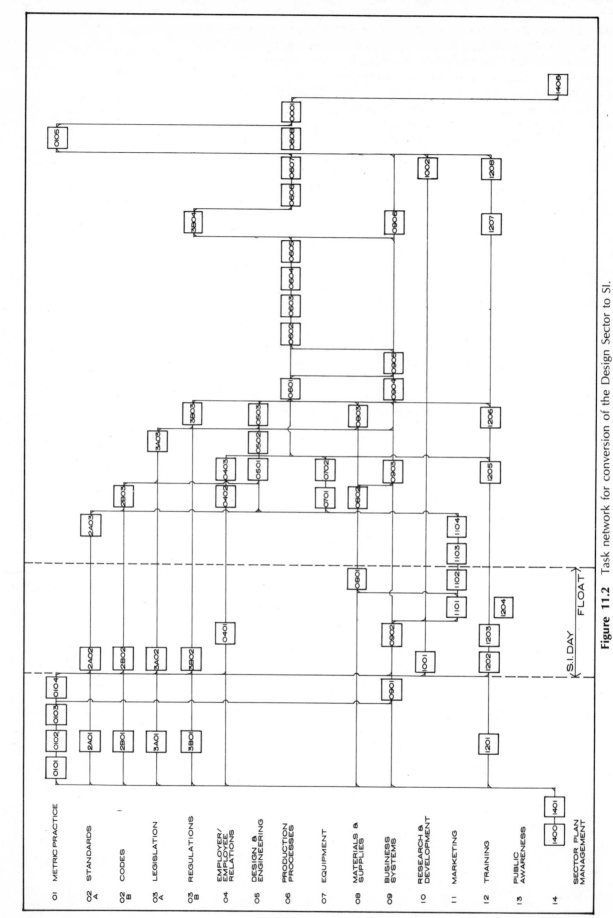

Figure 11.2 Task network for conversion of the Design Sector to SI.

Figure 11.2 *(Continued)*
3.01 DESIGN SECTOR

01 Metric Practice
1 Select Units & Ratios for Use in Design
2 Establish Preferred Dimensions for Design
3 Develop Measurement Rules & Drawing Practice
4 Develop Supplemental Metric Practice Guide for Design
5 Revise Supplemental Metric Practice Guide as Required

02A Standards
1 Identify Metric Standards Related to Design
2 Monitor Standards Development with Input on Priorities, Conversion & Rationalization
3 Obtain Necessary Standards

02B Codes
1 Identify Building Codes & References that are Measurement Sensitive
2 Monitor Code Development with Input on Priorities, Opportunity for Reform & Rationalization
3 Obtain Necessary Codes

03A Legislation
1 Identify Measurement Sensitive Legislation Related to Design
2 Monitor Legislation Progress, Determine Impact on Sector
3 Obtain Enabling Interim (if required) or Permanent Legislation

03B Regulations
1 Identify Measurement Sensitive Regulations Related to Design
2 Monitor Regulatory Process, Determine Impact on Sector
3 Obtain Metric Regulations
4 Obtain Building Permits for Metric Contract Documents

04 Employer/Employee Relations
1 Identify Measurement Sensitive Employment Agreements
2 Negotiate Necessary Changes & Establish Time Frames for Implementation
3 Implement Revised Employment Agreements

05 Design & Engineering
1 Begin Conceptual Design in Metric Terms
2 Begin Design Development & Engineering in Metric Terms
3 Obtain Surveys, Property & Legal Descriptions in Metric

06 Production Processes
1 Prepare Contract Documents in Metric Terms
2 Obtain Client Approval to Let Documents for Bid
3 Put Contract Documents Out to Bid
4 Receive & Evaluate Proposals from Contractors
5 Award Contracts in Metric Terms
6 Start Construction on Metric Project
7 Complete Construction of Metric Project

07 Equipment
1 Identify Metric Equipment Needs
2 Procure and/or Modify Equipment, Scales, etc.

08 Materials & Supplies
1 Obtain Metric Product Literature from Suppliers
2 Obtain Cost Data in Metric Terms from Suppliers
3 Obtain Data on Availability of Metric Materials & Supplies

09 Business Systems
1 Identify Business Activities Affected by Metric Conversion
2 Identify Units to be Used in Cost Estimating
3 Develop Unit Cost Data for Estimating
4 Convert Data Processing Activities & Programs to Metric
5 Develop Cost Estimates for Work in Progress in Metric Terms
6 Process Information on Costs Received from Bids for Future Estimating

10 Research & Development
1 Identify Areas of Research & Development Needs
2 Revise & or Identify Necessary R&D Based on Completed Cycle Information

11 Marketing
1 Initiate Marketing Feasibility Studies for Metric Projects
2 Prepare Designer-Client Documents in Metric Terms
3 Prepare Client Briefing on Construction in Metric Terms
4 Obtain Contract for Construction & Design in Metric Terms

12 Training
1 Identify Training Needs for Design Sector
2 Develop or Obtain Handbooks, Aids & Documents
3 Train Top Echelon Design Professionals
4 Develop Metric Education Programs with Universities, Technical Schools & Colleges
5 Train Technical Production Staff Personnel
6 Train Administrative, Accounting & Clerical Personnel
7 Train On Site Personnel
8 Assist in Training of Users Personnel as Required

13 Public Awareness

14 Sector Plan Management
1 Organize Sector
2 Develop Policies & Strategies
3 Dissolve Sector Committee
4 Metric Conversion Complete

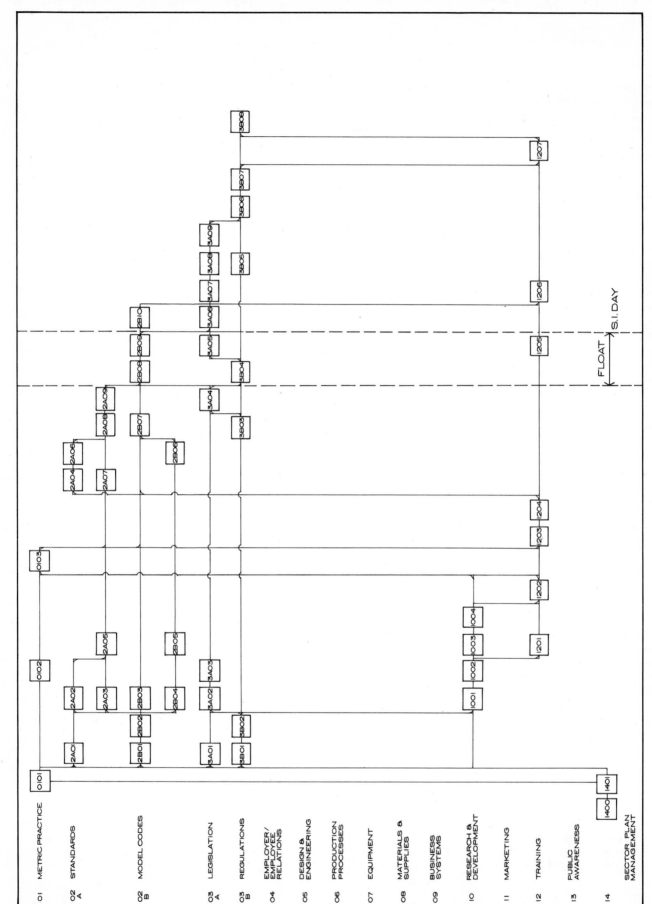

Figure 11.3 Task network for the conversion of the Codes and Standards Sector to SI.

Figure 11.3 *(Continued)*

3.02 CODES AND STANDARDS SECTOR

01 Metric Practice
1 Develop Guidelines for Metrication of Codes & Standards
2 Obtain Consensus from Sectors on Metric Practice Guide
3 Publish Metric Practice Guide for the Construction Industry

02A Standards
1 Establish Metric Standards Objectives
2 Identify New Metric Standards Needed
3 Identify Existing Standards Requiring Conversion
4 Develop Basic Metric Standards Needed
5 Establish Priorities for Standards Development or Conversion
6 Publish Basic Metric Standards
7 Establish Development/Conversion Program with Standards Sources
8 Develop Metric Standards
9 Publish Metric Standards

02B Model Codes
1 Establish Metric Model Code Objectives
2 Identify Standards Referenced in Model Codes
3 Identify Independent Provisions Established by Model Codes
3 Identify Independent Provisions Established by Model Codes
4 Identify Product/System Approval Listings
5 Establish Priorities for Conversion of Approvals
6 Establish Conversion Program with Approval Sources
7 Convert Provisions not Covered by Standards
8 Draft Model Code Changes
9 Obtain Consensus on Model Codes
10 Publish Metric Model Codes

03A Legislation
1 Establish Metric Legislation Objectives
2 Identify All Existing Legislation Affecting Construction Regulation
3 Identify All Legislation Needing Conversion
4 Consult with Affected Construction Industry Sectors
5 Develop Model Legislation
6 Develop Enabling Legislation for Transitional Period (As Needed)
7 Enact Enabling Legislation
8 Propose Effective Dates for Metric Regulations
9 Establish Dates for Withdrawal of Non-Metric Regulations

03B Regulators
1 Establish Metric Building Regulatory Objectives
2 Identify All Existing Regulations for Construction
3 Separate Out Regulations Originated by Issuing Organizations
4 Decide on Metric Action on Unilateral Regulations
5 Draft Metric Regulations
6 Coordinate Effective Dates with other Sectors and Regions
7 Promulgate Metric Building Regulations
8 Accept Plans in Metric & Issue Building Permits

04 Employer/Employee Relations

05 Design & Engineering

06 Production Processes

07 Equipment

08 Materials & Supplies

09 Business Systems

10 Research & Development
1 Develop Procedures for Metric Rationalization
2 Assess Relevant International Precedent
3 Research Technical Aspects Affected by Metrication
4 Assess Alternative Approaches to Codes & Standards Metrication

11 Marketing

12 Training
1 Establish Metric Training Objectives
2 Identify Training Needs of Sector
3 Develop Training Literature & Program
4 Train Standards Writers & Professionals
5 Train Professional Code Officials
6 Train Building Officials (Plan Evaluators)
7 Train Building Officials (Site Inspectors)

13 Public Awareness

14 Sector Plan Management
1 Organize Sector
2 Develop Metric Standards and Codes Objectives and Metrication Program

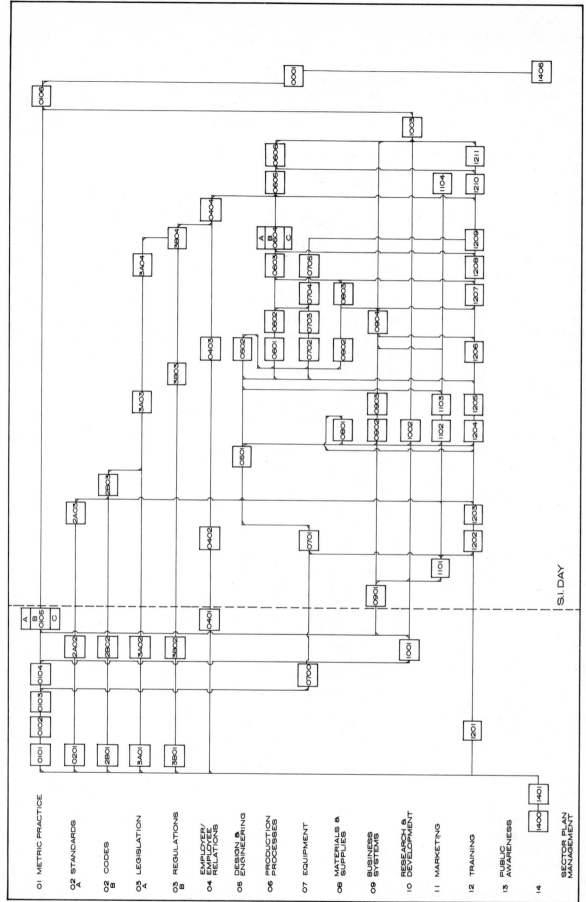

Figure 11.4   Task network for the conversion of the Construction Products Sector to SI.

Figure 11.4 *(Continued)*

3.03 CONSTRUCTION PRODUCTS SECTOR

01 Metric Practice

1 Determine Units & Ratios for S.I. Use in Sector
2 Develop Measurement Rules
3 Develop Metric Practice Guide
4 Major Review of Products and Components Sizes
  A–New
  B–Soft Conversion
  C–Hard Conversion
5 Determine S.I. Product Sizes
  A–New
  B–Soft Conversion
  C–Hard Conversion
6 Revise Metric Practice Guide

02A Standards

1 Identify Measurement Sensitive Standards
2 Monitor Revisions to Measurement Sensitive Standards
3 Obtain Necessary Product Standards

02B Codes

1 Identify Measurement Sensitive Codes
2 Monitor Revisions to Measurement Sensitive Codes
3 Obtain Necessary Model Codes

03A Legislation

1 Identify Measurement Sensitive Legislation
2 Monitor Revisions to Measurement Sensitive Legislation
3 Obtain Measurement Sensitive Legislation Related to Production
4 Obtain Construction Legislation

03B Regulations

1 Identify Measurement Sensitive Regulations
2 Monitor Revisions to Measurement Sensitive Regulations
3 Obtain Measurement Sensitive Regulations Related to Production
4 Obtain Construction Regulations

04 Employer/Employee Relations

1 Identify Measurement Sensitive Labor Agreements
2 Monitor Revisions to Measurement Sensitive Labor Agreements
3 Obtain Revised Shop Labor Agreements
4 Obtain Field Labor Agreements

05 Design & Engineering

1 Initiate Conceptual Design for Metric Products
2 Prepare Shop Drawings

06 Production Processes

1 Review Production Processes
2 Revise Shop Layouts and Production Processes as Required
3 Produce Metric Product
4 Deliver Metric Products to
  A–Warehouse (inventory)
  B–Construction Site
  C–Dealers or Suppliers
5 Install Equipment or Product on Site
6 Maintain thru Warranty Period

07 Equipment

0 Produce Metric Scales and Drawing Instruments & Equipment
1 Obtain Metric Scales and Drawing Instruments & Equipment
2 Order Necessary Production Equipment
3 Obtain and Install Product Equipment
4 Obtain Shop Measurement Tools and Instruments
5 Produce Technical Literature

08 Materials & Supplies

1 Develop and Distribute Product Literature
2 Order Necessary Production Materials and Supplies
3 Obtain Materials and Supplies for Production

09 Business Systems

1 Establish Unit Quantities and Costs for Estimating
2 Develop Unit Costs for Estimating
3 Revise Business Systems
4 Implement Revised Business Systems

10 Research & Development

1 Implement R&D on Product Sizes
2 Complete R&D for Initial Product
3 R&D Based on Initial Experience Recycle as Required

11 Marketing

1 Marketing Feasibility Studies
2 Trial Market Testing of New Product
3 Market and Price Metric Product
4 Market Maintenance Contracts if Required

12 Training

1 Identify & Plan Training Needs for Sector
2 Develop or Obtain Training Aids
3 Train Professional Product Designers and Consultants
4 Train Sales Personnel
5 Train Technicians & Technologists
6 Train Administrative Personnel
7 Train Production Personnel
8 Train Warehouse & Shipping & Receiving Personnel
9 Train Installation Mechanics
10 Train Maintenance Personnel
11 Train Users Personnel

13 Public Awareness

14 Sector Plan Management

1 Organize Sector
2 Identify Policies and Strategies for Conversion
3 Dissolve Sector Committee

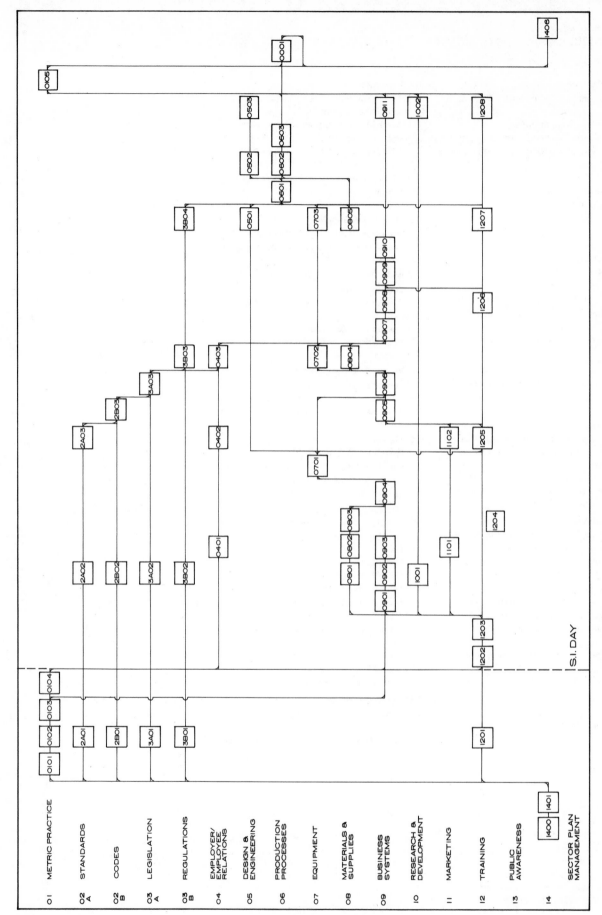

Figure 11.5 Task network for the conversion of the Contractors Sector to SI.

Figure 11.5 *(Continued)*
3.04 CONTRACTORS SECTOR

01 Metric Practice
1 Select Units & Ratios for Use in Contracting
2 Establish Preferred Units for Contracting
3 Develop Measurement Rules & Contracting Practice
4 Develop Supplemental Metric Practice Guide for Contracting
5 Revise Supplemental Metric Practice Guide as Required

02A Standards
1 Identify Measurement Sensitive Standards Relating to Contractors
2 Monitor Standards Development with Input on Priorities, Conversion & Rationalization
3 Obtain Necessary Metric Standards

02B Codes
1 Identify Building Codes & References that are Measurement Sensitive
2 Monitor Code Development with Input on Priorities
3 Obtain Necessary Metric Building Codes

03A Legislation
1 Identify Measurement Sensitive Legislation Related to Contracting
2 Monitor Legislation Progress, Determine Impact on Sector
3 Obtain Enabling Interim (if required) or Permanent Legislation

03B Regulations
1 Identify Measurement Sensitive Regulations Relating to Contracting
2 Monitor Regulatory Process, Determine Impact on Sector
3 Obtain Metric Regulations
4 Obtain Building Permits

04 Employer/Employee Relations
1 Identify Measurement Sensitive Employment Agreements
2 Negotiate Necessary Changes & Establish Time Frames for Implementation
3 Obtain Revised Employment Agreements

05 Design & Engineering
1 Layout, Formwork & Field Drawings in Metric
2 Maintain Record Drawings in Metric
3 Submit Record Drawings to Architect/ Engineer

06 Production Processes
1 Start Construction on Metric Project
2 Incorporate Metric Products on Project
3 Complete Construction on Metric Project

07 Equipment
1 Obtain Metric Scales and Instruments for Office
2 Identify Metric Tool & Equipment Needs for Field
3 Procure and/or Modify Equipment for Field

08 Materials & Supplies
1 Obtain Metric Product Literature from Suppliers
2 Develop Registry of Metric Supplies & Suppliers
3 Obtain Cost Data in Metric Terms from Suppliers
4 Obtain Proposals from Suppliers in Metric Terms
5 Order Metric Materials & Supplies

09 Business Systems
1 Identify Business Activities Affected by Metric Conversion
2 Identify Units to be Used in Cost Estimating
3 Revise Estimating Procedures as Required
4 Develop Estimating Data in Metric Terms
5 Revise Business Systems
6 Obtain Metric Contract Documents
7 Submit Bid in Metric
8 Receive Contract for Metric Project
9 Implement Revised Business Systems
10 Award Contracts to Sub Contractors & Suppliers
11 Revise Estimating Data for Future Projects Based on Project Experience

10 Research & Development
1 Identify Areas of Research & Development Needs
2 Revise and/or Identify Necessary R&D Based on Completed Cycle Information

11 Marketing
1 Initiate Marketing Feasibility Studies for Metric Projects
2 Register to Bid Metric Projects

12 Training
1 Identify Training Needs for Contractors Sector
2 Develop or Obtain Handbooks, Aids & Materials
3 Train Management & Professionals
4 Develop Metric Education Programs with Unions & Technical Schools
5 Train Contractors Technical Staff Personnel
6 Train Administrative, Accounting & Clerical Personnel
7 Train On-Site Personnel
8 Assist in Training Users Personnel as Required

13 Public Awareness

14 Sector Plan Management
1 Organize Sector
2 Develop Policies & Strategies
3 Dissolve Sector Committee

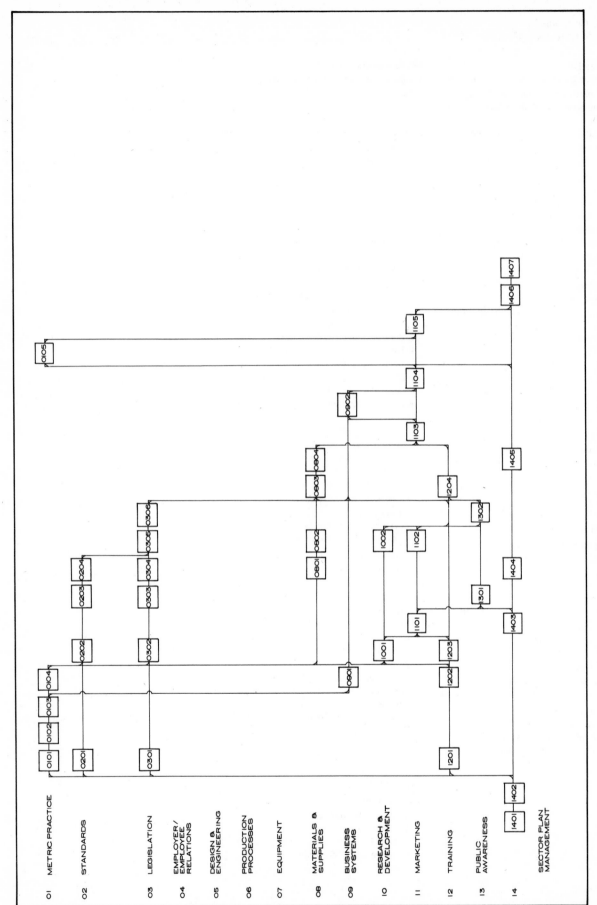

Figure 11.6   Task network for the conversion of the Real Estate Sector to SI.

Figure 11.6 *(Continued)*
3.06 REAL ESTATE SECTOR

01 Metric Practice

1 Select Units & Ratios for Use in Real Estate

2 Establish Preferred Dimensions for Real Estate

3 Develop Measurement Rules & Practices

4 Develop Supplemental Metric Practice Guide for Real Estate

5 Revise Metric Practice Guide as Required

02 Codes & Standards

1 Identify Metric Standards Related to Real Estate

2 Monitor Standards Development with Input on Priorities, Conversion & Rationalization

3 Obtain Necessary Metric Standards

4 Adopt Revised Standards

03 Legislation & Regulations

1 Identify Measurement Sensitive Legislation & Regulations Related to Real Estate

2 Monitor Legislative & Regulatory Progress and Determine Impact on Sector

3 Consult Government Officials

4 Recommend Priorities for Change

5 Monitor Changes

6 Obtain Enabling Interim (if Required) or Permanent Legislation

04 Employer/Employee Relations

05 Design & Engineering

06 Production Processes

07 Equipment

08 Materials & Supplies

1 Identify Materials & Supplies to be Changed

2 Evaluate Methods for Changing

3 Consult Suppliers

4 Procure Metric Materials & Supplies, Including Land Surveys, Construction Documents, etc.

09 Business Systems

1 Identify Business Systems & Activities Affected by Metric Conversion

2 Implement Revised Systems & Programs

10 Research & Development

1 Identify Measurement Sensitive Research Activities

2 Develop Metric Texts, Tables etc.

11 Marketing

1 Initiate Marketing Feasibility Studies for Use of Metric Terms in Real Estate

2 Develop Advertising Programs, Texts & Publications in Metric Terms

3 Land Transactions in Metric Terms

4 Real Estate Transactions (in Addition to Land) in Metric Terms

5 All Real Estate Transactions in Metric Terms

12 Training

1 Determine Training Requirements for Real Estate Sector

2 Develop Curricula

3 Develop Aids, Texts & Training Materials

4 Implement Training Programs & Seminars

13 Public Awareness

1 Develop Industry-Wide Awareness Program

2 Disseminate Information to Concerned Public

14 Sector Plan Management

1 Organize Sector

2 Develop Policies & Strategies

3 Schedule & Recommend Plan for Publication

4 Develop Liaison with Related Sectors

5 Monitor Sector Conversion Progress

6 Dissolve Sector Committee

7 Metric Conversion Complete

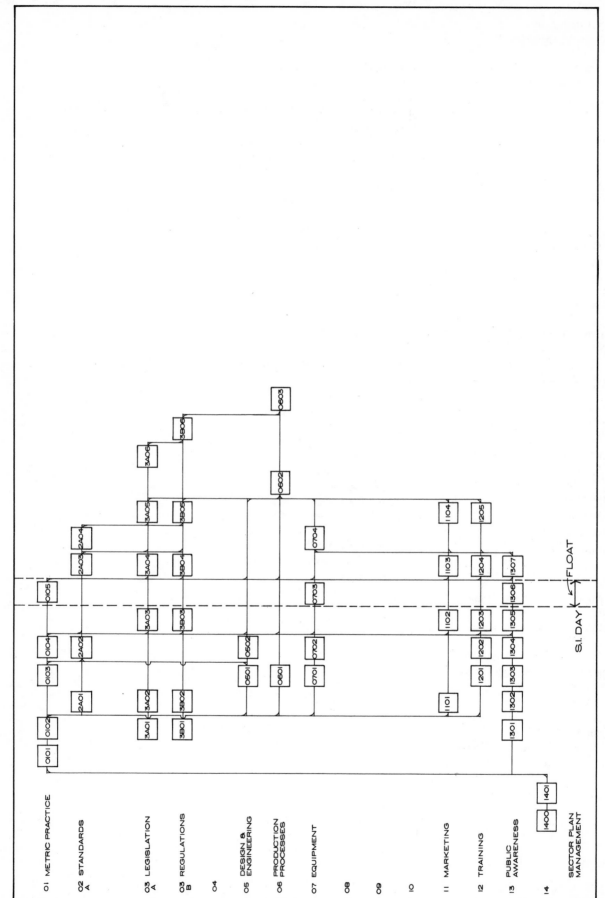

Figure 11.7   Task network for the conversion of the Surveying and Mapping Sector to SI.

Figure 11.7 *(Continued)*

3.08 SURVEYING AND MAPPING SECTOR

01 Metric Practice
1 Identify Customary Units of Measurement
2 Specify SI Equivalents for Customary Base Units
3 Liaison with Related Sectors
4 Prepare Supplementary Practice Guide Texts and Tables
5 Publish Supplementary Practice Guide, Texts and Tables

02A Standards
1 Identify Standards to be Changed
2 Liaise with other Sectors
3 Publish Standards & Specifications
4 Establish Data Banks and National Cadastre

02B Codes

03A Legislation
1 Identify Types of Measurement & Recordation Sensitive Legislation
2 Specify General Changes Required
3 Consult Government (Federal, state, county) Officials
4 Recommend Priorities for Change
5 Monitor Changes in Legislation
6 Enact Legislation

03B Regulators
1 Identify Types of Measurement & Recordation Sensitive Regulations
2 Specify General Changes Required
3 Consult Government (Federal, state, county) Officials
4 Recommend Priorities for Change
5 Monitor Changes in Regulations
6 Publish Regulations

04 Employer/Employee Relations

05 Design & Engineering
1 Identify Fields Affected
2 Liaise with Related Sectors

06 Production Processes
1 Identify Areas Affected
2 Coordinate Production Modifications
3 Metric Units (SI) Fully Applied

07 Equipment
1 Identify Surveying, Drafting, Printing, etc. Equipment Involved
2 Specify Changes
3 Consult Suppliers
4 Procure Equipment

08 Materials & Supplies

09 Business Systems

10 Research & Development

11 Marketing
1 Identify Markets Affected
2 Specify Products Affected by Changeover
3 Consult Customer Sectors
4 Implement Changes

12 Training
1 Identify Training Requirements
2 Specify Training Activities
3 Assign Priorities for Training
4 Develop Training Programs
5 Train Personnel

13 Public Awareness
1 Identify Needs
2 Specify Resource Requirements
3 Consult Related Organizations
4 Specify Priorities
5 Develop Programs
6 Implement Programs
7 Awareness, Consensus and Acceptance of Plan

14 Sector Plan Management
1 Organize Sector
2 Identify Policies and Strategies for Conversion
3 Dissolve Sector Committee

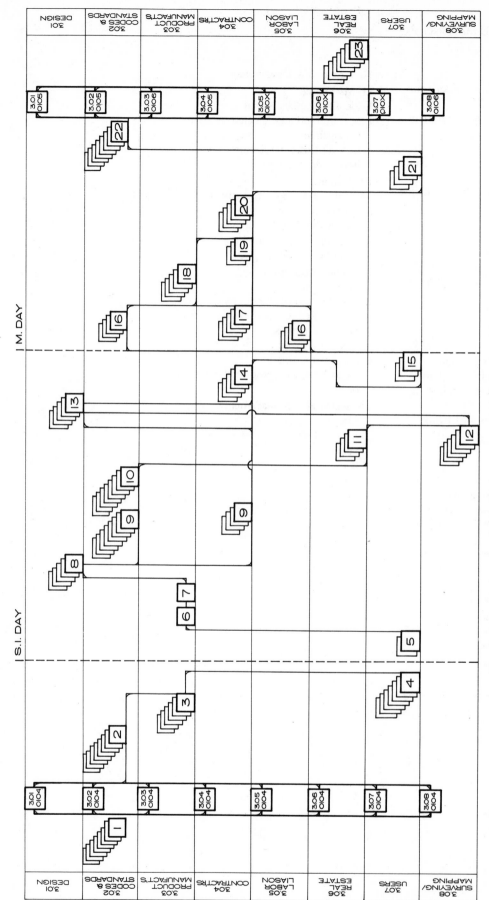

Figure 11.8   Task network for the conversion of the Construction Industry to SI.

Figure 11.8 *(Continued)*
THE CONSTRUCTION INDUSTRY

1 Publish Metric Practice Guide for Construction Industry (3.02, 3.01, 3.03, 3.04, 3.05, 3.06, 3.07, 3.08)
2 Develop Necessary Basic Metric Standards (3.02, 3.01, 3.03, 3.04, 3.05, 3.06, 3.07, 3.08)
3 Determine Product Sizes in SI Units (3.03, 3.01, 3.02, 3.04, 3.05, 3.07)
4 Decision to Build Metric Building (3.07, 3.06, 3.01, 3.02, 3.03, 3.04, 3.05)
5 Award Design Contract (3.07, 3.01)
6 Develop and Distribute Product Literature (3.03)
7 Produce Metric Measuring Equipment (3.03)
8 Begin Conceptual Design in Metric Terms (3.01, 3.07, 3.03, 3.02, 3.04)
9 Publish Model Codes in Metric (3.02, 3.01, 3.03, 3.04, 3.05, 3.06, 3.07, 3.08)
9 Develop Preliminary Metric Estimating System (3.04, 3.03, 3.01, 3.07)
10 Enact Enabling Legislation (3.02, 3.01, 3.03, 3.04, 3.05, 3.06, 3.07, 3.08)
11 Land Transactions in Metric (3.06, 3.08, 3.02, 3.07)
12 Produce Property Survey in Metric (3.08, 3.01, 3.02, 3.04, 3.06, 3.07)
13 Begin Design Development and Engineering (3.01, 3.07, 3.03, 3.02, 3.04)
14 Estimate and Bid on Metric Documents (3.04, 3.03, 3.01, 3.05, 3.02)
15 Award Construction Contract (3.07, 3.01, 3.04)
16 Accept Plans in Metric and Issue Building Permits (3.02, 3.01, 3.07, 3.04)
16 Obtain Labor Agreements in Metric Terms (3.05, 3.04, 3.03, 3.07)
17 Begin Construction of Metric Building (3.04, 3.07, 3.01, 3.03, 3.05)
18 Deliver Metric Products to Supplier and Site (3.03, 3.04, 3.01, 3.02, 3.05)
19 Install Metric Products (3.04, 3.03, 3.02)
20 Complete Construction (3.04, 3.01, 3.02, 3.03, 3.07)
21 Occupy and Maintain Metric Building (3.07, 3.03, 3.04, 3.01)
22 Revise Metric Practice Guide (3.02, 3.01, 3.03, 3.04, 3.05, 3.06, 3.07, 3.08)
23 Real Estate Transactions in Metric (3.06, 3.07, 3.01, 3.02, 3.04, 3.08, 3.05)

Note: Key events listed occur sequentially as shown in the chart. The numbers in parentheses indicate sector involvement in each task.

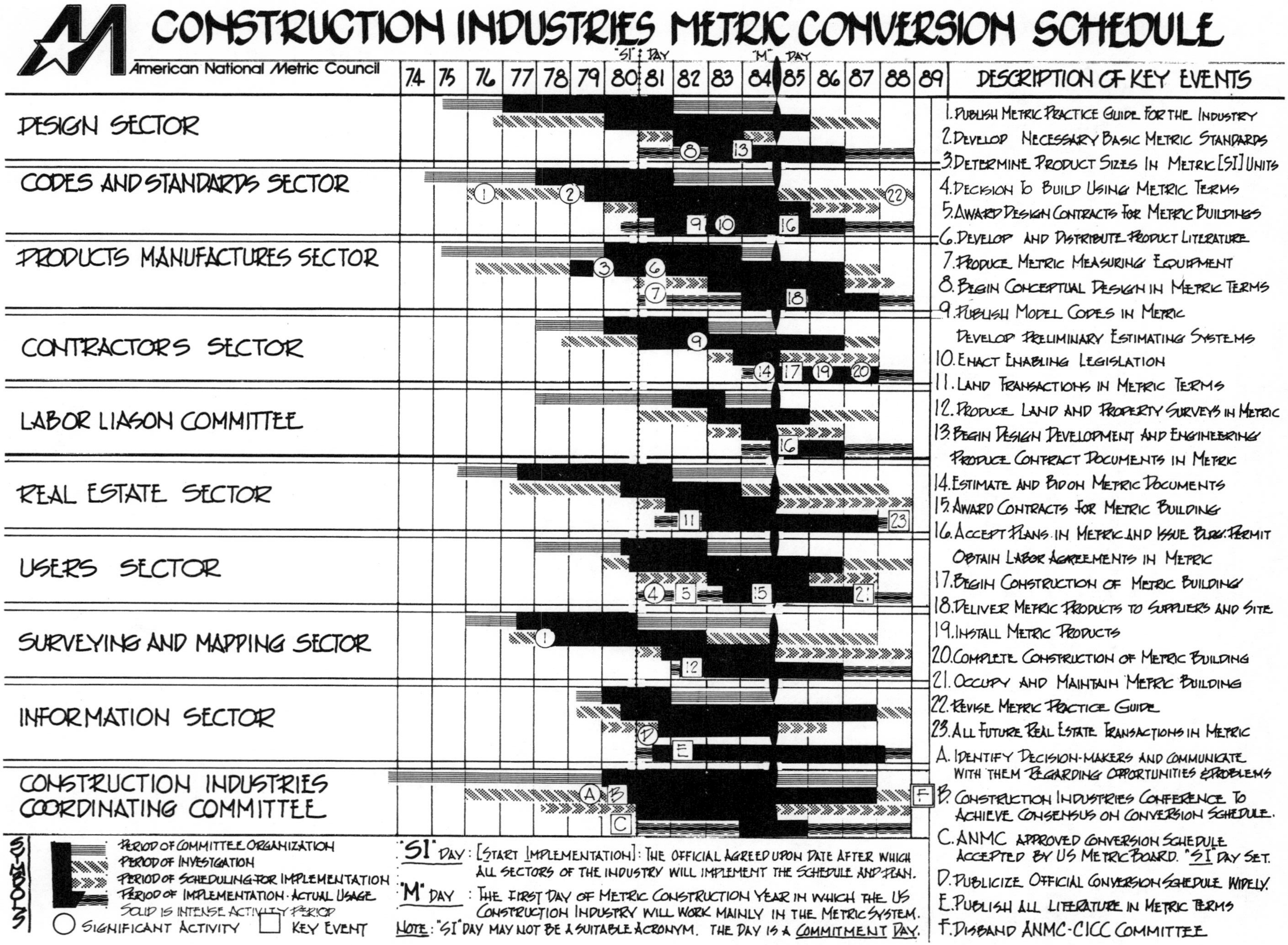

Figure 11.9 Master conversion schedule for the different sectors of the construction industry.

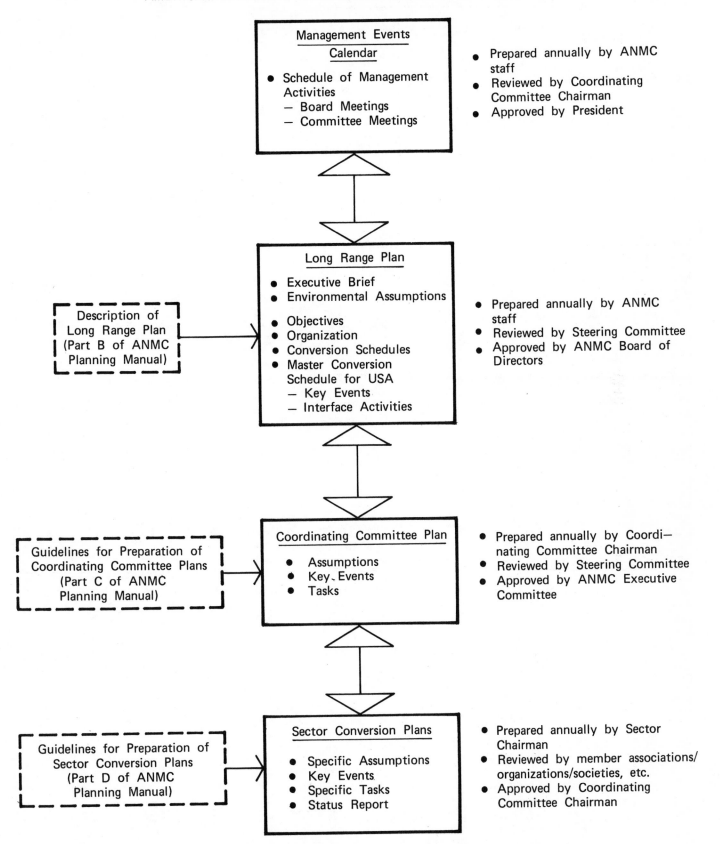

Figure 11.10 A graphic explanation of the actual ANMC planning process, identifying those responsible for preparation and approval activity.

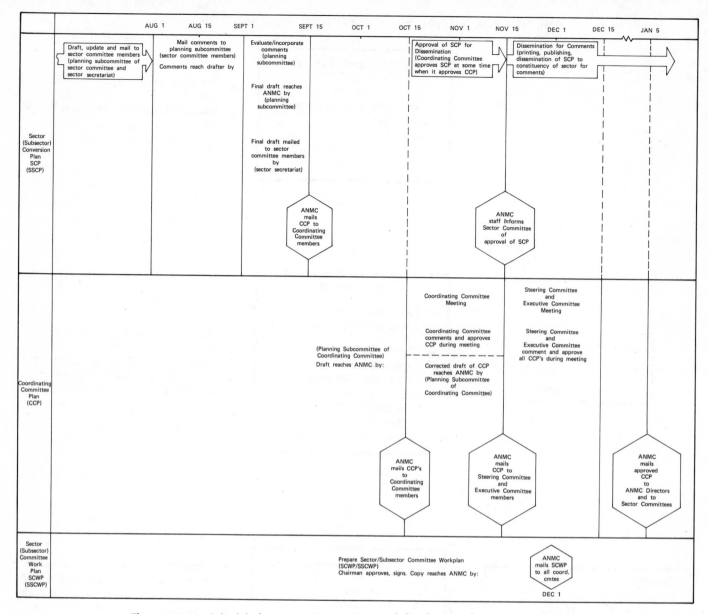

Figure 11.11 Schedule for preparation, review, and distribution of metrication plans.

APPENDIX 1

THE METRIC CONVERSION ACT

Public Law 94-168
94th Congress, H. R. 8674
December 23, 1975

An Act

To declare a national policy of coordinating the increasing use of the metric system in the United States, and to establish a United States Metric Board to coordinate the voluntary conversion to the metric system.

Be it enacted by the Senate and House of Representatives of the United States of America in Congress assembled, That this Act may be cited as the "Metric Conversion Act of 1975".

Sec. 2. The Congress finds as follows: Metric Conversion Act of 1975. 15 USC 205a note. 15 USC 205a.

(1) The United States was an original signatory party to the 1875 Treaty of the Meter (20 Stat. 709), which established the General Conference of Weights and Measures, the International Committee of Weights and Measures and the International Bureau of Weights and Measures.

(2) Although the use of metric measurement standards in the United States has been authorized by law since 1866 (Act of July 28, 1866; 14 Stat. 339), this Nation today is the only industrially developed nation which has not established a national policy of committing itself and taking steps to facilitate conversion to the metric system.

Sec. 3. It is therefore declared that the policy of the United States shall be to coordinate and plan the increasing use of the metric system in the United States and to establish a United States Metric Board to coordinate the voluntary conversion to the metric system. 15 USC 205b.

Sec. 4. As used in this Act, the term— Definitions. 15 USC 205c.

(1) "Board" means the United States Metric Board, established under section 5 of this Act;

(2) "engineering standard" means a standard which prescribes (A) a concise set of conditions and requirements that must be satisfied by a material, product, process, procedure, convention, or test method; and (B) the physical, functional, performance and/or conformance characteristics thereof;

(3) "international standard or recommendation" means an engineering standard or recommendation which is (A) formulated and promulgated by an international organization and (B) recommended for adoption by individual nations as a national standard; and

(4) "metric system of measurement" means the International System of Units as established by the General Conference of Weights and Measures in 1960 and as interpreted or modified for the United States by the Secretary of Commerce.

Sec. 5. (a) There is established, in accordance with this section, an independent instrumentality to be known as a United States Metric Board. United States Metric Board. Establishment. 15 USC 205d. Membership.

(b) The Board shall consist of 17 individuals, as follows:

(1) the Chairman, a qualified individual who shall be appointed by the President, by and with the advice and consent of the Senate;

(2) sixteen members who shall be appointed by the President, by and with the advice and consent of the Senate, on the following basis—

(A) one to be selected from lists of qualified individuals recommended by engineers and organizations representative of engineering interests;

(B) one to be selected from lists of qualified individuals recommended by scientists, the scientific and technical community, and organizations representative of scientists and technicians;

(C) one to be selected from a list of qualified individuals recommended by the National Association of Manufacturers or its successor;

(D) one to be selected from lists of qualified individuals recommended by the United States Chamber of Commerce, or its successor, retailers, and other commercial organizations;

(E) two to be selected from lists of qualified individuals recommended by the American Federation of Labor and Congress of Industrial organizations or its successor, who are representative of workers directly affected by metric conversion, and by other organizations representing labor;

(F) one to be selected from a list of qualified individuals recommended by the National Governors Conference, the National Council of State Legislatures, and organizations representative of State and local government;

(G) two to be selected from lists of qualified individuals recommended by organizations representative of small business;

(H) one to be selected from lists of qualified individuals representative of the construction industry;

(I) one to be selected from a list of qualified individuals recommended by the National Conference on Weights and Measures and standards making organizations;

(J) one to be selected from lists of qualified individuals recommended by educators, the educational community, and organizations representative of educational interests; and

(K) four at-large members to represent consumers and other interests deemed suitable by the President and who shall be qualified individuals.

Term of office. As used in this subsection, each "list" shall include the names of at least three individuals for each applicable vacancy. The terms of office of the members of the Board first taking office shall expire as designated by the President at the time of nomination; five at the end of the 2d year; five at the end of the 4th year; and six at the end of the 6th year. The term of office of the Chairman of such Board shall be 6 years. Members, including the Chairman, may be appointed to an additional term of 6 years, in the same manner as the original appointment. Successors to members of such Board shall be appointed in the same manner as the original members and shall have terms of office expiring 6 years from the date of expiration of the terms for which their predecessors were appointed. Any individual appointed to fill a vacancy occurring prior to the expiration of any term of office shall be appointed for the remainder of that term. Beginning 45 days after **Quorum.** the date of incorporation of the Board, six members of such Board shall constitute a quorum for the transaction of any function of the Board.

(c) Unless otherwise provided by the Congress, the Board shall have no compulsory powers.

(d) The Board shall cease to exist when the Congress, by law, determines that its mission has been accomplished.

Policy implementation. SEC. 6. It shall be the function of the Board to devise and carry out **15 USC 205e.** a broad program of planning, coordination, and public education, consistent with other national policy and interests, with the aim of implementing the policy set forth in this Act. In carrying out this program, the Board shall—

(1) consult with and take into account the interests, views, and conversion costs of United States commerce and industry, including small business; science; engineering; labor; education; consumers; government agencies at the Federal, State, and local level; nationally recognized standards developing and coordinating organizations; metric conversion planning and coordinating groups; and such other individuals or groups as are considered appropriate by the Board to the carrying out of the purposes of this Act. The Board shall take into account activities underway in the private and public sectors, so as not to duplicate unnecessarily such activities;

(2) provide for appropriate procedures whereby various groups, under the auspices of the Board, may formulate, and recommend or suggest, to the Board specific programs for coordinating conversion in each industry and segment thereof and specific dimensions and configurations in the metric system and in other measurements for general use. Such programs, dimensions, and configurations shall be consistent with (A) the needs, interests, and capabilities of manufacturers (large and small), suppliers, labor, consumers, educators, and other interested groups, and (B) the national interest;

(3) publicize, in an appropriate manner, proposed programs and provide an opportunity for interested groups or individuals to submit comments on such programs. At the request of interested parties, the Board, in its discretion, may hold hearings with regard to such programs. Such comments and hearings may be considered by the Board;

(4) encourage activities of standardization organizations to develop or revise, as rapidly as practicable, engineering standards on a metric measurement basis, and to take advantage of opportunities to promote (A) rationalization or simplification of relationships, (B) improvements of design, (C) reduction of size variations, (D) increases in economy, and (E) where feasible, the efficient use of energy and the conservation of natural resources;

(5) encourage the retention, in new metric language standards, of those United States engineering designs, practices, and conventions that are internationally accepted or that embody superior technology;

(6) consult and cooperate with foreign governments, and intergovernmental organizations, in collaboration with the Department of State, and, through appropriate member bodies, with private international organizations, which are or become concerned with the encouragement and coordination of increased use of metric measurement units or engineering standards based on such units, or both. Such consultation shall include efforts, where appropriate, to gain international recognition for metric standards proposed by the United States, and, during the United States conversion, to encourage retention of equivalent customary units, usually by way of dual dimensions, in international standards or recommendations;

(7) assist the public through information and education programs, to become familiar with the meaning and applicability of metric terms and measures in daily life. Such programs shall include—

Comments and hearings.

Consultation and cooperation.

Public information and education programs.

(A) public information programs conducted by the Board, through the use of newspapers, magazines, radio, television, and other media, and through talks before appropriate citizens' groups, and trade and public organizations;

(B) counseling and consultation by the Secretary of Health, Education, and Welfare; the Secretary of Labor; the Administrator of the Small Business Administration; and the Director of the National Science Foundation, with educational associations, State and local educational agencies, labor education committees, apprentice training committees, and other interested groups, in order to assure (i) that the metric system of measurement is included in the curriculum of the Nation's educational institutions, and (ii) that teachers and other appropriate personnel are properly trained to teach the metric system of measurement;

(C) consultation by the Secretary of Commerce with the National Conference of Weights and Measures in order to assure that State and local weights and measures officials are (i) appropriately involved in metric conversion activities and (ii) assisted in their efforts to bring about timely amendments to weights and measures laws; and

(D) such other public information activities, by any Federal agency in support of this Act, as relate to the mission of such agency;

(8) collect, analyze, and publish information about the extent of usage of metric measurements; evaluate the costs and benefits of metric usage; and make efforts to minimize any adverse effects resulting from increasing metric usage;

Surveys. Recommendations to Congress and President.

(9) conduct research, including appropriate surveys; publish the results of such research; and recommend to the Congress and to the President such action as may be appropriate to deal with any unresolved problems, issues, and questions associated with metric conversion, or usage, such problems, issues, and questions may include, but are not limited to, the impact on workers (such as costs of tools and training) and on different occupations and industries, possible increased costs to consumers, the impact on society and the economy, effects on small business, the impact on the international trade position of the United States, the appropriateness of and methods for using procurement by the Federal Government as a means to effect conversion to the metric system, the proper conversion or transition period in particular sectors of society, and consequences for national defense;

Report to Congress and President.

(10) submit annually to the Congress and to the President a report on its activities. Each such report shall include a status report on the conversion process as well as projections for the conversion process. Such report may include recommendations covering any legislation or executive action needed to implement the the programs of conversion accepted by the Board. The Board may also submit such other reports and recommendations as it deems necessary; and

Report to Congress and President.

(11) submit to the Congress and to the President, not later than 1 year after the date of enactment of the Act making appropriations for carrying out this Act, a report on the need to provide an effective structural mechanism for converting customary units to metric units in statutes, regulations, and other laws at all levels of government, on a coordinated and timely basis, in response to voluntary conversion programs adopted and implemented by various sectors of society under the auspices and with the approval

of the Board. If the Board determines that such a need exists, such report shall include recommendations as to appropriate and effective means for establishing and implementing such a mechanism.

SEC. 7. In carrying out its duties under this Act, the Board may—

(1) establish an Executive Committee, and such other committees as it deems desirable;

Committees, establishment. 15 USC 205f.

(2) establish such committees and advisory panels as it deems necessary to work with the various sectors of the Nation's economy and with Federal and State governmental agencies in the development and implementation of detailed conversion plans for those sectors. The Board may reimburse, to the extent authorized by law, the members of such committees;

(3) conduct hearings at such times and places as it deems appropriate;

Hearings.

(4) enter into contracts, in accordance with the Federal Property and Administrative Services Act of 1949, as amended (40 U.S.C. 471 et seq.), with Federal or State agencies, private firms, institutions, and individuals for the conduct of research or surveys, the preparation of reports, and other activities necessary to the discharge of its duties;

Contracts.

(5) delegate to the Executive Director such authority as it deems advisable; and

(6) perform such other acts as may be necessary to carry out the duties prescribed by this Act.

SEC. 8. (a) The Board may accept, hold, administer, and utilize gifts, donations, and bequests of property, both real and personal, and personal services, for the purpose of aiding or facilitating the work of the Board. Gifts and bequests of money, and the proceeds from the sale of any other property received as gifts or bequests, shall be deposited in the Treasury in a separate fund and shall be disbursed upon order of the Board.

Gifts and bequests. 15 USC 205g.

(b) For purpose of Federal income, estate, and gift taxation, property accepted under subsection (a) of this section shall be considered as a gift or bequest to or for the use of the United States.

(c) Upon the request of the Board, the Secretary of the Treasury may invest and reinvest, in securities of the United States, any moneys contained in the fund authorized in subsection (a) of this section. Income accruing from such securities, and from any other property accepted to the credit of such fund, shall be disbursed upon the order of the Board.

(d) Funds not expended by the Board as of the date when it ceases to exist, in accordance with section 5(d) of this Act, shall revert to the Treasury of the United States as of such date.

Unexpended funds.

SEC. 9. Members of the Board who are not in the regular full-time employ of the United States shall, while attending meetings or conferences of the Board or while otherwise engaged in the business of the Board, be entitled to receive compensation at a rate not to exceed the daily rate currently being paid grade 18 of the General Schedule (under section 5332 of title 5, United States Code), including travel-time. While so serving, on the business of the Board away from their homes or regular places of business, members of the Board may be allowed travel expenses, including per diem in lieu of subsistence, as authorized by section 5703 of title 5, United States Code, for persons employed intermittently in the Government service. Payments under this section shall not render members of the Board employees or officials of the United States for any purpose. Members of the Board who are in the employ of the United States shall be entitled to travel expenses when traveling on the business of the Board.

Compensation. 15 USC 205h.

5 USC 5332 note. Travel expenses.

Executive
Director,
appointment.
15 USC 205i.

SEC. 10. (a) The Board shall appoint a qualified individual to serve as the Executive Director of the Board at the pleasure of the Board. The Executive Director, subject to the direction of the Board, shall be responsible to the Board and shall carry out the metric conversion program, pursuant to the provisions of this Act and the policies established by the Board.

5 USC 5101
et seq.
5 USC 5331.

(b) The Executive Director of the Board shall serve full time and be subject to the provisions of chapter 51 and subchapter III of chapter 53 of title 5, United States Code. The annual salary of the Executive Director shall not exceed level III of the Executive Schedule under section 5314 of such title.

(c) The Board may appoint and fix the compensation of such staff personnel as may be necessary to carry out the provisions of this Act in accordance with the provisions of chapter 51 and subchapter III of chapter 53 of title 5, United States Code.

Experts and
consultants.

(d) The Board may (1) employ experts and consultants or organizations thereof, as authorized by section 3109 of title 5, United States Code; (2) compensate individuals so employed at rates not in excess of the rate currently being paid grade 18 of the General Schedule under section 5332 of such title, including traveltime; and (3) may allow such individuals, while away from their homes or regular places of business, travel expenses (including per diem in lieu of subsistence) as authorized by section 5703 of such title 5 for persons in the Government service employed intermittently: *Provided, however,* That contracts for such temporary employment may be renewed annually.

Financial
and adminis-
trative
services.
15 USC 205j.

SEC. 11. Financial and administrative services, including those related to budgeting, accounting, financial reporting, personnel, and procurement, and such other staff services as may be needed by the Board, may be obtained by the Board from the Secretary of Commerce or other appropriate sources in the Federal Government. Payment for such services shall be made by the Board, in advance or by reimbursement, from funds of the Board in such amounts as may be agreed upon by the Chairman of the Board and by the source of the services being rendered.

Appropriation
authorization.
15 USC 205k.

SEC. 12. There are authorized to be appropriated such sums as may be necessary to carry out the provisions of this Act. Appropriations to carry out the provisions of this Act may remain available for obligation and expenditure for such period or periods as may be specified in the Acts making such appropriations.

Approved December 23, 1975.

LEGISLATIVE HISTORY:

HOUSE REPORT No. 94-369 (Comm. on Science and Technology).
SENATE REPORT No. 94-500 (Comm. on Commerce).
CONGRESSIONAL RECORD, Vol. 121 (1975):
    Sept. 5, considered and passed House.
    Dec. 8, considered and passed Senate, amended, in lieu of S. 100.
    Dec. 11, House concurred in Senate amendment.
WEEKLY COMPILATION OF PRESIDENTIAL DOCUMENTS, Vol. 11, No. 52:
    Dec. 23, Presidential statement.

APPENDIX 2

RECOMMENDED METRIC UNITS IN CONSTRUCTION

Recommended Metric Units for Use in Design and Construction
The use of SI units is preferred. Non-SI units that may be used with SI are shown in parentheses. In general, units are shown in ascending order of magnitude.

Application	SI Unit (Derivation)	Working Units	Replaced Customary Units and Non-SI Units
Design			
General Applications			
Linear measurement	m	mm, m, km	in, ft, yd, mi
Area	m²	mm², m², (ha), km²	in², ft², yd², acre, mi²
Volume, capacity	m³	mm³, m³, (mL), (L)	in³, ft₂, yd³, board foot, fl. oz, qt. gal
Plane angle	rad	rad, (decimal degree)	deg, min, sec (°, ', ")
Solid angle	sr	sr	sr (*unchanged*)
Time, time interval	s	s, (h), (d)	s, min, h, d
Frequency	Hz (1/s)	Hz, kHz	c.p.s (= Hz)
Velocity, speed	m/s	m/s, (km/h)	ft/s, ft/min, mi/h (mph)
Acceleration	m/s²	m/s²	ft/s²
Volume rate of flow	m³/s	m³/s, (L/s)	ft³/s, ft³/min, gal/min (gpm), gal/h, million gal/d
Temperature interval temperature value	K	°C, K	°F
Mass	kg	g, kg, (t = Mg)	oz, lb, slug, ton (2000 lb)
Mass per unit length	kg/m	g/m, kg/m	oz/ft, lb/ft, lb/mi
Mass per unit area	kg/m²	g/m², kg/m²	oz/yd², oz/ft², lb/yd², lb/ft²
Density, mass per unit volume	kg/m³	kg/m³, (t/m³)	lb/yd³, lb/ft³, ton/yd³
Mass per unit time	kg/s	kg/s, (t/h)	lb/min, lb/s, ton/h
Engineering design			
Section modulus	m³	mm³, m³	in³
Second moment of area torsional constant	m⁴	mm⁴, m⁴	in⁴
Warping constant	m⁶	mm⁶, m⁶	in⁶
Moment of inertia	kg·m²	kg·m²	lb·ft²
Force	N (kg · m/s²)	N, kN	lbf, poundal, kip, tonf
Force per unit length	N/m	N/m, kN/m	lbf/ft, lbf/in, kip/ft, tonf/ft
Moment of force, torque	N·m	N·m, kN·m, MN·m	lbf·ft, lbf·in, kip·ft, tonf·ft
Pressure, stress, modulus of elasticity	Pa (N/m²)	Pa, kPa, MPa, GPa	lbf/ft², lbf/in² (psi), kip/ft², tonf/ft², kip/in², tonf/in², in Hg, in H₂O, ft H₂O; bar, mbar
Compressibility	1/Pa	1/Pa, 1/kPa	ft²/tonf, in²/lbf
Dynamic viscosity	Pa·s	mPa·s, Pa·s	lbf·s/in²
Kinematic viscosity	m²/s	mm²/s, m²/s	in²/s, ft²/s

Table (*Continued*)

Application	SI Unit (Derivation)	Working Units	Replaced Customary Units and Non-SI Units
Engineering design			
Energy, work, quantity of heat	J (N·m) (W·s)	J, kJ, MJ, (kWh)	ft · lbf, ft · poundal, kWh, Btu, therm; cal, kcal
Impact strength	J/m²	J/m², kJ/m²	lbf/ft, kip/ft, ton/ft
Specific energy, specific latent heat	J/kg	kJ/kg, MJ/kg	Btu/lb
Energy density	J/m³	kJ/m³, MJ/m³	Btu-ft³
Heat capacity, entropy	J/K	J/K, kJ/K J/°C, kJ/°C	Btu/°F
Specific heat capacity, specific entropy	J/kg·K	J/kg·K, kJ/kg·K	Btu-lb·°F
Power, heat flow rate	W (J/s) (V/A)	W, kW, MW	W, kW, MW, hp, ft · lbf/min, ft · lbf/s, Btu/h, Btu/min, Btu/s ton (refrigeration); cal/s, kcal/s
Heat flux density, irradiance	W/m²	W/m², kW/m²	Btu/ft²·h, Btu/ft²·min, Btu/ft²·s
Heat release rate	W/m³	W/m³, kW/m³	Btu/ft³·h, Btu/ft³·min, Btu/ft³·s
Thermal conductivity k-value	W/m·K	W/m·K (= W/m·°C)	Btu·in/ft²·h·°F
Coefficient of heat transfer, U-value	W/m²·k	W/m²·K (= W/m²·°C)	Btu/ft²·h·°F
Thermal resistivity	m·k/W	m·K/W (= m·°C/W)	ft²·h·°F/Btu·in
Thermal insulance, R-value	m²·K/W	m²·K/W (= m²·°C/W)	ft²·h·°F/Btu
Electricity and Illumination			
Electric current	A	mA, A, kA	mA, A, kA (*unchanged*)
Electric charge	C (A·s)	mC, C, kC	mC, C, kC (*replaces A·h*)
Electric potential, potential difference	V (W/A)	mV, V, kV	mV, V, kV (*unchanged*)
Electric resistance	Ω (V/A)	mΩ, Ω, kΩ, MΩ	mΩ, Ω, kΩ, MΩ (*unchanged*)
Electric conductance	S (1/Ω)	mS, S, kS	S (*replaces mho*)
Luminous intensity	cd	cd, kcd	cd (*unchanged*)
Luminous flux	lm (cd·sr)	lm, klm	lm (*unchanged*)
Quantity of light	lm·s	lm·s, (lm·h)	lm·s, lm·h
Luminance	cd/m²	cd/m², kcd/m²	cd/in², cd/ft², lambert, footlambert; stilb
Illuminance (illumination)	lx (lm/m²)	lx, klx	lm/ft²
Luminous efficacy	lm/W	lmW	lm/W (*unchanged*)

Note: For a comprehensive tabulation of SI Units for use in design and construction, including typical applications and remarks, refer to NBS Technical Note 938, Section 8, Tables G to M (pages 10–21), or ANSI/ASTM E621-78, Section 8 and Tables 7 to 12 (pages 4/5, and 18–30).

Metric Units for Building Materials and Components

Units are shown in order of: length, area, volume (capacity), mass, other quantities.

Materials and Components	Metric Working Units	Replaced Customary Units
Basic materials		
Asphalt, cutback liquids	m^3, L; t (Mg)	ft^3, gal; ton (2000 lb)
Bagged materials	m^3; kg, t	ft^3, yd^3; lb, ton
Bituminous concrete	m^2; t	ft^2; ton
Concrete		
Admixtures	mL, L; g, kg	fl. oz, qt, gal; oz, lb
Aggregates	m^3; t	yd^3; ton
Cement	m^3; kg, t	lb, cwt, bbl, ton
Concrete volume	m^3	ft^3, yd^3
Concrete mass	kg, t	lb, ton
Concentration	kg/m^3	lb/ft^3
Slump	mm	in
Water	L	gal, ft^3
Bulk insulation	mm, m; m^2; kg	in, ft; ft^2, square (100 ft^2); lb
Coverage: liquids	L/m^2	gal/ft^2, gal/yd^2
Coverage: solids	kg/m^2	lb/ft^2, lb/yd^2
Lime	kg, t	lb, ton
Mortar	m^3; kg	ft^3; lb
Plaster	m^2; m^3; kg, t	ft^2, yd^2; ft^3; lb, ton
Stone, riprap	m^2; m^3; t	ft^2, yd^2; ft^3, yd^3; ton
Timber	m; m^3	ft; board foot, cunit, cord
Fabricated Products		
Boards, panels, tiles	mm, m; m^2; kg	in, ft; ft^2; lb
Bricks, blocks	mm; kg	in, ft; lb
Coverings: floor, wall	mm; m^2	in, ft; ft^2, yd^2
Equipment	mm, m; kg, t	in, ft; lb, ton
Fasteners (nails, screws, bolts, etc.)	mm; g, kg	in; pennyweight, oz, lb
Lumber	mm, m; m^2; m^3	in, ft; ft^2; board foot, ft^3
Reinforcing steel		
Wire, bars	mm, m; kg, t	in, ft; lb, ton
Mesh	mm; m^2; kg, t	in; ft^2; lb, ton
Roofing	mm, m; m^2; kg	in, ft; ft^2, yd^2, square; lb
Sheets (membranes, flashing, glass, metal, etc.)	mm, m; m^2; kg; g/m^2, kg/m^2	in, ft; ft^2, yd^2; oz, lb; oz/ft^2, lb/ft^2
Siding, shingles	mm, m^2	in, ft^2
Structural steel	mm, m; mm^2; kg, t; kg/m	in, ft; in^2; lb, ton; lb/ft

CONVERSION FACTORS

Conversion factors are taken to <u>six</u> significant figures, where appropriate.   <u>Underlined</u> values denote <u>exact</u> conversions.

METRIC TO CUSTOMARY   CUSTOMARY TO METRIC

LENGTH

1 km	= 0.621 371	mile (international)	1 mile (international)	= <u>1.609 344</u>	km
	= 49.7096	chain	1 chain	= 20.1168	m
1 m	= 1.093 61	yd	1 yd	= <u>0.9144</u>	m
	= 3.280 84	ft	1 ft	= <u>0.3048</u>	m
1 mm	= 0.039 370 1	in		= <u>304.8</u>	mm
			1 in	= <u>25.4</u>	mm
			(1 U.S. survey foot	= 0.304 800 6	m)

AREA

1 km^2	= 0.386 101	mile^2 (U.S. survey)	1 mile^2 (U.S. survey)	= 2.590 00	km^2
1 ha	= 2.471 04	acre (U.S. survey)	1 acre (U.S. survey)	= 0.404 687	ha
1 m^2	= 1.195 99	yd^2		= 4046.87	m^2
	= 10.7639	ft^2	1 yd^2	= 0.836 127	m^2
1 mm^2	= 0.001 550	in^2	1 ft^2	= 0.092 903	m^2
			1 in^2	= <u>645.16</u>	mm^2

VOLUME, MODULUS OF SECTION

1 m^3	= 0.810 709 x 10^{-3}	acre feet	1 acre ft	= 1233.49	m^3
	= 1.307 95	yd^3	1 yd^3	= 0.764 555	m^3
	= 35.3147	ft^3	100 board ft	= 0.235 974	m^3
	= 423.776	board ft	1 ft^3	= 0.028 316 8	m^3
1 mm^3	= 61.0237 x 10^{-6}	in^3		= 28.3168	L (dm^3)
			1 in^3	= 16 387.1	mm^3
				= 16.3871	mL (cm^3)

(FLUID) CAPACITY

1 L	= 0.035 314 7	ft^3	1 gal (U.S. liquid)**	= 3.785 41	L
	= 0.264 172	gal (U.S.)	1 qt (U.S. liquid)	= 946.353	mL
	= 1.056 69	qt (U.S.)	1 pt (U.S. liquid)	= 473.177	mL
1 mL	= 0.061 023 7	in^3	1 fl oz (U.S.)	= 29.5735	mL
	= 0.033 814	fl oz (U.S.)			

** 1 gal(UK) approx. 1.2 gal(US)

SECOND MOMENT OF AREA

1 mm^4	= 2.402 51 x 10^{-6}	in^4	1 in^4	= 416 231	mm^4
				= 0.416 231 x 10^{-6}	m^4

PLANE ANGLE

1 rad	= 57° 17' 45"	(degree)	1° (degree)	= 0.017 453 3	rad
	= 57.2958°	(degree)		= 17.4533	mrad
	= 3437.75'	(minute)	1' (minute)	= 290.888	µrad
	= 206 265"	(second)	1" (second)	= 4.848 14	µrad

VELOCITY, SPEED

1 m/s	= 3.280 84	ft/s	1 ft/s	= <u>0.3048</u>	m/s
	= 2.236 94	mile/h	1 mile/h	= <u>1.609 344</u>	km/h
1 km/h	= 0.621 371	mile/h		= <u>0.447 04</u>	m/s

Data from NBS Technical Note 938, Recommended Practice for the Use of Metric (SI) Units in Building Design and Construction, National Bureau of Standards, 1977.

ACCELERATION

| 1 m/s^2 | = 3.280 84 | ft/s^2 | 1 ft/s^2 | = 0.3048 | m/s^2 |

VOLUME RATE OF FLOW

1 m^3/s	= 35.3147	ft^3/s	1 ft^3/s	= 0.028 316 8	m^3/s
	= 22.8245	million gal/d	1 ft^3/min	= 0.471 947	L/s
	= 0.810 709 x 10^{-3}	acre ft/s	1 gal/min	= 0.063 090 2	L/s
1 L/s	= 2.118 88	ft^3/min	1 gal/h	= 1.051 50	mL/s
	= 15.850 3	gal/min	1 million gal/d	= 43.8126	L/s
	= 951.022	gal/h	1 acre ft/s	= 1233.49	m^3/s

TEMPERATURE INTERVAL

| 1 °C | = 1 K | = 1.8 °F | 1 °F | = 0.555 556 | °C or K |
| | | | | = 5/9 °C = 5/9 K | |

EQUIVALENT TEMPERATURE VALUE   ($t_C = T_K - 273.15$)

| $t°C$ | = 5/9 (t_F − 32) | | t_F | = 9/5 $t°C$ + 32 | |

MASS

1 kg	= 2.204 62	lb (avoirdupois)	1 ton (short)***	= 0.907 185	metric ton
	= 35.2740	oz (avoirdupois)		= 907.185	kg
1 metric	= 1.102 31	ton (short, 2000 lb)	1 lb	= 0.453 592	kg
ton	= 2204.62	lb	1 oz	= 28.3495	g
1 g	= 0.035 274	oz	1 pennyweight	= 1.555 17	g
	= 0.643 015	pennyweight			

***(1 long ton (2240 lb) = 1016.05 kg)

MASS PER UNIT LENGTH

| 1 kg/m | = 0.671 969 | lb/ft | 1 lb/ft | = 1.488 16 | kg/m |
| 1 g/m | = 3.547 99 | lb/mile | 1 lb/mile | = 0.281 849 | g/m |

MASS PER UNIT AREA

1 kg/m^2	= 0.204 816	lb/ft^2	1 lb/ft^2	= 4.882 43	kg/m^2
1 g/m^2	= 0.029 494	oz/yd^2	1 oz/yd^2	= 33.9057	g/m^2
	= 3.277 06 x 10^{-3}	oz/ft^2	1 oz/ft^2	= 305.152	g/m^2

DENSITY (MASS PER UNIT VOLUME)

1 kg/m^3	= 0.062 428	lb/ft^3	1 lb/ft^3	= 16.0185	kg/m^3
	= 1.685 56	lb/yd^3	1 lb/yd^3	= 0.593 276	kg/m^3
1 t/m^3	= 0.842 778	ton/yd^3	1 ton/yd^3	= 1.186 55	t/m^3

MOMENT OF INERTIA

| 1 kg·m^2 | = 23.7304 | lb·ft^2 | 1 lb·ft^2 | = 0.042 140 1 | kg·m^2 |
| | = 3417.17 | lb·in^2 | 1 lb·in^2 | = 292.640 | kg·mm^2 |

MASS PER UNIT TIME

| 1 kg/s | = 2.204 62 | lb/s | 1 lb/s | = 0.453 592 | kg/s |
| 1 t/h | = 0.984 207 | ton/h | 1 ton/h | = 1.016 05 | t/h |

FORCE

1 MN	= 112.404	tonf (ton-force)	1 tonf (ton-force)	= 8.896 44	kN
1 kN	= 0.112 404	tonf	1 kip (1000 lbf)	= 4.448 22	kN
	= 224.809	lbf (pound-force)	1 lbf (pound-force)	= 4.448 22	N
1 N	= 0.224 809	lbf			

MOMENT OF FORCE, TORQUE

1 N·m	= 0.737 562	lbf·ft	1 lbf·ft	= 1.355 82	N·m
	= 8.850 75	lbf·in	1 lbf·in	= 0.112 985	N·m
1 kN·m	= 0.368 781	tonf·ft	1 tonf·ft	= 2.711 64	kN·m
	= 0.737 562	kip·ft	1 kip·ft	= 1.355 82	kN·m

FORCE PER UNIT LENGTH

1 N/m	= 0.068 521 8	lbf/ft	1 lbf/ft	= 14.5939	N/m
1 kN/m	= 0.034 260 9	tonf/ft	1 lbf/in	= 175.127	N/m
			1 tonf/ft	= 29.187 8	kN/m

PRESSURE, STRESS, MODULUS OF ELASTICITY (FORCE PER UNIT AREA) ($1\ Pa = 1\ N/m^2$)

1 MPa	= 0.072 518 8	$tonf/in^2$	$1\ tonf/in^2$	= 13.7895	MPa
	= 10.4427	$tonf/ft^2$	$1\ tonf/ft^2$	= 95.7605	kPa
	= 145.038	lbf/in^2	$1\ kip/in^2$	= 6.894 76	MPa
1 kPa	= 20.8854	lbf/ft^2	$1\ lbf/in^2$	= 6.894 76	kPa
			$1\ lbf/ft^2$	= 47.8803	Pa

WORK, ENERGY, HEAT ($1\ J = 1\ N·m = 1\ W·s$)

1 MJ	= 0.277 778	kWh	1 kWh (550 ft·lbf/s)	= 3.6	MJ
1 kJ	= 0.947 817	Btu	1 Btu (Int. Table)	= 1.055 06	kJ
1 J	= 0.737 562	ft·lbf		= 1055.06	J
			1 ft·lbf	= 1.355 82	J

POWER, HEAT FLOW RATE

1 kW	= 1.341 02	hp (horsepower)	1 hp	= 0.745 700	kW
1 W	= 3.412 14	Btu/h		= 745.700	W
	= 0.737 562	ft·lbf/s	1 Btu/h	= 0.293 071	W
			1 ft·lbf/s	= 1.355 82	W

HEAT FLUX DENSITY

$1\ W/m^2$	= 0.316 998	$Btu/(ft^2·h)$	$1\ Btu/(ft^2·h)$	= 3.154 59	W/m^2

COEFFICIENT OF HEAT TRANSFER

$1\ W/(m^2·K)$	= 0.176 110	$Btu/(ft^2·h·°F)$	$1\ Btu/(ft^2·h·°F)$	= 5.678 26	$W/(m^2·K)$

THERMAL CONDUCTIVITY

$1\ W/(m·K)$	= 0.577 789	$Btu/(ft·h·°F)$	$1\ Btu/(ft·h·°F)$	= 1.730 73	$W/(m·K)$

	METRIC TO CUSTOMARY		CUSTOMARY TO METRIC		

CALORIFIC VALUE (MASS AND VOLUME BASIS)

1 kJ/kg (1 J/g)	= = 0.429 923	Btu/lb	1 Btu/lb	(= 2.326 = 2.326	kJ/kg (J/g)
1 kJ/m^3	= 0.026 839 2	Btu/ft^3	1 Btu/ft^3	= 37.2589	kJ/m^3

THERMAL CAPACITY (MASS AND VOLUME BASIS)

1 kJ/(kg·K)	= 0.238 846	Btu/(lb·°F)	1 Btu/(lb·°F)	= 4.1868	kJ/(kg·K)
1 kJ/(m^3·K)	= 0.014 910 7	Btu/(ft^3·°F)	1 Btu/(ft^3·°F)	= 67.0661	kJ/(m^3·K)

ILLUMINANCE

1 lx (lux)	= 0.092 903	lm/ft^2 (footcandle)	1 lm/ft^2 (footcandle)	= 10.7639	lx (lux)

LUMINANCE

1 cd/m^2	= 0.092 903 = 0.291 864	cd/ft^2 footlambert	1 cd/ft^2 1 footlambert	= 10.7639 = 3.426 26	cd/m^2 cd/m^2
1 kcd/m^2	= 0.314 159	lambert	1 lambert	= 3.183 01	kcd/m^2

CONVERSION TABLES

Table 1 Inches and fractions to millimeters (1 in = 25.4 mm)

	0	1	2	3	4	5	6	7	8	9	10	11
Inches							millimeters (mm)					
0	. . .	25.40	50.80	76.20	101.60	127.00	152.40	177.80	203.20	228.60	254.00	279.40
1/16	1.59	26.99	52.39	77.79	103.19	128.59	153.99	179.39	204.79	230.19	255.59	280.99
1/8	3.18	28.58	53.98	79.38	104.78	130.18	155.58	180.98	206.38	231.78	257.18	282.58
3/16	4.76	30.16	55.56	80.96	106.36	131.76	157.16	182.56	207.96	233.36	258.76	284.16
1/4	6.35	31.75	57.15	82.55	107.95	133.35	158.75	184.15	209.55	234.95	260.35	285.75
5/16	7.94	33.34	58.74	84.14	109.54	134.94	160.34	185.74	211.14	236.54	261.94	287.34
3/8	9.53	34.93	60.33	85.73	111.13	136.53	161.93	187.33	212.73	238.13	263.53	288.93
7/16	11.11	36.51	61.91	87.31	112.71	138.11	163.51	188.91	214.31	239.71	265.11	290.51
1/2	12.70	38.10	63.50	88.90	114.30	139.70	165.10	190.50	215.90	241.30	266.70	292.10
9/16	14.29	39.69	65.09	90.49	115.89	141.29	166.69	192.09	217.49	242.89	268.29	293.69
5/8	15.88	41.28	66.68	92.08	117.48	142.88	168.28	193.68	219.08	244.48	269.88	295.28
11/16	17.46	42.86	68.26	93.66	119.06	144.46	169.86	195.26	220.66	246.06	271.46	296.86
3/4	19.05	44.45	69.85	95.25	120.65	146.05	171.45	196.85	222.25	247.65	273.05	298.45
13/16	20.64	46.04	71.44	96.84	122.24	147.64	173.04	198.44	223.84	249.24	274.64	300.04
7/8	22.23	47.63	73.03	98.43	123.83	149.23	174.63	200.03	225.43	250.83	276.23	301.63
15/16	23.81	49.21	74.61	100.01	125.41	150.81	176.21	201.61	227.01	252.41	277.81	303.21

Table 2 Feet and inches to millimeters (1 ft = 304.8 mm; 1 in = 25.4 mm)

Inches	0	1	2	3	4	5	6	7	8	9	10	11
milli-meters	...	25	51	76	102	127	152	178	203	229	254	279

Feet	0	1	2	3	4	5	6	7	8	9
					millimeters (mm)					
0	...	305	610	914	1 219	1 524	1 829	2 134	2 438	2 743
10	3 048	3 353	3 658	3 962	4 267	4 572	4 877	5 182	5 486	5 791
20	6 096	6 401	6 706	7 010	7 315	7 620	7 925	8 230	8 534	8 839
30	9 144	9 449	9 754	10 058	10 363	10 668	10 973	11 278	11 582	11 887
40	12 192	12 497	12 802	13 106	13 411	13 716	14 021	14 326	14 630	14 935
50	15 240	15 545	15 850	16 154	16 459	16 764	17 069	17 374	17 678	17 983
60	18 288	18 593	18 898	19 202	19 507	19 812	20 117	20 422	20 726	21 031
70	21 336	21 641	21 946	22 250	22 555	22 860	23 165	23 470	23 774	24 079
80	24 384	24 689	24 994	25 298	25 603	25 908	26 213	26 518	26 882	27 127
90	27 432	27 737	28 042	28 346	28 651	28 956	29 261	29 566	29 870	30 175
100	30 480	30 785	31 090	31 394	31 699	32 004	32 309	32 614	32 918	33 223
110	33 528	33 833	34 138	34 442	34 747	35 052	35 357	35 662	35 966	36 271
120	36 576	36 881	37 186	37 490	37 795	38 100	38 405	38 710	39 014	39 319
130	39 624	39 929	40 234	40 538	40 843	41 148	41 453	41 758	42 062	42 367
140	42 672	42 977	43 282	43 586	43 891	44 196	44 501	44 806	45 110	45 415
150	45 720									

Table 3 Feet to meters (1 ft = 0.304 8 m)

Feet	0	1	2	3	4	5	6	7	8	9
					meters (m)					
0	...	0.305	0.610	0.914	1.219	1.524	1.829	2.134	2.438	2.743
10	3.048	3.353	3.658	3.962	4.267	4.572	4.877	5.182	5.486	5.791
20	6.096	6.401	6.706	7.010	7.315	7.620	7.925	8.230	8.534	8.839
30	9.144	9.449	9.754	10.058	10.363	10.668	10.973	11.278	11.582	11.887
40	12.192	12.497	12.802	13.106	13.411	13.716	14.021	14.326	14.630	14.935
50	15.240	15.545	15.850	16.154	16.459	16.764	17.069	17.374	17.678	17.983
60	18.288	18.593	18.898	19.202	19.507	19.812	20.117	20.422	20.726	21.031
70	21.336	21.641	21.946	22.250	22.555	22.860	23.165	23.470	23.774	24.079
80	24.384	24.689	24.994	25.298	25.603	25.908	26.213	26.518	26.822	27.127
90	27.432	27.737	28.042	28.346	28.651	28.956	29.261	29.566	29.870	30.175
100	30.480	30.785	31.090	31.394	31.699	32.004	32.309	32.614	32.918	33.223
110	33.528	33.833	34.138	34.442	34.747	35.052	35.357	35.662	35.966	36.271
120	36.576	36.881	37.186	37.490	37.795	38.100	38.405	38.710	39.014	39.319
130	39.624	39.929	40.234	40.538	40.843	41.148	41.453	41.758	42.062	42.367
140	42.672	42.977	43.282	43.586	43.891	44.196	44.501	44.806	45.110	45.415
150	45.720	46.025	46.330	46.634	46.939	47.244	47.549	47.854	48.158	48.463
160	48.768	49.073	49.378	49.682	49.987	50.292	50.597	50.902	51.206	51.511
170	51.816	52.121	52.426	52.730	53.035	53.340	53.645	53.950	54.254	54.559
180	54.864	55.169	55.474	55.778	56.083	56.388	56.693	56.998	57.302	57.607
190	57.912	58.217	58.522	58.826	59.131	59.436	59.741	60.046	60.350	60.655
200	60.960									

Table 4   Miles to kilometers (1 mi = 1.609 344 km)

Miles	0	1	2	3	4	5	6	7	8	9
					kilometers (km)					
0	...	1.609	3.219	4.828	6.437	8.047	9.656	11.265	12.875	14.484
10	16.093	17.703	19.312	20.921	22.531	24.140	25.750	27.359	28.968	30.578
20	32.187	33.796	35.406	37.015	38.624	40.234	41.843	43.452	45.062	46.671
30	48.280	49.890	51.499	53.108	54.718	56.327	57.936	59.546	61.155	62.764
40	64.374	65.983	67.592	69.202	70.811	72.420	74.030	75.639	77.249	78.858
50	80.467	82.077	83.686	85.295	86.905	88.514	90.123	91.733	93.342	94.951
60	96.561	98.170	99.779	101.389	102.998	104.607	106.217	107.826	109.435	111.045
70	112.654	114.263	115.873	117.482	119.091	120.701	122.310	123.919	125.529	127.138
80	128.748	130.357	131.966	133.576	135.185	136.794	138.404	140.013	141.622	143.232
90	144.841	146.450	148.060	149.669	151.278	152.888	154.497	156.106	157.716	159.325
100	160.934	162.544	164.153	165.762	167.372	168.981	170.590	172.200	173.809	175.418
110	177.028	178.637	180.247	181.856	183.465	185.075	186.684	188.293	189.903	191.512
120	193.121	194.731	196.340	197.949	199.559	201.168	202.777	204.387	205.996	207.605
130	209.215	210.824	212.433	214.043	215.652	217.261	218.871	220.480	222.089	223.699
140	225.308	226.918	228.527	230.136	231.746	233.355	234.964	236.574	238.183	239.792
150	241.402	243.011	244.620	246.230	247.839	249.448	251.058	252.667	254.276	255.866
160	257.495	259.104	260.714	262.323	263.932	265.542	267.151	268.760	270.370	271.979
170	273.588	275.198	276.807	278.417	280.026	281.635	283.245	284.854	286.463	288.073
180	289.682	291.291	292.901	294.510	296.119	297.729	299.338	300.947	302.557	304.166
190	305.775	307.385	308.994	310.603	312.213	313.822	315.431	317.041	318.650	320.259
200	321.869									

Table 5   Square inches to square millimeters (1 in^2 = 645.16 mm^2)

Square Inches	0	1	2	3	4	5	6	7	8	9
					square millimeters (mm^2)					
0	...	645	1 290	1 935	2 581	3 226	3 781	4 516	5 161	5 806
10	6 452	7 097	7 742	8 387	9 032	9 677	10 323	10 968	11 613	12 258
20	12 903	13 548	14 194	14 839	15 484	16 129	16 774	17 419	18 064	18 710
30	19 355	20 000	20 645	21 290	21 935	22 581	23 226	23 871	24 516	25 161
40	25 806	26 452	27 097	27 742	28 387	29 032	29 677	30 323	30 968	31 613
50	32 258	32 903	33 548	34 193	34 839	35 484	36 129	36 774	37 419	38 064
60	38 710	39 355	40 000	40 645	41 290	41 935	42 581	43 226	43 871	44 516
70	45 161	45 806	46 452	47 097	47 742	48 387	49 032	49 677	50 322	50 968
80	51 613	52 258	52 903	53 548	54 193	54 839	55 484	56 129	56 774	57 419
90	58 064	58 710	59 355	60 000	60 645	61 290	61 935	62 581	63 226	63 871
100	64 516	65 161	65 806	66 451	67 097	67 742	68 387	69 032	69 677	70 322
110	70 968	71 613	72 258	72 903	73 548	74 193	74 839	75 484	76 129	76 774
120	77 419	78 064	78 710	79 355	80 000	80 645	81 290	81 935	82 580	83 226
130	83 871	84 516	85 161	85 806	86 451	87 097	87 742	88 387	89 032	89 677
140	90 322	90 968	91 613	92 258	92 903					

Table 6 Square feet to square meters (1 ft^2 = 0.0929 m^2)

Square feet	0	1	2	3	4	5	6	7	8	9
Square meter	. . .	0.09	0.19	0.28	0.37	0.46	0.56	0.65	0.74	0.84

Square Feet	0	10	20	30	40	50	60	70	80	90
	square meters (m^2)									
0	. . .	0.93	1.86	2.79	3.72	4.65	5.57	6.50	7.43	8.36
100	9.29	10.22	11.15	12.08	13.01	13.94	14.86	15.79	16.72	17.65
200	18.58	19.51	20.44	21.37	22.30	23.23	24.15	25.08	26.01	26.94
300	27.87	28.80	29.73	30.66	31.59	32.52	33.45	34.37	35.30	36.23
400	37.16	38.09	39.02	39.95	40.88	41.81	42.74	43.66	44.59	45.52
500	46.45	47.38	48.31	49.24	50.17	51.10	52.03	52.95	53.88	54.81
600	55.74	56.67	57.60	58.53	59.46	60.39	61.32	62.25	63.17	64.10
700	65.03	65.96	66.89	67.82	68.75	69.68	70.61	71.54	72.46	73.39
800	74.32	75.25	76.18	77.11	78.04	78.97	79.90	80.83	81.75	82.68
900	83.61	84.54	85.47	86.40	87.33	88.26	89.19	90.12	91.04	91.97
1000	92.90	93.83	94.76	95.69	96.62	97.55	98.48	99.41	100.34	101.26
1100	102.19	103.12	104.05	104.98	105.91	106.84	107.77	108.70	109.63	110.55
1200	111.48	112.41	113.34	114.27	115.20	116.13	117.06	117.99	118.92	119.84
1300	120.77	121.70	122.63	123.56	124.49	125.42	126.35	127.28	128.21	129.14
1400	130.06	130.99	131.92	132.85	133.78	134.71	135.64	136.57	137.50	138.43
1500	139.35									

Table 7 Acres to hectares (1 acre = 0.404 685 6 ha)

Acres	0	1	2	3	4	5	6	7	8	9
hectares	. . .	0.40	0.81	1.21	1.62	2.02	2.43	2.83	3.24	3.64

Acres	0	10	20	30	40	50	60	70	80	90
	hectares (ha)									
0	. . .	4.05	8.09	12.14	16.19	20.23	24.28	28.33	32.37	36.42
100	40.47	44.52	48.56	52.61	56.66	60.70	64.75	68.80	72.84	76.89
200	80.94	84.98	89.03	93.08	97.12	101.17	105.22	109.27	113.31	117.36
300	121.41	125.45	129.50	133.55	137.59	141.64	145.69	149.73	153.78	157.83
400	161.87	165.92	169.97	174.01	178.06	182.11	186.16	190.20	194.25	198.30
500	202.34	206.39	210.44	214.48	218.53	222.58	226.62	230.67	234.72	238.76
600	242.81	246.86	250.91	254.95	259.00	263.05	267.09	271.14	275.19	279.23
700	283.28	287.33	291.37	295.42	299.47	303.51	307.56	311.61	315.65	319.70
800	323.75	327.80	331.84	335.89	339.94	343.98	348.03	352.08	356.12	360.17
900	364.22	368.26	372.31	376.36	380.40	384.45	388.50	392.55	396.59	400.64
1000	404.69									

Table 8 Cubic feet to cubic meters (1 ft³ = 0.0283 m³)

Cubic Feet	0	1	2	3	4	5	6	7	8	9
					Cubic meters (m³)					
0	. . .	0.028	0.057	0.085	0.113	0.142	0.170	0.198	0.227	0.255
10	0.283	0.311	0.340	0.368	0.396	0.425	0.453	0.481	0.510	0.538
20	0.566	0.595	0.623	0.651	0.680	0.708	0.736	0.765	0.793	0.821
30	0.850	0.878	0.906	0.934	0.963	0.991	1.019	1.048	1.076	1.104
40	1.133	1.161	1.189	1.218	1.246	1.274	1.303	1.331	1.359	1.386
50	1.416	1.444	1.472	1.501	1.529	1.557	1.586	1.614	1.642	1.671
60	1.699	1.727	1.756	1.784	1.812	1.841	1.869	1.897	1.926	1.954
70	1.982	2.010	2.034	2.067	2.095	2.124	2.152	2.180	2.209	2.237
80	2.265	2.293	2.322	2.350	2.379	2.407	2.435	2.464	2.492	2.520
90	2.549	2.577	2.605	2.633	2.662	2.690	2.718	2.747	2.775	2.803
100	2.832	2.860	2.888	2.917	2.945	2.973	3.002	3.030	3.058	3.087
110	2.115	3.143	3.171	3.200	3.228	3.256	3.285	3.313	3.341	3.370
120	3.398	3.426	3.455	3.483	3.511	3.540	3.568	3.596	3.625	3.653
130	3.681	3.710	3.738	3.766	3.794	3.823	3.851	3.879	3.908	3.936
140	3.964	3.993	4.021	4.049	4.078	4.106	4.134	4.163	4.191	4.219
150	4.248	4.276	4.304	4.332	4.361	4.389	4.417	4.446	4.474	4.502
160	4.531	4.559	4.587	4.616	4.644	4.672	4.701	4.729	4.757	4.786
170	4.814	4.482	4.870	4.899	4.927	4.955	4.984	5.012	5.040	5.069
180	5.097	5.125	5.154	5.182	5.210	5.239	5.267	5.295	5.324	5.352
190	5.380	5.409	5.437	5.465	5.493	5.522	5.550	5.578	5.606	5.635
200	5.663									

Note: 1 cubic meter (m³) equals 1000 liters (L). Cubic feet can be converted to liters by shifting the decimal point three places to the right; for example, 125 cubic feet = 3.540 m³ = 3540 L.

Table 9 Gallons to liters (1 gal [U.S.] = 3.7841 L)

Gallons	0	1	2	3	4	5	6	7	8	9
					Liters (L)					
0	. . .	3.79	7.57	11.36	15.14	18.93	22.71	26.50	30.28	34.07
10	37.85	41.64	45.42	49.21	53.00	56.78	60.57	64.35	68.14	71.92
20	75.71	79.49	83.28	87.06	90.85	94.64	98.42	102.21	105.99	109.78
30	113.56	117.35	121.13	124.92	128.70	132.49	136.27	140.06	143.85	147.63
40	151.42	155.20	158.99	162.77	166.56	170.34	174.13	177.91	181.70	185.49
50	189.27	193.06	196.84	200.63	204.41	208.20	211.98	215.77	219.55	223.34
60	227.12	230.91	234.70	238.48	242.27	246.05	249.84	253.62	257.41	261.19
70	264.98	268.76	272.55	276.34	280.12	283.91	287.69	291.48	295.26	299.05
80	302.83	306.62	310.40	314.19	317.97	321.76	325.55	329.33	333.12	336.90
90	340.69	344.47	348.26	352.04	355.83	359.61	363.40	367.18	370.97	374.76

	0	10	20	30	40	50	60	70	80	90
100	378.5	416.4	454.2	492.1	530.0	567.8	605.7	643.5	681.4	719.2
200	757.1	794.9	832.8	870.6	908.5	946.4	984.2	1022.1	1059.9	1097.8
300	1135.6	1173.5	1211.3	1249.2	1287.0	1324.9	1362.7	1400.6	1438.5	1476.3
400	1514.2	1552.0	1589.9	1627.7	1665.6	1703.4	1741.3	1779.1	1817.0	1854.9
500	1892.7	1930.6	1968.4	2006.3	2044.1	2082.0	2119.8	2157.7	2195.5	2233.4
600	2271.2	2309.1	2347.0	2384.8	2422.7	2460.5	2498.4	2536.2	2574.1	2611.9
700	2649.8	2687.6	2725.5	2763.4	2801.2	2839.1	2876.9	2914.8	2952.6	2990.5
800	3028.3	3066.2	3104.0	3141.9	3179.7	3217.6	3255.5	3293.3	3331.2	3369.0
900	3406.9	3444.7	3482.6	3520.4	3558.3	3596.1	3634.0	3671.8	3709.7	3747.6
1000	3785.4									

Table 10   Pounds to kilograms (1 lb = 0.453 592 kg)

Pounds	0	1	2	3	4	5	6	7	8	9
						kilograms (kg)				
0	. . .	0.45	0.91	1.36	1.81	2.27	2.72	3.18	3.63	4.08
10	4.54	4.99	5.44	5.90	6.35	6.80	7.26	7.71	8.16	8.62
20	9.07	9.53	9.98	10.43	10.89	11.34	11.79	12.25	12.70	13.15
30	13.61	14.06	14.52	14.97	15.42	15.88	16.33	16.78	17.24	17.69
40	18.14	18.60	19.05	19.50	19.96	20.41	20.87	21.32	21.77	22.23
50	22.68	23.13	23.59	24.04	24.49	24.95	25.40	25.85	26.31	26.76
60	27.22	27.67	28.12	28.58	29.03	29.48	29.94	30.39	30.84	31.30
70	31.75	32.21	32.66	33.11	33.57	34.02	34.47	34.93	35.38	35.83
80	36.29	36.74	37.19	37.65	38.10	38.56	39.01	39.46	39.92	40.37
90	40.82	41.28	41.73	42.18	42.64	43.09	43.54	44.00	44.45	44.91
100	45.36	45.81	46.27	46.72	47.17	47.63	48.08	48.53	48.99	49.44
110	49.90	50.35	50.80	51.26	51.71	52.16	52.62	53.07	53.52	53.98
120	54.43	54.88	55.34	55.79	56.25	56.70	57.15	57.61	58.06	58.51
130	58.97	59.42	59.87	60.33	60.78	61.24	61.69	62.14	62.60	63.05
140	63.50	63.96	64.41	64.86	65.32	65.77	66.22	66.68	67.13	67.59
150	68.04	68.49	68.95	69.40	69.85	70.31	70.76	71.21	71.67	72.12
160	72.57	73.03	73.48	73.94	74.39	74.84	75.30	75.75	76.20	76.66
170	77.11	77.56	78.02	78.47	78.93	79.38	79.83	80.29	80.74	81.19
180	81.65	82.10	82.55	83.01	83.46	83.91	84.37	84.82	85.28	85.73
190	86.18	86.64	87.09	87.54	88.00	88.45	88.90	89.36	89.81	90.26
200	90.72	91.17	91.63	92.08	92.53	92.99	93.44	93.89	94.35	94.80

Table 11   U.S. short tons (2000 lb) to metric tons (1 ton = 0.907 185 t)

Short Tons	0	1	2	3	4	5	6	7	8	9
						metric tons (t)				
0	. . .	0.907	1.814	2.722	3.629	4.536	5.443	6.350	7.257	8.165
10	9.072	9.979	10.886	11.793	12.701	13.608	14.515	15.422	16.329	17.237
20	18.144	19.051	19.958	20.865	21.772	22.680	23.587	24.494	25.401	26.308
30	27.216	28.123	29.030	29.937	30.844	31.751	32.659	33.566	34.473	35.380
40	36.287	37.195	38.102	39.009	39.916	40.823	41.731	42.638	43.545	44.452
50	45.359	46.266	47.174	48.081	48.988	49.895	50.802	51.710	52.617	53.524
60	54.431	55.338	56.245	57.153	58.060	58.967	59.874	60.781	61.689	62.596
70	63.503	64.410	65.317	66.225	67.132	68.039	68.946	69.853	70.760	71.668
80	72.575	73.482	74.389	75.296	76.204	77.111	78.018	78.925	79.832	80.739
90	81.647	82.554	83.461	84.368	85.275	86.183	87.090	87.997	88.904	89.811
100	90.718									

Note: 1 metric ton (t) equals 1000 kilograms (kg). U.S. short tons can be converted to kilograms by shifting the decimal point three places to the right; for example, 48 short tons = 43.545 t = 43 545 kg (rounded to the nearest kilogram).

Table 12   Pounds per cubic foot to kilograms per cubic meter (1 lb/ft³ = 16.018 46 kg/m³)

Pounds per cubic foot	0	1	2	3	4	5	6	7	8	9
	kilograms per cubic meter (kg/m³)									
0	. . .	16.0	32.0	48.1	64.1	80.1	96.1	112.1	128.1	144.2
10	160.2	176.2	192.2	208.2	224.3	240.3	256.3	272.3	288.3	304.4
20	320.4	336.4	352.4	368.4	384.4	400.5	416.5	432.5	448.5	464.5
30	480.6	496.6	512.6	528.6	544.6	560.6	576.7	592.7	608.7	624.7
40	640.7	656.8	672.8	688.8	704.8	720.8	736.8	752.9	768.9	784.9
50	800.9	816.9	833.0	849.0	865.0	881.0	897.0	913.1	929.1	945.1
60	961.1	977.1	993.1	1009.2	1025.2	1041.2	1057.2	1073.2	1089.3	1105.3
70	1121.3	1137.3	1153.3	1169.3	1185.4	1201.4	1217.4	1233.4	1249.4	1265.5
80	1281.5	1297.5	1313.5	1329.5	1345.6	1361.6	1377.6	1393.6	1409.6	1425.6
90	1441.7	1457.7	1473.7	1489.7	1505.7	1521.8	1537.8	1553.8	1569.8	1585.8
100	1601.8	1617.9	1633.9	1649.9	1665.9	1681.9	1698.0	1714.0	1730.0	1746.0
110	1762.0	1778.0	1794.1	1810.1	1826.1	1842.1	1858.1	1874.2	1890.2	1906.2
120	1922.2	1938.2	1954.3	1970.3	1986.3	2002.3	2018.3	2034.3	2050.4	2066.4
130	2082.4	2098.4	2114.4	2130.5	2146.5	2162.5	2178.5	2194.5	2210.5	2226.6
140	2242.6	2258.6	2274.6	2290.6	2306.7	2322.7	2338.7	2354.7	2370.7	2386.8
150	2402.8	2418.8	2434.8	2450.8	2466.8	2482.9	2498.9	2514.9	2590.9	2546.9
160	2563.0	2579.0	2595.0	2611.0	2627.0	2643.0	2659.1	2675.1	2691.1	2707.1
170	2723.1	2739.2	2755.2	2771.2	2787.2	2803.2	2819.2	2835.3	2851.3	2867.3
180	2883.3	2899.3	2915.4	2931.4	2947.4	2963.4	2979.4	2995.4	3011.5	3027.5
190	3043.5	3059.5	3075.5	3091.6	3107.6	3123.6	3139.6	3155.6	3171.7	3187.7
200	3203.7									

Table 13 Pound-force to newtons (1 lbf = 4.448 22 N)

Pound-force	0	1	2	3	4	5	6	7	8	9
					newtons (N)					
0	· · ·	4.45	8.90	13.34	17.79	22.24	26.69	31.14	35.59	40.03
10	44.48	48.93	53.38	57.83	62.28	66.72	71.17	75.62	80.07	84.52
20	88.96	93.41	97.86	102.31	106.76	111.21	115.65	120.10	124.55	129.00
30	133.45	137.89	142.34	146.79	151.24	155.69	160.14	164.58	169.03	173.48
40	177.93	182.38	186.83	191.27	195.72	200.17	204.62	209.07	213.51	217.96
50	222.41	226.86	231.31	235.76	240.20	244.65	249.10	253.55	258.00	262.45
60	266.89	271.34	275.79	280.24	284.69	289.13	293.58	298.03	302.48	306.93
70	311.38	315.82	320.27	324.72	329.17	333.62	338.06	342.51	346.96	351.41
80	355.86	360.31	364.75	369.20	373.65	378.10	382.55	387.00	391.44	395.89
90	400.34	404.79	409.24	413.68	418.13	422.58	427.03	431.48	435.93	440.37

	0	10	20	30	40	50	60	70	80	90
100	444.8	489.3	533.8	578.3	622.8	667.2	711.7	756.2	800.7	845.2
200	889.6	934.1	978.6	1023.1	1067.6	1112.1	1156.5	1201.0	1245.5	1290.0
300	1334.5	1378.9	1423.4	1467.9	1512.4	1556.9	1601.4	1645.8	1690.3	1734.8
400	1779.3	1823.8	1868.3	1912.7	1957.2	2001.7	2046.2	2090.7	2135.1	2179.6
500	2224.1	2268.6	2313.1	2357.6	2402.0	2446.5	2491.0	2535.5	2580.0	2624.5
600	2668.9	2713.4	2757.9	2802.4	2846.9	2891.3	2935.8	2980.3	3024.8	3069.3
700	3113.8	3158.2	3202.7	3247.2	3291.7	3336.2	3380.6	3425.1	3469.6	3514.1
800	3558.6	3603.1	3647.5	3692.0	3736.5	3781.0	3835.5	3870.0	3914.4	3958.9
900	4003.4	4047.9	4092.4	4136.8	4181.3	4225.8	4270.3	4314.8	4359.3	4403.7
1000	4448.2	4492.7	4537.2	4581.7	4626.1	4670.6	4715.1	4759.6	4804.1	4848.6
1100	4893.0	4937.5	4982.0	5026.5	5071.0	5115.5	5159.9	5204.4	5248.9	5293.4
1200	5337.9	5382.3	5426.8	5471.3	5515.8	5560.3	5604.8	5649.2	5693.7	5738.2
1300	5782.7	5827.2	5871.7	5916.1	5960.6	6005.1	6049.6	6094.1	6138.5	6183.0
1400	6227.5	6272.0	6316.5	6361.0	6405.4	6449.9	6494.4	6538.9	6583.4	6627.8
1500	6672.3	6716.8	6761.3	6805.8	6850.3	6894.7	6939.2	6983.7	7028.2	7072.7
1600	7117.2	7161.6	7206.1	7250.6	7295.1	7339.6	7384.0	7428.5	7473.0	7517.5
1700	7562.0	7606.5	7650.9	7695.4	7739.9	7784.4	7828.9	7873.3	7917.8	7962.3
1800	8006.8	8051.3	8095.8	8140.2	8184.7	8229.2	8273.7	8318.2	8362.7	8407.1
1900	8451.6	8496.1	8540.6	8585.1	8629.5	8674.0	8718.5	8763.0	8807.5	8852.0
2000	8896.4									

Note: 1000 newtons (N) equal 1 kilonewton (1 kN). The lower portion of the table could also have been shown in kilonewtons; for example, 4893.0 N = 4.8930 kN. The table can also be used for the conversion of kips (1000 lbf) to kilonewtons (kN), since a multiplier of 1000 applies to both measurement units.

Table 14 Pounds-force per square root to kilopascals (kPa) (1 lbf/ft$_2$ = 0.047 88 kN/m²)

Pounds-force per square foot	0	10	20	30	40	50	60	70	80	90
	kilonewtons per square meter (kN/m² = kPa)									
0	· · ·	0.479	0.958	1.436	1.915	2.394	2.873	3.352	3.830	4.309
100	4.788	5.267	5.746	6.224	6.703	7.182	7.661	8.140	8.618	9.097
200	9.576	10.055	10.534	11.013	11.491	11.970	12.449	12.928	13.406	13.886
300	14.364	14.843	15.322	15.800	16.279	16.758	17.237	17.716	18.195	18.673
400	19.152	19.631	20.110	20.589	21.067	21.546	22.025	22.504	22.983	23.461
500	23.940	24.419	24.898	25.377	25.855	26.334	26.813	27.292	27.771	28.249
600	28.728	29.207	29.686	31.165	30.643	31.122	31.601	32.080	32.559	33.037
700	33.516	33.995	34.474	34.953	35.431	35.910	36.389	36.868	37.347	37.825
800	38.304	38.783	39.262	39.741	40.219	40.698	41.177	41.656	42.135	42.613
900	43.092	43.571	44.050	44.529	45.007	45.486	45.965	46.444	46.923	47.401
1000	47.880									

Table 15 Pounds-force per square inch (psi) to megapascals (MPa) (1 psi = 0.006 895 MPa)

Pounds-force per square inch	0	10	20	30	40	50	60	70	80	90
	megapascals (MPa)									
0	· · ·	0.069	0.138	0.207	0.276	0.345	0.414	0.483	0.552	0.621
100	0.689	0.758	0.827	0.896	0.965	1.034	1.103	1.172	1.241	1.310
200	1.379	1.448	1.517	1.586	1.655	1.724	1.793	1.862	1.931	1.999
300	2.068	2.137	2.206	2.275	2.344	2.413	2.482	2.551	2.620	2.689
400	2.758	2.827	2.896	2.965	3.034	3.103	3.172	3.241	3.309	3.378
500	3.447	3.516	3.585	3.654	3.723	3.792	3.861	3.903	3.999	4.068
600	4.137	4.206	4.275	4.344	4.413	4.482	4.551	4.619	4.688	4.757
700	4.826	4.895	4.964	5.033	5.102	5.171	5.240	5.309	5.378	5.447
800	5.516	5.585	5.654	5.723	5.792	5.861	5.929	5.998	6.067	6.136
900	6.205	6.274	6.343	6.412	6.481	6.550	6.619	6.688	6.757	6.826

	0	100	200	300	400	500	600	700	800	900
1000	6.895	7.584	8.274	8.963	9.653	10.342	11.032	11.721	12.411	13.100
2000	13.790	14.479	15.168	15.858	16.547	17.237	17.926	18.616	19.305	19.995
3000	20.684	21.374	22.063	22.753	23.442	24.132	24.821	25.511	26.200	26.890
4000	27.579	28.269	28.958	29.647	30.337	31.026	31.716	32.405	33.095	33.784
5000	34.474	35.163	35.853	36.542	37.232	37.921	38.611	39.300	39.990	40.679
6000	41.369	42.058	42.747	43.437	44.126	44.816	45.505	46.195	46.884	47.574
7000	48.263	48.953	49.642	50.332	51.021	51.711	52.400	53.090	53.779	54.469
8000	55.158	55.848	56.537	57.226	57.916	58.605	59.295	59.984	60.674	61.363
9000	62.053	64.742	63.432	64.121	64.811	65.500	66.190	66.879	67.569	68.258
10 000	68.948									

Note: 1 megapascal (MPa) is equal to 1 meganewton per square meter (MN/m²) and to 1 newton per square millimeter (N/mm²).

Lumens per square foot	0	1	2	3	4	5	6	7	8	9
					lux (lm/m²)					
0	· · ·	10.8	21.5	32.3	43.1	53.8	64.6	75.3	86.1	96.9
10	107.6	118.4	129.2	139.9	150.7	161.5	172.2	183.0	193.8	204.5
20	215.3	226.0	236.8	247.6	258.3	269.1	279.9	290.6	301.4	312.2
30	322.9	333.7	344.4	355.2	366.0	376.7	387.5	398.3	409.0	419.8
40	430.6	441.3	452.1	462.8	473.6	484.4	495.1	505.9	516.7	527.4
50	538.2	549.0	559.7	570.5	581.3	592.0	602.8	613.5	624.3	635.1
60	645.8	656.6	667.4	678.1	688.9	699.7	710.4	721.2	731.9	742.7
70	753.5	764.2	775.0	785.8	796.5	807.3	818.1	828.8	839.6	850.3
80	861.1	871.9	882.6	893.4	904.2	914.9	925.7	936.5	947.2	958.0
90	968.8	979.5	990.3	1001.0	1011.8	1022.6	1033.3	1044.1	1054.9	1065.6

	0	10	20	30	40	50	60	70	80	90
					kilolux (1000 lux)					
100	1.076	1.184	1.292	1.399	1.507	1.615	1.722	1.830	1.938	2.045
200	2.153	2.260	2.368	2.476	2.583	2.691	2.799	2.906	3.014	3.122
300	3.229	3.337	3.444	3.552	3.660	3.767	3.875	3.983	4.090	4.198
400	4.306	4.413	4.521	4.628	4.736	4.844	4.951	5.059	5.167	5.274
500	5.382	5.490	5.597	5.705	5.813	5.920	6.028	6.135	6.243	6.351
600	6.458	6.566	6.674	6.781	6.889	6.997	7.104	7.212	7.319	7.427
700	7.535	7.642	7.750	7.858	7.965	8.073	8.181	8.288	8.396	8.503
800	8.611	8.719	8.826	8.934	9.042	9.149	9.257	9.365	9.472	9.580
900	9.688	9.795	9.903	10 010	10.118	10.226	10.333	10.441	10.549	10.656
1000	10.764									

METRIC BIBLIOGRAPHY

American Society for Testing and Materials (ASTM)

1916 Race St., Philadelphia, PA 19103.
ASTM E 380-76, *Standard for Metric Practice* (to be reissued, with amendments, in 1979).

American National Metric Council (ANMC)

1625 Massachusetts Ave., N.W., Washington, DC 20036.
ANSI/ASTM E 621-78, *Standard Practice for the Use of Metric (SI) Units in Building Design and Construction.*

ANMC Metric Editorial Guide, 3rd. ed., 1977.

National Bureau of Standards (NBS)

Publications obtainable from Superintendent of Documents, U.S. Government Printing Office, Washington, DC 20402, by quoting Stock No.
Technical Note 938, *Recommended Practice for the Use of Metric (SI) Units in Building Design and Construction* (SD Stock No. 003-003-01761-2).
Technical Note 976, *International Trends and Development of Importance to the Metrication Plans of the US Construction Community* (SD Stock No. 003-003-01937-2).
Technical Note 990, *The Selection of Preferred Metric Values for Design and Construction* (SD Stock No. 003-003-02001-0).
Special Publication 330, *The International System of Units (SI)—1977 Edition* (SD Stock No. 003-003-01784-1).
Special Publication 458, *Metrication and Dimensional Coordination—A Selected Bibliography (up to 1976)* (SD Stock No. 003-003-01684-5).
Special Publication 504, *Metric Dimensional Coordination—The Issues and Precedent* (SD Stock No. 003-003-01887-2). Edited Proceedings of a Joint Conference (ANMC Design and Construction Products Sector) on Metrication and Dimensional Coordination.
Special Publication 530, *Metrication in Building Design, Production and Construction* (SD Stock No. 003-003-01971-2). Compendium of 10 papers on various aspects of metrication.

Canadian Standards Association

178 Rexdale Boulevard, Rexdale, Ont. Canada, M9W 1R3.
Can3-B78.3-M77, *Building Drawings.*
Can3-A31.M-75, *Series of Standards for Metric Dimensional Coordination in Building.*

National Research Council of Canada, Ottawa

Montreal Road, Building M-20, Ottawa, Canada, K1A ORG.
Special Technical Publication No. 3 of the Division of Building Research, NRC 15234, *Manual on Metric Building Drawing Practice* (April 1976).

INDEX